The Information Society

Issues and Illusions

DAVID LYON

Polity Press

Copyright © David Lyon 1988

First published 1988 by Polity Press
in association with Basil Blackwell.

Editorial Office:
Polity Press, Dales Brewery, Gwydir Street,
Cambridge CB1 2LJ, UK

Basil Blackwell Ltd
108 Cowley Road, Oxford OX4 1JF, UK

Basil Blackwell Inc.
432 Park Avenue South, Suite 1503
New York, NY 10016, USA

British Library Cataloguing in Publication Data

Lyon, David, *1948–*
    The Information society: issues and
    illusions.
    1. Technology—Social aspects
    2. Information storage and retrieval systems
    —Social aspects
    I. Title
    303.4′83   T14.5
ISBN 0–7456–0260–6
ISBN 0–7456–0369–6 Pbk

Typeset in 11 on 12½ pt Bembo
by Joshua Associates Limited, Oxford
Printed in Great Britain by Billing & Sons Ltd, Worcester

Contents

But we are delivered to [technology] in the worst possible way when we regard it as something neutral; for this conception of it, to which today we particularly like to do homage, makes us utterly blind to the essence of technology.

Martin Heidegger, The question concerning technology (1955)

The search for justice before God, the measuring of technique by other criteria than those of technique itself – these were the great obstacles that Christianity opposed to technical progress.

Jacques Ellul, The technological society (1954)

Preface

'Information technology is changing the world!'

Little doubt exists among many popular commentators that the advanced nations are entering a new phase: the information society. Forecasts abound of the massive social impacts of new information technologies of computing and telecommunications. Time-honoured social institutions and lifestyles are said to be undergoing transformation. Remote cashless shopping, homeworking, robotic manufacture, the automated office, television broadcast direct via satellite and desktop publishing are just a few of the electronic agents of change. Work-patterns, family life, leisure and entertainment and even the ways we view ourselves as humans are all vulnerable to alteration as information technology ('IT') is diffused throughout society. So general is this displacement of tradition and taken-for-granted social arrangements that the 'information society' concept is invoked to sum up what is happening.

This book offers an assessment of such forecasts. Information techno-logy does indeed have extensive social consequences, and thus raises fundamental questions about the future shaping of society. But the kinds of vision conjured up by the information society phrase are often too good to be true. Of course, many people have good cause to be grateful for the effects of the silicon chip. Machines which use microelectronics aid the disabled, reduce the drudgery and danger of some occupations, speed medical diagnosis, crime detection or welfare benefits payments, help to conserve scarce natural resources and to anticipate disasters such as crop failures or earthquakes. Along with many other writers, I frankly enjoy the flexibility and time-saving of my word-processor. But it is a mistake to jump from specific social benefits to the assumption that all IT's effects are equally benign.

Here, then, are two common beliefs about the social impact of IT: first, a total social transformation is predicted ('information society' is coming); and secondly, this transformation is generally a good and progressive movement. What is wrong with such beliefs? I shall argue, in different ways, that the main problem is the one-way relationship expressed in the idea of 'social impacts of technology'. For it suggests that technology is somehow 'outside' society, impinging upon it. An alternative view, which I illustrate throughout the book, is that the 'social' and the 'technological' cannot be separated in this way. New technology is as much a social product as the shape of society is a technological product. There is a constant interplay between 'technology' and 'society'.

The technologically shaped future is mistaken because it fails to take account of at least two factors. For one thing, IT has *social origins* (in military research for instance) which are seldom laid bare, but which have decisively guided its development. For another, new technology is not always accepted and assimilated passively. Consumers may decline to buy new gadgets (cable television is a case in point); workers may oppose the installation of new machines (think of newspaper printers). At the same time, I do not wish to replace technological with social determinism. IT has many unforeseen social consequences, and must be treated as a relatively independent factor within some specific circumstances. The technical convergence between computing and telecommunications does have ramifications which are quite unintended (examples in the book include state surveillance, middle management and global communications grids).

To foresee the emergence of a new kind of society is to exaggerate the novelty of IT's social consequences and to neglect familiar factors and processes – such as the built-in inequalities of the market system – which continue to be highly significant. At the same time, I do wish to stress that many of the social changes related to IT are truly far-reaching, and do raise basic questions for social theory. The great classical social theorists – Karl Marx, Max Weber and Emile Durkheim – took as their starting point the evident transformations of the Western world, in which industrialism and capitalism played a central role. Computerized systems are today affecting the very organization of industry, while simultaneously helping to alter aspects of capitalism, so old concepts and theories must be re-appraised. The part played by governments is also important here (in ways underestimated by classical sociology), and they too are implicated in the current computerization processes.

It is assumed that the 'new kind of society' brought about by IT is also generally desirable. This sort of optimism (not unknown in the history of technology!) is not warranted, or so I shall argue. Let me also say quickly that the alternative to such optimism is not scepticism or pessimism, still less despair. Such optimism about the socially beneficial effects of new technology is a distraction. It serves simply to sidestep crucial questions about the *ways* that IT is developed and introduced. In other words, the social analytical question (are we entering an information society?) is inseparable from the social ethical or normative question (what counts as good, right and just technology?).

In what follows, therefore, the analytical and the normative tasks are considered as vitally linked, though distinguishable. It is not possible clinically to isolate social analysis from (often implicit) beliefs about the 'good society'. So I endorse some insights of both 'critical theory' and 'public philosophy', which in different ways explicitly connect analysis and ethics, although I would not align myself entirely with either tradition.[1] In weighing and choosing between theories I try to be guided both by empirical constraint and by convictions rooted in Christian social thought.[2] This, for me, is how the analytical and the normative come together. At certain points this is particularly important. Rather than labouring them later I highlight them here.

First, the fact that human beings are active reflexive creatures has to be incorporated within any explanation of our patterns of human relationship. This is neglected both in some accounts where technology apparently has the capacity to shape society in some autonomous fashion, and also in some critiques of new technology which ignore the role of human response and resistance. While not for a moment denying ways in which social and technological arrangements constrain and limit human action, this perspective rejects all forms of determinism.

Secondly, human action does not take place in some normless vacuum. We are valuing creatures, and any attempt to explain social relationships and processes itself involves valuation. If this normative dimension is taken seriously, then, for example, technological optimism is exposed in all its superficiality and concepts such as 'responsibility' become much more relevant. Social analysis guided by a commitment to 'responsible technology' may play a constructive role within policy decisions in boardrooms, educational institutions, labour unions, in the local community or wherever.

Thirdly, while it is true that many of new technology's most significant aspects are first felt in the workplace, this does not necessarily mean that the most vital clues about the relation of technology to society are dicovered in the sphere of material production. For humans are cultural creatures, engaged in a chronic quest for meaning. Thus, for instance, I make no apology for introducing the biblical category of idolatry to denote a misplaced faith in the power of technology to provide meaning or to resolve the human condition.

In mentioning these things I am aware that others may well share some of these views, but from a different perspective. That is fine. I am not pretending that they are idiosyncratic to me. Mentioning them may also help the reader to see ways in which this book may be distinguished from others which cover similar ground. The Luddite analysis of Frank Webster and Kevin Robins, for instance, while arguing well the crucial point that technology 'incorporates social values' ends on a fairly dismal note. 'Centralized corporate capital', usually in collusion with the 'disciplinary state', 'extends and consolidates its hold in society'.[3] In my view this version of Luddism puts too little weight both on other factors such as gender relations or military institutions, and on the moral critique that was strongly implied in early Luddism and is still relevant today.

The idea that an information society is emerging does raise important questions. At the same time it invites critique. By surveying what has been discovered so far about the social impacts of new technology and connecting this with social theory I try to put a spotlight on those important questions. By way of critique, I focus attention on three matters. One, IT *is* socially significant, but is it so for the reasons that 'information society' theorists think? New technologies are playing a central role in the restructuring of the advanced economies, but do we understand their real contribution to social change? Two, examining the information society thesis unavoidably involves normative questions and ethical choice. Has this dimension been obscured in a world where even political discourse is often dominated by technique? Three, if the information society idea also expresses social aspirations, is it best seen as a utopian goal or as an ideological smokescreen? Or does it in fact contain strong traces of each?

A note on terms

The information society concept has gained currency across national borders despite the fact that terms describing the new technologies vary from country to country. In the USA, the parallel terms 'computing technologies' or 'communications technologies' still tend to be used, whereas British use of the clumsier term 'information technology' expresses the convergence of the two older fields (as does the German, *Informationstechnik*). In France, the simpler *l'informatique* holds sway, referring mainly to computing, and often used in conjunction with *la télématique*. I shall use mainly the British abbreviation 'IT', and for variety's sake, the anglicized 'informatics' and 'telematics'.

Acknowledgements

I am very grateful for the practical help and encouragement of several people. Those who commented on a complete draft are Peter Bramham, Howard Davis, Bill Dutton – whose observations on American examples were particularly helpful – Anne Goldthorpe and Mark Gregory. Shirley Dex, Arthur Francis, Donald MacKenzie and John Street helped with specific chapters. James Carey, Rob Kling, Judy Larsen and Quin Schultze drew my attention to important sources, while Jay Blumler helped provide context and direction. Tony Giddens, whose theoretical ideas are a constant stimulus, gave early guidance to the project and also waited patiently for the final text. Both the Shaftesbury Project IT Study Group, in Britain, and discussions with friends in Silicon Valley in 1986, have helped to earth my research in the 'real worlds' of IT and also to hammer home the urgency of finding an adequate normative approach. Bradford and Ilkley College released me from teaching duties in 1984–5, during which time much of the background research was done. While sincerely thanking all the above named I should stress that remaining mistakes and poor judgements are my fault, not theirs.

Needless to say I have also relied on the loving forbearance of Sue and our children. I am striving to be a less preoccupied participant in the 'distractions' of model-building, music-making, biking and the other things we like to do together.

Chapter 1 is in part a revised version of 'From postindustrialism to information society: a new social transformation?' published in *Sociology*, 20 (4), November 1986, and appears by permission. The diagram on p. 46 is reproduced by permission of the Department of Trade and Industry, London.

1

Introduction: the roots of the information society idea

> People started getting together and exploring the idea that there was going to be a revolution in technology which was going to change society so drastically.
>
> *Steve Wozniak (1986)*[1]

Suddenly, success in just about any field has become impossible without information technology. In farming, manufacture, education, policing, medicine, entertainment, banking or whatever, IT is apparently set to change everything that human beings do in advanced societies. Steve Wozniak, of Apple computers fame, sees the real revolution as putting personal computers into the home. Others see it in direct broadcasting by satellite, automated work opening up new vistas for freed time, or in the potential for push-button democracy. While differing over details, though, many seem to agree that bringing together computing with telecommunications spells the start of a new age.

It appears that this is the only way forward. Initiation in the processes of information handling, transmission, storage and retrieval is the key to future prosperity and to qualitatively different ways of life. Failure to proceed in this direction carries dire consequences. Punishment for national laggards, according to a British National Economic Development Office report, will be relegation to 'Third World' status.[2]

Not surprisingly, this 'one way forward' is greeted by others with some sense of foreboding. Cheerful book-titles such as *Silicon Civilization* and *The Mighty Micro* are answered in *Electronic Nightmare* and *Electronic Illusions*.[3] And fears of being sucked into a new transnational empire or being technologically dependent upon the USA or Japan are greater, for some smaller countries, than the threat of impending 'Third World' status. Nevertheless, for better or for worse, the arrival of the information society is felt to be imminent.

Are we at the threshold of a new kind of society? Discussions of the 'wired society' or of the 'wealth of information' certainly imply this.[4] Alvin Toffler's well-known 'third wave' concept is perhaps the clearest example.[5] The first 'wave' is agricultural, the second industrial, and the third, information society. Sociological debate has not yet crystallized around this single concept – the information society – but it is in sufficiently popular and social scientific use to make it the focus of this study. It finds a ready home in accounts of the 'social impact of new technology', is frequently referred to in policy studies, and is strongly related to other emerging concepts such as that of the 'information worker'. But should it be used as a basic means of characterizing 'society' today? That is what this book is about.

Despite appearances, the idea of the information society is not entirely new. It has its roots in the literature of 'postindustrialism', a popular social science notion of the 1960s and 1970s which heralded the end of the industrial capitalist era and the arrival of a 'service' or 'leisure' society. Although postindustrialism has been subject to damaging criticism, its resilience is shown by the fact that it can be re-cycled as 'the information society'. This chapter starts by asking what the two concepts have in common, but also the points at which the information society goes beyond postindustrialism. There is more than 'recycling' here. I also set the scene for subsequent chapters by proposing which analytical avenues are worth following, and what pitfalls must be avoided.

From postindustrialism to information society

The roots of the information society idea are intertwined in a complex manner. It is hard to disentangle the diverse strands of attempted social prediction, government policy, futuristic speculation and empirical social analysis. For instance, a Canadian government report, *Planning Now for the Information Society*[6] is clearly geared to identifying a national technology strategy in microelectronics. But it depends upon social scientific concepts such as the 'information economy', indulges briefly in quoted 'predictions' (for instance that by the year 2000 'smart' highways for semi-automated driving will enter development), and refers to empirical studies of the impact of microelectronics on, among other things, women's work.

One readily identifiable strand, on which hopeful accounts of information society often rely, is the idea of postindustrialism, especially the version associated with Daniel Bell. This is the view that, just as agrarian was replaced by industrial society as the dominant economic emphasis shifted from the land to manufacturing, so postindustrial society develops as a result of the economic tilt towards the provision of services. The increased part played by science in the productive process, the rise to prominence of professional, scientific and technical groups, plus the introduction of what is now called information technology, all bear witness to a new 'axial principle' at the core of the economy and society. This axial principle, 'the energising principle that is the logic for all the others', is the centrality of 'theoretical knowledge'.[7]

Bell argues that the information society is developing in the context of postindustrialism. He forecasts the growth of a new social framework based on telecommunications which 'may be decisive for the way economic and social exchanges are conducted, the way knowledge is created and retrieved, and the character of work and occupations in which men [sic] are engaged'. The computer plays a pivotal role in this 'revolution'.[8]

Bell also sketches other significant features of the information society. IT, by shortening labour time and diminishing the production worker, actually replaces labour as the source of 'added value' in the national product. Knowledge and information supplant labour and capital as the 'central variables' of the economy. He comments on the way that information is being treated as a commodity, with a price-tag on it, and how the 'possession' of information increasingly confers power on its owner. Unlike some postindustrialists, Bell recognizes some of the ambiguities involved in identifying a 'service sector' and proposes that economic sectors be divided into 'extractive, fabrication and information activities'. This way, he claims, one may monitor the penetration of information activities into more traditional areas of agriculture, manufacturing and services.

Bell underlines ways in which these areas are expanding in the wake of IT development. He foresees major social changes resulting from the establishment of new telecommunications infrastructures. Such huge changes will occur as 'the merging technologies of telephone, computer, facsimile, cable television and video discs lead to a vast reorganization in the modes of communication between persons; the transmission of data;

the reduction if not the elimination of paper in transactions and exchanges; new modes of transmitting news, entertainment and knowledge[9] and so on. These in turn will intensify concern about population distribution, national planning, centralization, privacy and so on. For Bell, the 'fateful question', or, one might say, the consumerist question, is whether the promise will be realized that 'instrumental technology' will open 'the way to alternative modes of achieving individuality and variety within a vastly increased output of goods'.[10]

Without doubt, Bell asks many of the right questions, and indicates worthwhile lines of inquiry. This is why his work deserves to be taken seriously. But it also demands serious critique because, as I shall show, Bell's attempt to find a thoroughgoing alternative to Marxian class analysis underestimates both the resilience of some familiar features of modern societies, and the extent to which new conflicts and struggles could arise within this 'information society'.

Those 'familiar features' include military, commercial and government power. No small significance lies in the fact that it was military requirements which gave birth to modern computers. The massive mainframe, ENIAC, built in 1946 in the electrical engineering department of the University of Pennsylvania, was intended to assist the aiming of guns, and was soon involved in calculations for the atomic bomb. Neither is it irrelevant to note that huge forces of international capitalist commerce are today locked in mortal combat to capture markets and conquer opposition within the lucrative high technology field. Nor is it an accident that governments are so active in promoting IT and purchasing its products. IT is a powerful tool for monitoring and supervising people's activities. In other words, one does not have to look far before this question comes to mind: Does IT bring about a new society without precedent, or does it rather help to intensify certain processes in today's society of which we are all too aware?

What of 'new conflicts and struggles'? Are we entering an era, not of Bell's rather smoothly harmonious information society, but of new social frictions and power alignments within a divided and contradictory 'information society'? Around the same time as Bell's work on post-industrialism a European contribution appeared which took account of the same social and economic trends: Alain Touraine's *La Société post-industrielle*.[11]

Touraine's study took a quite different tack from Bell's. He challenged the bland postindustrial assumption that class struggle was a thing of the past, although he argued that many class images are too bound up with the 'era of capitalist industrialisation'. He invited readers to consider the 'fundamental importance of class situations conflicts and movements in the programmed society'. In particular he had in mind a major cleavage between technocrats and a more disparate grouping whose livelihood and lifestyles are governed by them. Property ownership is less a bone of contention than the opposition brought about because 'the dominant classes dispose of knowledge and control information'.[12]

So do changing technologies and shifts in educational qualification and skill lead to novel class alignments? This issue is tackled in chapter 3. But this question still concentrates upon the workplace and on production. The analyses of Touraine and others hint at wider movements of power. The use of IT within governments, education, the media and the domestic sphere as well as in the workplace means that more and more social relationships are mediated by machines. What does this imply for power? Mark Poster suggests that because 'new forms of social interaction based on electronic communications devices are replacing older types of social relations',[13] we should speak of a new 'mode of information'. He too is questioning the relevance today of some Marxian assumptions but for very different reasons from Daniel Bell's.

Social forecasters and social planners

The roots of the information society idea are found not only in sociology. Futurists and 'social impact of technology' commentators also contribute. They tend to share the belief that technology 'shapes' social relationships. One of the many cheerful social forecasts comes from Tom Stonier. 'Living in a postindustrial world', he avers, 'means that not only are we more affluent, more resourceful and less likely to go to war, but also more likely to democratise'.[14] Increasing prosperity is a common information society theme. By 'more resourceful', Stonier means that IT will enable us to overcome the environmental and ecological problems associated with industrialism. Again he touches on a common theme. James Martin, in *The Wired Society*, also stresses the 'non-polluting, non-destructive' quality of IT as a major point in its favour.[15]

New communications technologies hold out the next promise – the demise of war ('as slavery disappeared in the industrial era', says Stonier[16]). Some even hold this out as a 'stage' beyond information society:

'communication society'.[17] Lastly, IT ushers in the world of computer democracy. More information availability, plus push-button referenda, open the door for the first time to genuinely responsive participatory government. This, along with the burden of administration being thoroughly automated, is the contented futurist's world of information society.

A short step away from the futurist's vision is the forecaster's proposal. Japan was the first country to produce such a proposal, in the shape of *The plan for information society: a national goal toward the year 2000*.[18] Lacking natural energy resources, the Japanese were acutely aware of the fragility of their economy in the face of recession. Yoneji Masuda's work, *The information society as postindustrial society*[19] played a significant part in establishing a 'national plan'. He gives the idea of 'computopia' concrete shape, connecting futurist dreams – 'the goal . . . is a society that brings about a general flourishing state of human intellectual creativity, instead of affluent material consumption'[20] – with actual 'new towns' in Japan and 'information society infrastructures' elsewhere.

Japan's Tama New Town, with its built-in network of co-axial cables, Canada's *Telidon* (videotex) programme, and Sweden's *Terese* project, which monitors regional development using new telecommunications, are cited as relevant examples of such infrastructures. They are significant to Masuda as portending 'a new type of human society' in the information society. For him, 'production of information values and not material values will become the driving force'. At the same time, past experiences within industrial society may be used as an 'historical analogical model of future society'.[21]

This assumption, that the history of industrial society may be used as an analogy for what will happen in information society, brings us back to the core of the sociological question. Is it legitimate to claim that the steam engine (or more properly the clock) was to industrial society what the computer is to information society, so that one, the new technology shapes the resulting social and political relations, and two, a qualitatively different kind of society emerges?

Within the same sociological question lies the problem of exactly what are the social origins and social consequences of the diffusion of information technologies. Though their immediate genesis is important, the roots of the so-called information society are more properly sought in what James Beniger calls the 'control revolution', analysed at the turn of the century by theorists of bureaucracy such as Max Weber.[22] Putting new technologies in a longer historical context helps us understand non-technical aspects of their origins and relativizes claims that technologies themselves cause change.

On the other hand, even if one remains sceptical about the capacity of silicon chips and fibre optics to transform the world in quite the way envisaged by a Stonier or a Masuda, it is clear that IT is a major phenomenon with a broad potential social impact. It is a 'heartland' technology, one which enables the development of many others, more and more cheaply, and using components of shrinking size and expanding power.[23]

Critical comments about futurism and social forecasting should not be understood as a denial either that some view of the 'good society' ought to be connected with the social analysis of new technology, or that attempts to discern the direction of social-technological trends are worthwhile. On the contrary. The problem is rather the lack of realism, the items missing from accounts of the information society. Eyes focused on the tremendous technological potential of IT frequently fail to see that countervailing processes – loss of skills, privacy or personal contact, for instance – unceremoniously puncture confident predictions.

In other words, social factors of several different kinds tend to be neglected. The nature of Japanese post-war reconstruction, and its reliance upon the experience of other advanced societies, has guided the direction of IT development there. In Britain, the 'Alvey' programme of IT research, weighted in favour of commerce rather than the universities, has served to give a distinct flavour to the sorts of work carried out. And so on. In fact, the further one moves from grand national IT plans and from futuristic forecasts of conditions prevailing within the 'informatizing' society, and the nearer one gets to actual social analysis in which technology is not perceived as a quasi-autonomous force acting upon society, the more questionable the information society concept appears.

The information society as problematic

So what are the prospects for the information society concept? The answer is not straightforward. For one thing, more than one image of the information society is available. The popular image of a social transformation along 'Third Wave' lines is not the same as the fuzzier image produced within more careful social analysis of societies coming to terms with a range of more and less profound political, economic and cultural effects of information technology. In his 'information society' essay Daniel Bell himself has become silent about the affluence and leisure he once associated with postindustrialism. Another complicating factor is that both popular and serious versions of the information society thesis either rely upon or provoke genuine questions of tremendous importance.

The idea of an information society is more than recycled postindustrialism. To be sure, the two concepts do share a number of common features, not to mention several common flaws. Popular versions of information society forecasting, often giddy with the astonishing progress of microelectronics since the late 1970s, are infused with the same technological determinism that informed much postindustrialism. While strong currents of critical social investigation cause some ripples, much present-day research focuses on social *adaptation to* IT, rather than how IT may be designed to suit people, which betrays the extent to which technologically determinist views have been accepted.

This book is an assessment of various images of the information society. Although the sharpest critique is reserved for the overblown promotional versions that masquerade as serious social analysis or that sometimes influence policy, a number of more serious sociological and economic claims are also criticized. Several chapters start by outlining important features of one or another aspect of the information society idea which are then sifted in order to retain what *is* significant or contrasted with alternative interpretations.

I choose this method because I see little point in summarily discarding the information society as the rotten fruit of futurist fancy or as ideology in the guise of social analysis. Rather, the information society should be granted the status of 'problematic'. According to Philip Abrams, a problematic is a 'rudimentary organization of a field of phenomena which yields problems for investigation'.[24] Without succumbing to the sociological simplism which sees the information society as a 'Third Wave' of evolutionary progress, it is nevertheless true to say that some of the most significant changes in late twentieth-century society are those inherent in, related to, or consequent upon IT. The information society concept points to that cluster of issues and its better exponents already use it in this sense.

As a problematic its components refer to changes in the workplace and employment and also the political, cultural and global aspects of the diffusion of IT. Whether the sum of these changes amounts to a shift beyond industrial capitalism, militarism or male dominance is highly questionable. Important continuities, such as the chronic persistence of inequalities and the growth of state power using IT, seem to suggest that changes may be more of degree than kind. In important respects many supposed changes highlighted by information society theorists originated well before information technology!

At the same time the category of information is undoubtedly becoming vitally important as an economic factor in its own right. The phenomenon of insider dealing on international stock markets is an obvious illustration. While it may not be supplanting property as a key to the social structure of modern societies, information is proving to be a crucially important element in our understanding of social relationships. Certainly at present it lacks adequate definition, let alone incorporation within a coherent theory of contemporary social change. Yet the new technologies which handle and process information simultaneously influence diverse but significant aspects of social, cultural and political reality.

Let me note two other features of the information society problematic. One is that social analysis must grapple with the ramifications of the *fusion* of technologies which comprise IT. Conventional distinctions between communication and media studies, on the one hand, and studies of the social aspects of computing, on the other, are eroded. For example, implications of the decline in public service broadcasting now extend far beyond traditional concerns for broadcasting as such. In the USA, the dissemination of government data, once a public function, is under increasing pressure as private profit-seeking firms compete to sell repackaged data. Burgeoning communication between computers and the coming of the commercial database brings 'public service' questions into the heartland of computing.

The other noteworthy feature is that as social analysis exposes alternative options in the adoption of new technology that are in fact available to government, industry and the public, discussions of the strategy for shaping new technologies become more relevant. Do government-sponsored slogans such as 'automate or liquidate' represent genuine choices? Is it 'data' or 'persons' that ought to be protected by law? How does one decide what counts as an appropriate technology where microelectronics is concerned? Social analysis can serve to indicate the conditions under which ethical considerations and social hopes might be realized.

Information society: the major themes

The information society concept inherits several symptoms of the troubles that beset postindustrialism. The postindustrialists largely failed to justify the significance granted to trends such as the growth of theoretical knowledge and of services. A leisured society based on automated manufacture, a vast array of services and a culture of self-expression, political participation and an emphasis on the quality of life does not seem to have materialized – at least, not for the majority of the populations of the advanced societies.

Will this hereditary syndrome prove fatal for the information society? The answer depends upon careful investigation in the following areas.

Information workers in an information economy

It is clear from job advertisements at least that in the late 1980s one's chances of obtaining employment are enhanced by the possession of qualifications in microelectronics, computing, systems analysis, tele-communications, operational research, software design, fibre optics, expert systems and so on. But what does this proliferation of new job descriptions mean? Those that Tom Stonier refers to as 'information operatives' seem to appear in all manner of workplaces. The big questions are: who are these 'operatives', and what contribution do their activities make to the pattern of social relationship?

Central to much information society discourse is the contention that 'information workers' are rising to a majority within the labour forces of the advanced societies. As early as 1967, claims Marc Porat, 50 per cent of American workers were engaged in the 'information sector', and they received just over 50 per cent of total employee remuneration. But just who are these information workers? Unfortunately, because he does not actually explain what 'information' is (he only defines it as 'data that have been organized and communicated') the categories are blurred. Judges and rent-collectors find themselves in this sector, but doctors, for instance, have an 'ambiguous occupation', straddling 'service' and 'information' sectors.[25]

Few studies of 'information work' comment on its purpose, function, or content. Without this, however, we cannot know who makes decisions, on what basis, or with what effect. Masses of computer-generated information confers no power whatsoever on those who use it, whereas at certain points within organizations it may be crucial to the maintenance of power. As it happens, postindustrialism also glossed over questions of information, knowledge and power, especially with regard to the social significance of research and development (R&D). The sheer amount of R&D in any given society tells us little. We learn nothing about the social role of scientific and technical knowledge, the price put on it, and the power of those who manipulate it. The fact that R&D is often financed for political rather than social reasons, and developed for military rather than economic purposes, pulls the rug from beneath the (Bell-inspired) idea that universities are crucibles of power in the modern world.[26] The current squeeze on university funding and the politicizing of technology policy makes the idea laughable.

That said, changes are occurring in the occupational structure of the advanced societies. While the relabelling process noted in Krishan Kumar's critique of postindustrialism still occurs – though today it is programmers becoming software architects rather than plumbers becoming heating engineers – there is expansion at managerial, professional and technical levels. There is, moreover, a strong link between innovation and economic growth; hence the frequently expressed British worries about the lack of domestic R&D funding relative to other countries.

Two major questions are raised by the 'discovery' of information work and an information sector in the economy. First, are the apparently new categories of work and occupation leading to shifts in power? Is there an emerging information 'technocracy' which is wresting power from previously dominant classes? What opportunities for women are opened by the spread of IT? What is the likely effect of IT on industrial relations? When British Rail computerized its freight system, for instance, many 'middle managers' found their positions were simply redundant, and personnel in subordinate positions actually discovered they had new powers of control over the work process.[27]

The other question is this: how accurate is the idea of an 'information sector', and is there an historical 'march through the sectors'[28] as agrarianism gives way to industrialism, and industrialism to information society? This point affects not only the advanced societies but also those to which the promise is alluringly held out that they may be able to jump straight from a non-industrial to an information society. Is this really possible, or does 'informatizing' depend upon an already 'advanced' situation?

These questions are discussed mainly in chapters 3 and 4.

Political and global aspects

Echoes of postindustrialism are again heard with respect to the political and global aspects of information society. A common feature of each is that opportunities for political choice and participation will increase. The difference, however, is that the means of implementing these is now visible, particularly in the possibilities of two-way, interactive electronic networks. The extreme case is that of an 'instant referendum' in which voters' views are canvassed via cable television which allows people to receive as well as transmit signals from their living rooms. More soberly, IT is seen as a means of enabling an electorate to be more informed, or for decision-making to be more decentralized.[29]

Those committed to ideals of democratic participation on both the right and the left of the political spectrum may advocate the harnessing of new technologies to such ends. Without adequate access to modern means of communication, any idea of a just political community is indeed a chimera. But a number of important questions are raised by this, not least how the necessary telecommunications infrastructure is to be set up. While France is establishing a national *télématique* system which could in principle serve such ends, Britain has experienced some difficulties persuading domestic subscribers to pay for a suitable cable television network, whereas in the USA only local experimental systems have been tried. In the absence of a coherent policy which is intended to ensure equal access of all to such a communications network it is difficult to imagine how dreams of electronic democracy could be translated into realities.

The prominent source of anxiety, however, is the threat of an Orwellian society. Does the widespread political and administrative use of extensive databases which allow for the easy storage, retrieval and transmission of personal information portend a future fraught with the dangers of electronic eavesdropping? On the one hand police, defence, social security and other personnel reassure the public that no innocent person need have any worries about improper prying into their private lives. On the other, cases of wrongful dismissal or arrest which are traced to erroneous computer files serve to fuel fears that in fact 'ordinary citizens' may well be at risk.

But are these computerized forms of surveillance an intrinsically new departure? Or do they rather represent an extension of state garnering of information on citizens which has been occurring for many decades? Is it merely the use of these databases by law-and-order agencies which creates potential perils for citizens? Or is a deeper process at work in which more generalized forces of social control achieve more power by computerization? And what exactly are the risks involved, against which 'data protection' laws and policies are directed? Is wrongful arrest the tip of an iceberg, the submerged portion of which conceals a fundamental issue of invaded privacy and impugned integrity?

This of course, is only one aspect of the state-and-IT connection. As I have already mentioned, the connections between government activity and economic-technological developments are numerous and significant. Whereas postindustrialist Bell insisted upon the relatively independent operation of economic and political spheres, this position is exceedingly hard to justify. It is quite clear that polity and economy are interdependent, and that the relationship between the two is far from simple.

Bringing the global situation into focus, however, other connections between the political and the economic become clear. The IT industry, as others, is dominated by giant transnational corporations – IBM, Exxon, Mitsubishi, AT&T, Philips, Siemens and so on – which often call the political tune. Many countries find their national sovereignty, not to mention the position of their workers, threatened by the activities of these 'stateless' economic interests. Such companies increasingly rely upon the free flow of data across national boundaries for financial reporting and management, marketing, distribution, R&D, and order processing.

Labour unions may debate the future of plants in vain if the crucial decisions are made on another continent. National governments may find their attempts to change direction thwarted, as when in 1985 Australian prime minister Bob Hawke tried to stop Australian bases being used to monitor MX missile tests. Dismayed financial and transnational corporate interests withdrew capital, putting pressure on the economy and thus the government.[30] It would appear that Walter Wriston (who seems not to treat this as a matter for regret) is right to claim that 'the ancient and basic concept of sovereignty which has been discussed since the time of Plato is being profoundly changed by information technology'.[31]

Of course it is not only the national sovereignty of the larger and more powerful countries which is challenged by the power of transnational corporations. The phenomenon of 'deindustrialization', for example, often viewed in the northern hemisphere in terms of the shrinking proportion of the labour force involved in manufacturing, may be equally well understood as the partial relocation of workers to 'offshore' plants in the south. The information society is not inaccurately depicted as a global phenomenon. The current expansion and development of microelectronics-related industries require a world market.

There is no doubt that the technological potential for beneficial change – 'deserts that bloom' – is tremendous, and nothing in this book should be taken as denying or minimizing that fact. Tom Stonier, Alvin Toffler and Jacques Servan-Schrieber make a lot of this angle. Stonier reports great gains made in the Upper Volta village of Tangaye when a solar photovoltaic-powered grain mill and water pump were installed.[32] (This is an example of what he calls the 'second silicon revolution'.) Such advances, he states correctly, are dependent on technology and information transfer. That such changes will take place and that 'the postindustrial economy will produce the wealth of information to make it all happen' is rather more open to question.

At present, as a matter of fact, things are somewhat different. Despite dreams of poorer countries 'catching up' with richer ones, or 'leapfrogging' the industrial era, the situation is overwhelmingly not just one of interdependence, but of dependence. While the advanced societies produce silicon chips comprising hundreds of thousands of elements, in Africa only one person in eighteen has a radio. Far from narrowing the 'North-South' divide, the evidence suggests that IT helps to widen it. As Juan Rada sagely observes, 'Technological fixes of whatever nature are nothing but a drop of water in the sea of reality'.[33]

No treatment of the political and global aspects of IT can afford to ignore the connections between new technology and the continuing Cold War. Like earlier postindustrialists, Stonier's focus is on the 'wealth of information' that spells 'unprecedented affluence both at the private level and in the public sector'.[34] But as Krishan Kumar laconically notes, 'the science-based "welfare" state can be rapidly reclassified as the science-based "warfare" state, and with greater respect for the actual history of the last fifty years'.[35]

For example, the Japanese 'Fifth Generation' computer project, which aims to introduce the world to ordinary language-recognizing 'artificial intelligence' during the 1990s, is ostensibly civil and commercial. But American responses relate to military supremacy. As Feigenbaum and McCorduck put it, 'the Defense Department needs the ability to shape technology to conform to its needs in military systems. A Fujitsu or a Hitachi marches to a different drummer from a Rockwell or a Lockheed. Our defense industry must obtain and retain a strong position in the new advanced computer technologies'.[36] It goes without saying that these are not the kinds of 'needs' which those concerned for a 'welfare state' – or world welfare – have in mind.

An information culture?

The notion of a 'fifth generation' of computers raises another set of questions besides those of military prowess. Unlike previous technological artifacts which typically have augmented human energy with improved sources of power, those spawned by IT augment – and, according to some, transcend – the human capacity to think and to reason. Needless to say, some references to machine intelligence are no more sophisticated than those associated with Hal, the 'thinking' computer from the film *2001, A Space Odyssey*. Others, however, are pointers to a series of profound cultural issues whose analysis could have far-reaching implications.

It must be said, though, that while debate over the workplace and employment aspects of IT is widespread, and awareness of the political and global dimensions is beginning to make itself felt, the cultural questions have not as yet received the attention they deserve. In what follows, therefore, I can do no more than set the scene.

Once again, Bell's thoughts on postindustrial culture make a suitable starting point. For him, 'a new kind of modernity' has been created by the 'revolutions in transportation and communication that have banded together the world society into one great *Oikoumene*'. It represents a break with the past, thus replacing continuity with variety, tradition with syncretism. Its agent is technology, which by 'introducing a new metric and enlarging our control over nature' has 'transformed our social relationships and our ways of looking at the world'.[37]

Bell maintains that technology has been the 'chief engine' of raised living standards and reduced inequalities, created a 'new class' of engineers and technicians who plan work-tasks rather than actually performing them, brought about a new functional and quantitative way of thinking, created 'new economic dependencies and new social interactions', and altered aesthetic perceptions of time and space. While he believes that cultural issues are of the utmost importance, he partially disconnects analysis of them from political or social life. Each sphere has a different 'axial principle'; that of contemporary culture being the desire for fulfilment and enhancement of the self.[38]

Of course, when writing of postindustrialism (in the 1960s) Bell could have had little clear idea of the rapidity with which the technologies of computing and telecommunications would move to centre stage (hence his later work on the information society). But other theorists have taken further these kinds of ideas about the relation of IT to culture. Where Bell limited himself to comments about concepts of 'speed' or the 'view from the air' unknown to pre-moderns, writers such as David Bolter have argued that the computer itself is the harbinger of novel cultural transformations including a new human sense of self.[39]

Bolter's argument is as follows. Just as the clock is the key symbol of the industrial era, as Lewis Mumford rightly held, so the computer is becoming the key symbol of the present. It is a 'defining technology' which by its impact on certain basic relationships – of knowledge to technical power, and mankind to the world of nature – occupies 'a special place in our cultural landscape'.[40] Thus humans begin to think of themselves as 'information processors' and nature as 'information to be processed'.[41]

Sceptical eyebrows may well be raised about such speculations. Are not those who define themselves as information processors likely to be only a tiny minority of a given population? By what process does the computer become a defining technology? Bolter's thesis is well worth attending to, though not, I shall argue, for the reasons he gives.

Three issues concerning the 'culture of information' are addressed in this book, mainly in the later chapters. First, I draw together questions about computing and telecommunications; the fact of technological 'convergence' is a significant one. While Bell's idea of the 'overflowing of all the world's traditions of art, music and literature into a new, universal container, accessible to all and obligatory upon all'[42] is somewhat inflated, it does flag an important phenomenon. A form of cultural 'synchronization' is indeed taking place, as new communications carrying essentially similar messages encircle the globe.[43] Who controls these messages, and what is their content? Does the ownership of the means of (increasingly computerized) communication lead to the cultural dominance of certain elite groups and societies over others?

Secondly, is the 'defining technology' idea an appropriate means of social and cultural analysis? Are the emerging technologies of information and communication indeed shaping the social and cultural experience of those societies affected by them? Do the new technologies not confer on those with access to them considerable power to control not only the processes of production, about which Marx was concerned, but also those of leisure and consumption? Is there more than passing significance in the rise of 'hackers' and computer gamesters, who get totally absorbed in their machines, or in the ways that computers may 'converse' with each other about human destinies (I am thinking of credit-worthiness or welfare-eligibility)?[44]

Thirdly, consideration of the so-called culture of information is incomplete without reference to its religious and ideological aspects. Do human beings remake themselves in the image of their technology? If so, then there are obvious implications for philosophical debates about the unique place of human beings in the cosmos. Furthermore, there is scope for critique along 'religious' lines, as evidenced by the denunciation of IT as 'silicon idolatry'.[45] It also brings us back, finally, to the over-riding question of this study: does IT usher us into a new kind of society? And at this point a further query is highlighted: what is the social *meaning* of the 'information society'? Is it better understood as a kind of 'myth' or 'utopia' than the social 'forecast' it is more frequently taken to be?

Critique of the information society

For the sake of clarity, and oversimplifying, let me make some distinctions. There are two kinds of information society thesis, each of which makes two kinds of claims. The view popularized in many media and policy accounts stresses the major social changes for the better that follow in the wake of IT. This popular version may well be buttressed by the 'findings of social science'. The other use of the information society concept is more cautious and open-ended. Here it is a 'problematic' rather than a descriptive term. The two images of information society overlap.

The claims made are both analytical and evaluative, and the two kinds of claim are interrelated. Thus both kinds of information society thesis try to anticipate the *sorts of social change* which can be expected as IT is diffused through different economic, political and cultural spheres. And both also provide at least strong clues as to whether such social changes are *desirable*. This book draws together evidence from a wide range of sources in an attempt to assess both the analytical and evaluative claims of each information society thesis.

The information society idea has both utopian and ideological aspects. I discuss these in the final chapter, but to put things in focus I comment on some of the dangers associated with using the information society concept, that is, its ideological aspects. Three are prominent.

Firstly, it obscures vested interests that are involved in IT and that in fact do much to shape its overall direction. The concept yields no clues as to who wields power. Repeatedly, for instance, the popular rhetoric assures us that 'everyone can own information' or 'the real revolution is personal computer ownership'. But information is not steadily diffused in a general way through all social echelons. As Cees Hamelink points out, some information is specialist and thus restricted to a few.[46] Intellectual and managerial skills are required to exploit information economically, and these are unevenly distributed in society. Advanced hardware and software for information processing are expensive, and therefore the few who can afford them are scarcely challenged by others using inferior machines.

Such inequalities are felt globally between north and south in the theatre of transnational corporations and military interests, and locally, whether with the word-processor operator's lack of control over her work or the suspected criminal's difficulty in gaining access to information held about him. 'Information power' is only a reality when access exists to the means of collecting, storing, retrieving and communicating the information.

Secondly, the inequalities and conflicts discernible on the surface are often related to underlying contradictions. These too may be disguised by the information society concept. Within capitalism, private gain is constantly set against efforts to 'socialize' production. In the late twentieth century, the latent potential for trade in information – for this entity to become a commodity – is being realized. While many undoubtedly gain from this process, others lose. Public libraries and public service broadcasting are both time-honoured concepts whose 'public' status is under threat as information has a price put on it. Likewise, new integrated services digital networks (ISDNs) mean more efficient information services, but higher costs for ordinary telephone subscribers.

Another discordant element, which may not qualify as a 'contradiction' in the same sense, is the collusion of military with microelectronic interests in the modern world. The same technologies whose avowed purposes (and actual achievement in many cases) are to reduce drudgery, increase efficiency, conserve resources and promote mutual communication are also dedicated to hostile, destructive and lethal ends. Regardless of any justifications which may legitimately be presented for expanding electronically a nation's 'defence' capabilities, most discussions of the information society conceal in the background the huge military impetus to IT research and development.

Thirdly, the arrival of the information society appears as an entirely natural event, the outcome of progressive tendencies within Western industrial societies. It may be 'revolutionary' in its consequences, such that it represents a new era in human history. But it is simultaneously the obvious and logical way forward. Witness the postures struck against any who dare question the ways in which IT is implemented! The chairman of the British Manpower Services Commission provided a clear illustration in a 1986 speech which recommended 'embracing wholeheartedly the new technologies'. He complained that 'We still have latter-day Luddites around in all parts of our society. They threaten our future, and the attitudes they reflect must go'.[47]

Very extravagant claims are often made for IT - 'Athens without the slaves' and so on - which suggest that the aura surrounding new technology is not merely that of the 'gee-whiz' variety. Perhaps, as Jacques Ellul and others have suggested,[48] new technologies are invested with a 'sacred' quality. The awe and veneration once accorded to the gods who supposedly controlled human destinies now belong to the machine. This dimension - which Michael Shallis refers to as 'silicon idolatry' - would tend to reinforce views of the information society as the obvious scenario.

Against the backdrop of the well-established Western belief in social progress via unlimited economic accumulation, the information society does indeed appear as a natural development. Information technology is its sacred guarantor. But granting it this 'natural' status forecloses debate over and action towards any alternatives to that dominant tendency. As such, it invites critique.

By arguing that the information society has significant ideological aspects I do not for a moment want to suggest that it is some kind of 'dominant ideology', accepted by the 'masses' of any given population.[49] On the contrary, there is plenty of evidence of coolness, fear and resignation towards, as well as sober and realistic acceptance of, the new technologies. Likewise it should be stressed that using the term 'ideological' does not mean that there is a deliberate conspiracy to 'deceive the general public' by using the information society slogan. If the above analysis is correct, however, the *effect* of using it is to disguise the reality of powerful interests and beliefs at work within it.

On the other hand, it is clear that notions like the information society have become a working 'reality' for many. Educational institutions meekly fall in line with pleas for closer ties with industry. Businesses do computerize, some most successfully, some soon discovering they are encumbered with digital white elephants. As Jennifer Slack admits, 'We are buying computers to have fun and to "keep up". And our children who do not learn to operate computers are "falling behind". And information is being developed to be bought and sold and protected like any other kind of commodity. And it *does* make a certain amount of "good sense" to try to "get by" in that world.'[50] The point is not to deny that it is happening, but rather to examine how it is orchestrated and by whom, to what purpose, and with what methods and effects.

Beyond liberal and Luddite critique

Just as there are different images of the information society, so critique comes from different angles. What might be called 'liberal' critiques, while refusing to be seduced by the siren songs of high-tech hype, still assume that 'things could go either way'. They issue warnings about the anti-social potential of some IT applications, but maintain that as long as people are alert to them, effective choices can be made to ensure that IT development will be appropriate and socially beneficial. For them, the information society is the outcome of an informed democratic process.

The Luddite would retort quickly that the liberal seems to have swallowed the idea of technological neutrality. The new technologies already express particular values and priorities. Far from choices being relatively free, they are in fact tightly constrained by dominant interest groups, above all by the power of capital. As for being 'informed', this is a sick joke. By insisting on the neutrality of technology, those dominant interests ensure that its 'real' effects and biases are effectively obscured. Thus the exposure of those dominant interests is of prime importance, before any choices can be made.

In so far as it stresses the importance of choice, and therefore of value, priorities and democratic participation, the liberal critique makes a valid contribution. Such an emphasis is a vital antidote to any technological determinism that forecasts that future society will be shaped by new technologies or that ignores social factors in technical change. On the other hand, the Luddite is correct to temper this by drawing attention to the ways in which choice is limited, often severely and systematically, by social, political and economic definition. But the negative image of Luddism is hard to live down. Luddism can be as pessimistic as the popular information society pundits are optimistic.[51] Their future may be similarly foreclosed.

The kind of critique to which this book aspires catches both the sense of potential for socially appropriate development of IT without pretending that it can occur without considerable struggle on several fronts, and the sober realism of the Luddite, without succumbing to sheer negativism or pessimism. I do not hide the fact that some alternatives with which I have sympathy – such as partnership between women and men from the design stage onwards, or innovations originating from users' needs rather than mere commercial potential – represents a radical departure from present practice. By placing them in the context of a normative and critical social analysis, however, I hope to show both the enormity of the obstacles to be overcome, and possible routes to their realization.

The yawning credibility gap between futuristic forecasts and fantasies and the hard realities of government, transnational and military involvement in IT demands a sense of urgency within the information society problematic. It also points up a vital role for serious social analysis within the policy-making process, analysis which is not simply shut up within either optimistic or pessimistic scenarios.

2

A marriage of convergence?
The shaping of IT

> The age of information technology – IT as we call it here – has arrived. I know of no other technological advantage which has brought together so many areas of rapid and exciting development. Computers and telecommunications are converging very rapidly, huge investments are being made, and the impact of information technology will be felt at every level in our society; in industry, in commerce, in our offices and in our homes.
>
> *Kenneth Baker (1982)*[1]

There is little doubt that the spread of computers and new communications systems is one of the most striking phenomena within the advanced societies of the late twentieth century. Few can fail to be aware of the proliferation of 'plastic money' in the form of credit cards, the number of computerized letters and bills which fall into our mailboxes, the arrival of computer-controlled machines in the workplace, the cellular telephones in cars and the promise of endless new forms of entertainment via video, cable television and direct satellite broadcasting. Each is an aspect of a marriage between computers and telecommunications hailed as an epoch-making technological convergence.

The quotation at the head of this chapter, a statement enthusiastically made by Britain's then minister for information technology, makes a good place to begin. The aim of this chapter is to tease out several popular assumptions embodied within it. Few would deny that 'technological advance' is seen in the 'convergence' of computing and telecommunications known as 'information technology'. The ideas that, firstly, this convergence spells the start of the 'age of information technology', and that, secondly, everyone would consider them 'exciting' are more questionable. But it is the implicit assumption that the relation between technology and society is best seen as technology's 'impact' on society to which I wish to draw particular attention.

The marriage: spontaneous or arranged?

At its simplest, the convergence of information technologies is explained (in an American context) by B. O. Evans: 'The merger of communications and computers was brought about because the demand for computing power quickly outpaced the productivity of computer installations, since operational procedures became inefficient'.[2] Data, or questions about data, used once to disappear for days on end into the computer room, while the operator (who alone could punch the cards) produced the desired results. The advantage of being able directly to communicate with the machine (made possible by the key-driven terminal) is obvious. Evans goes on to say that this marriage is a 'natural union' because of the common technical history of the partners.

That common history lies in solid state physics and electromagnetism, in switching theory and in stored program control. Evans quickly jumps from these to the 'applications' fields like data-entry (used for insurance claims or travel bookings for example), point-of-sale funds transfer (at filling stations, supermarkets and so on), automatic bank tellers and production control. He suggests that the growth of demand for computer applications led to the quests for new modes of transmission, given that the old telephone networks were really intended for voice rather than data. Hence the proliferation of data-lines, cable television, fibre optics and communications satellites. The enhancement of these leads in turn to further applications in business, education, medical diagnosis, administration, energy management, home shopping, and so on.

So what is 'new' and 'revolutionary'? Telephones have been with us for a hundred years, pulse-code modulation was invented in 1936, and digital computers have been around since the 1950s. Another ingredient was required to launch the 'IT revolution', namely microelectronics, with its common currency of digital operations. Plummeting costs and shrinking size of components – using the silicon chip – are, technically, behind the convergence. Or, in the romantic analogy of our title, microelectronics plays the part of Cupid.

This then is the 'techno-logic' of convergence. It makes sense, and the factors mentioned are all part of the IT story. The steps towards 'marriage' are vital, the applications are indeed appearing. They in turn stimulate the search for other forms of convergence and make their contribution to social change. But what is missing from such accounts? They give the impression that new technology is 'outside' society, impinging upon it, that the marriage is an entirely spontaneous technical affair which gives birth to an 'information society'. The missing factors are those which give the technologies their chance, and which contribute in different ways to their development.

Social impacts; social shaping

While it is already clear that the social impacts of IT are profound, though not necessarily for the reasons given by the more visionary technologists, to focus only on the 'impacts' is to take the new technologies and their 'convergence' as given. This neglects the equally important question of the *origins* of the technologies, and the non-technical reasons why they have converged. If the aim is to understand IT (in a social rather than merely technical sense) then it is crucial to distance analysis from that perspective which limits itself to 'social impacts'. There are at least three reasons for this.

Firstly, the social impacts are themselves poorly understood if no account is taken of the origins of new technologies. To take the most extreme example, several information society pundits anticipate that IT will reduce the likelihood of a global nuclear catastrophe. It is difficult, to say the least, to square this with the palpable fact that military and defence-oriented requirements and funding provide the biggest single thrust behind IT. This is one theme explored here. And beside military involvement is the role of commercial interests in IT – they wish to *sell* the new technologies to us – and the role of the state. Governments, whose activities are bound up both with military and commercial interests, also promote IT in specific ways. Technological 'impacts' are seen in clearer relief when social origins are laid bare.

Alongside these 'macro' level interests there are of course many 'micro' level movements, organizations and processes with which most of us are more immediately familiar. They mediate the bigger interests to the population at large, acting as social carriers of new technologies. The drive to put computers into schools, for instance, mediates government and commercial interests, while the *aficionados* of artificial intelligence help to legitimize military interests by demonstrating its civil applications. On the domestic front, crazes like computer games, the advertisers' promise of 'greater choice in entertainment', and the magazine racks laden with computer-related periodicals are obvious instruments of commercial interest.[3]

Secondly, a more theoretical point, the perspective which concentrates on social consequences of 'given' technology neglects the role of human action within the technological process. To give it its proper name, 'technological determinism' assumes that technology has a kind of 'life of its own', which then shapes our social existence. True enough, no one living in the nineteenth century could have guessed that the motor car would have contributed so deeply to twentieth-century lifestyles. Too often cities built with car transport in mind discourage pedestrians and cyclists, pollute the atmosphere, and oblige people to make many transactions – shopping, sporting, eating, and so on – at some distance from their homes. Moreover the car has been augmented[4] internally by modifications for luxury, safety and speed, and externally by generating new forms of support and service industry. It seems to have grown, almost autonomously.

But the point is that none of this occurred without people choosing, colluding, promoting or acquiescing in motor car development. Technology – whether we are talking about machines or systems or both together – possesses no life of its own. It is a human product, a social construction. As I have already indicated, its social shaping is achieved by very powerful forces, especially military, economic and political ones. But in these cases also it is clearer that active human agents are involved, people who are constantly (though often unwittingly) monitoring, evaluating, and justifying their activities.

Thirdly, and following from the last point, if we examine the interplay between the social shaping of technology and the technological shaping of society, then the door is opened for re-shaping, re-directing or simply resisting certain technological developments. The worst forms of hype present 'information society' as a *fait accompli* (and other milder versions come pretty close to this), a result of the social diffusion of IT. But in the perspective of this book there is nothing inevitable about it at all. To deny technological (or social) determinism is to abandon inevitability, and to clear a way for the consideration and promotion of alternative paths for IT development.

The rest of this chapter is about the social as well as the technical origins of IT, and of the ongoing convergence of computing and telecommunications. Two cautions are in order. One, I am not suggesting any sort of 'conspiracy' theory which will explain the arcane and sinister sources of today's technology. I am not impugning the integrity of electronics research workers, computer or communications companies, systems analysts or anyone else. Nor am I suggesting that a similar weighting of interests is discernible in every situation (the significance of the military factor, for instance, differs from country to country and waxes and wanes according to the current state of international relations). All I propose is that technical developments and innovations are not self-explanatory. They have to be put in a social and cultural context properly to be understood. Two, I am not suggesting that the 'redirection' of IT is in any sense easy or straightforward. It would be naive not to acknowledge that, for most of us, the power and opportunity to influence technological development are tightly limited.

The military factor

Without doubt, the experience of the Second World War did much to raise the status of science and technology in the Western world. The dependence – in a rather profound sense – of modern society upon technology came to be seen as a fact of life. Technological innovations such as radar had contributed to success in the war effort. Military leaders were now obliged to consult with scientists. As Braun and MacDonald put it: 'The Western world emerged from the war with a strong faith in a better and more prosperous tomorrow, and the tool to achieve it, the fulcrum of the effort, was to be science-based technology.'[5]

During the war, silicon had been used in radar installations, and scientists were keen to discover its properties and potential. The semiconductor industry, which was to make such massive strides using silicon, was to find its major scientific base at the huge and famous Bell Laboratories in New Jersey. This is significant, because Bell's research record related directly to long-term communications needs. But although the Bell scientists were searching for communications applications for their semi-conductors, the market for their most famous item – the transistor – was ensured by the development of the computer. And the transistor was immediately recognized at Bell as a breakthrough which would be of tremendous interest to the Defense Department. So much so that they kept its existence secret at first for fear that the military would want to classify it and thus slow the Russian military advance.[6] This is all part of the pre-history of the convergence between computing and telecommunications.

The experience of the USA provides the best illustration of the connection between military factors and the growth of today's microelectronic and IT industries. So that is where we begin. However, present trends in international relations means that Britain is increasingly drawn into parallel (if not identical) projects. Other European countries are similarly involved in research and development which relates defence and IT.

The war-time reliance on, and research into, radar, continued to spur growth in the young electronics industry. There is a direct lineage from war-time radar to today's microelectronics. In 1949 the Russians surprised the West by exploding their first atomic device, and the Americans were faced, for the first time in their history, with the possibility of devastating air attack.[7] This represented a threat far beyond what anyone had anticipated during the war itself, as one plane could create more damage than any mass bombings, and low-flying jet aircraft could remain undetected by conventional radar.

The solution proposed was that a large number of radars be deployed, each linked to a computer 'net' which would analyse all the signals. The prototype of this was the MIT 'Whirlwind' valve-based computer. But computer power was not the only difficulty. Communication power was also required, especially over the vast distances involved between American centres of population. The war-time British 'home chain' connecting radar stations had proved inadequate. It was manually operated, and used voice and teletype. The Americans decided to use the telephone lines, but to install massive digital processing equipment to convert the radar signals into communicable form. Here, not in the 1970s, we find the real beginnings of the 'convergence' of computing and telecommunications. Integrated circuits were to make IT a 'consumer' and 'domestic' technology, but the roots of the convergence lay elsewhere. Indeed, this defence decision had long-term impact in that the American Telephone and Telegraph Company (AT&T) was prompted by it to inaugurate a 'generally available, high-quality, digital data service'.[8]

The Russians had another surprise in store for the Americans. In 1957 they launched successfully their first 'sputnik'. It was immediately recognized that from then the accent had to be on miniaturization of components. Defence would increasingly depend on space technology. The world-renowned Silicon Valley in California had its genesis at this time. Although it is taken by many as a model of combining commercial enterprise with university research, it owed at least some of its early strength to the military factor. Following the sputnik, American attempts to catch up with the Russians entailed spending huge sums of money on microelectronics research. One of the areas which benefited was the Californian aerospace industry, for which semi-conductors were required. That is when activity in Santa Clara County shifted from fruit production to integrated circuits.[9]

Actual war engagement during the 1950s and 1960s also stimulated the American microelectronics industry. The Korean and Vietnam wars each created a demand for a steadily rising proportion of microelectronic components. By the late 1950s over half of American semi-conductor sales were for defence purposes.[10] Success in semi-conductor research and development was attributed in large part to the role of this government funding. After the successful launching of the Russian sputnik in 1957 it was said that all one had to do to obtain money was to 'wave a Russian threat'.[11]

The fortunes of microelectronics and IT research have varied with the extent of engagement in war, and also with the (related) space programme of NASA. The latter was temporarily halted in the mid-1970s, which event, coming not long after the impact of finishing the war in Vietnam, contributed significantly to a steep rise in unemployment figures in areas such as California. But the resumption of the NASA programmes has always been good news for those involved in these industries.

In the early 1980s, another boom for microelectronics and IT appeared to be promised in an ambitious new Defense Department plan for 'strategic computing'. In October 1983 the 'Defense Advanced Research Projects Agency' (DARPA) announced its $600 million plans to compete with the Japanese 'Fifth Generation' project. The aim is to develop computers capable of speech recognition, vision, and reasoning which would make possible unmanned armoured tanks and automated co-pilots which could understand the human voice. The 'electronic battlefield' was to become a reality on several fronts at once. As Marjorie Sun points out, one use of DARPA's fifth-generation computers 'conjures up visions from the recent movie *War games*. Like the "WOPR" computer in the film, the military's real version would alert commanders of impending problems during the battle, lay out operations in war strategy while factoring in uncertainties, carry out the preferred option, and monitor the results'.[12] Of course, film makers have no privileged insights. The R&D for today's 'novelties' has been germinating for several decades.

The capacity of the film industry to provide a crystal ball for defence analysts revealed itself again in the mid-1980s with President Reagan's 'Strategic Defense Initiative', popularly known as 'Star Wars'. This proposed system of anti-missile defence is based on powerful computers linked to orbiting sensors, which determine the nature of an attack and select a suitable strategy for response. The highest priority targets would then have orbiting battle stations, armed with lasers (or other weapons) assigned to them. Completing the SDI programme would entail building the largest computer software system ever.

The SDI project raises two questions worthy of further analysis. One concerns the role of nation-state in fostering and shaping the direction of IT research and development. We shall come to this below. The other issue is that the SDI project has provoked considerable incredulity and resistance from computer experts. At least one SDI Office scientist resigned in 1985.[13] British (and other European) scientists presented a case to Vice-President Bush that the SDI programme is unworkable. They argue that the 'Star Wars' concept imposes demands on computer systems which could never reliably be met. The danger of accidental nuclear war would thereby be heightened.[14] The extent to which such 'expert' resistance to high-tech military plans is succcessful remains to be seen.

The American administration is keen to encourage European involvement in projects such as SDI. British acquiescence in this caused deep dilemmas for computer scientists. On the one hand, in a time of recession-based research budget cuts, a boost for artificial intelligence and more general Fifth Generation work is very welcome. On the other, many fear for the eventual (intended or unintended) outcome of SDI research. At the same time, suspicions are expressed that even the European Economic Community's proposed cooperation on civilian IT research – the Eureka project – veils military intentions.[15]

This recent evidence calls in question the popular idea that the military impetus for microelectronics research gave way entirely to a commercial impetus during the 1960s. While it is true that during the boom of the 1950s and early 1960s the size of the potential military market may have been exaggerated (and the coming microelectronics consumer boom underestimated), it is misleading to imagine that the military factor is insignificant in the closing decades of the twentieth century. The defence budget remains a major source of funding for IT research, in Britain as in the USA. The largest part of government funding of electronics research and development in the UK comes through the defence industry.[16]

Many questions remain after this brief survey. While the connections between defence industries and IT continue to be strong in the USA and many other countries, it is neither a necessary nor a necessarily beneficial connection. Japan, for instance, does not link IT directly with military research; its programmes are civil ones, even though they have been responded to in relation to their military potential. The Soviet Union, on the other hand, with its commitment to high-tech military capacity, lacks the IT consumerism so vital to 'information societies' elsewhere. As to whether the connection is necessarily beneficial, quite apart from moral questions about automated armaments themselves, grave doubts have been expressed as to how many authentic civilian spin-offs are generated by military research.[17] Moreover, it has been argued that in a small country like Britain, a persistently high defence budget (of which much is devoted to high-tech research and development) could have disastrous long-term consequences for industry.[18]

The commercial factor

Before it was a decade old, IT was clearly a commercial winner – if one could corner the market. The spirit of classic entrepreneurial indivi-dualism was revived for the effort. Californian heroes of 'Apple' computers, Steven Wozniak and Steve Jobs, have been virtually canonized; Britain's first (then–rising) star Clive Sinclair, who launched the first cheap micro-computer, was knighted. Massive cut-throat competition between rival global-scale firms dominates the scene. Anxieties about 'silicon crises' serve simply to fuel further efforts aimed at controlling more aspects of the production processes and at managing the markets.

The convergence between computing and telecommunications is again extremely important, as it opens up numerous commercial opportunities. This does not just mean 'hardware' convergence, as it did in the early 1980s, but now also transmission, the link between equipment manufac-turers, customers and information providers.[19] Software has become the predominant cost in any system. Convergence, moreover, is not yet complete. More is to come, especially as public telephone networks become fully digital, consumer communications are computerized (as in the PC-phone or in cellular radio-phones), and so on. As one British commentator puts it, 'The stage now seems set for the full convergence of computers and IC [integrated circuit] technology into almost every home and business', adding for good measure, 'A revolution may be just around the corner'.[20]

Examples of this convergence proliferate. In Britain, the Nottingham Building Society was said to have gained an edge over others by pioneering the first home banking service. (Similar services are offered in North America.) Users rent a viewdata adaptor alongside their domestic TV sets, and from their armchairs check accounts, pay bills, or obtain computer-approved loans, 24 hours a day, seven days a week. In the USA, American Airlines similarly gained a lead over competition offering an on-line reservation system to travel agents. Their system, Sabre, captured 40 per cent more automated travel agents than any other, and increased their revenue by listing their flights before those of the other 400 airlines.

What these examples show from a commercial perspective is that for a growing number of companies IT has become a strategic resource. It does not merely process payroll and accounts, or generate management data, but can add value to products or create new ones, and forge ties between customers and distributors. From the production of the basic hardware through to the delivery of goods and services, several trends stand out. They include the increasing vertical and horizontal integration of companies, their transnationalization and their concern with manipulating consumption. The last-mentioned is particularly interesting, for IT provides new opportunities to blur the boundary between 'business' and 'leisure' as the domestic threshold is crossed. In what follows I shall comment on each of these in turn.

Companies which once concentrated upon one area – say, the manufacture of computer hardware – now attempt to hold together different aspects of the business, right through from the production of silicon chips to the (now complex) end-product. If a company can control component production, for example, it can control software design. This 'vertical' integration is one reason why the business news is constantly buzzing with some new merger, takeover, or commercial arrangement. The other reason is the 'horizontal' integration between companies re-grouping themselves around a coherent range of products, the most obvious example being compatible equipment for the so-called electronic office.

The struggle to dominate the market takes place in the main between giants including Mitsubishi, Exxon, Hitachi, Philips, Siemens, AT&T, Honeywell, GEC, Burroughs, RCA, Ericsson and above all IBM. Since the 1960s 'Big Blue' has held by far the largest market share in data processing worldwide. In Western Europe it supplies about 70 per cent of users, and until recently (given that IBM compatibles are under IBM's indirect control) held a monopoly of operating software. But IBM's response to technological convergence is to move into telecommunications, while telecommunications companies move into computing. Once-discrete operations now find themselves locked into battle with commercial enemies which they have no previous experience of facing.

Since the American giant AT&T was broken up in 1985, coincidentally with the expanding convergence of technologies, the escalating economic war between it and IBM has been shifted even more decisively into a global cockpit. However, IBM's advantage may be traced to modes of operation and personnel recruitment, not necessarily to superior technology. The focus of this particular conflict is a battle of standards; the Open Systems Interconnection (OSI), backed by European and Japanese manufacturers and AT&T, and the System Network Architecture (SNA) of IBM. If AT&T is invading the computer business, then IBM is wasting no time securing footholds in the telecommunications business. In 1985 it bought a 30 per cent share in MCI Communications (which itself needs capital to build telephone networks to rival AT&T's). The MCI share was bought with the assets of Satellite Business Systems, a long-distance 'phone subsidiary already belonging to IBM. Another strategic purchase by IBM gave it Rolm, which makes PBX exchange sytems, again strengthening its hand against AT&T. IBM have also entered the financial information market through links with Merrill Lynch, and have begun to establish videotex connections as well.[21]

While the American-based battle for electronic networking supremacy is the biggest global battle as well, the other big companies are playing the same game. Japan's NTT is cooperating with IBM to produce and market small IBM computers, and other Japanese companies are allying themselves with American ones to provide value-added networks. The British computer company ICL is entering the global network transmission field, collaborating extensively, especially in the stage between R&D and commercial application, while British Telecom, by taking over the Canadian firm Mitel, has shown its interest in telecommunications manufacture.

These different forms of integration and the creation of quasi-monopolies make it hard for other smaller companies to compete with the giants who can afford the necessary R&D, and have the capital to produce complete systems rather than isolated products. And the more they integrate, the more they are able to internationalize, as data processing and communications are precisely the tools required for international operations. The stakes are high; the prizes glittering. And it is the huge oligopolies which are best placed to reap the benefits.

On the other hand, things are far from plain sailing, even for the massive transnational corporations. More recently developed countries such as Korea present real challenges to the established ones. The lack of adequate infrastructure can badly hinder the exploitation of, for instance, information services production. And unexpected challenges can make a real difference to market conditions. An example of the latter is British Alan Sugar's Amstrad computer company, whose cheap word processors and IBM-compatible PCs have successfully penetrated the British market, and are intended to take their assault right into the USA, whose market represents 80 per cent of the world market.[22] Not surprisingly, Sugar is using some of his profits to buy shares in Direct Broadcasting by Satellite.

That said, there is much worry in Europe about the future of IT. Doom-laden headlines of 'Silicon Crisis' appear, and leading commentators may be heard bemoaning 'a sunrise industry that is being eclipsed before it has properly risen'.[23] Falling sales, job losses, financial insecurity and factory closures combine to create a gloomy atmosphere within governments and industry alike. The most commonly cited cause of European difficulties is the lack of entrepreneurial enthusiasm and a 'culture' of industry. Ian Mackintosh's *Sunrise Europe*, for instance, argues that while Europe has an unrivalled community of pure scientists, the application of science is neglected: 'If your whole training, work ethic and intellectual culture are targeted on creating new knowledge, you are unlikely to absorb the kind of *savoir faire* relevant to creating new enterprises.'[24]

Whatever the reason, it certainly is the case that those who succeed concentrate much energy on marketing. Research is one thing, development another, but in order to open up new fields, maintain competitiveness and generally to combat the hazards of haphazard and unpredictable occurrences in the IT field, marketing becomes a *sine qua non*. This represents a further development within capitalist enterprises. Whereas once attention was focused on the control of the productive process –

Henry Ford's assembly line and Frederick Taylor's scientific management – this has now been extended to attempts to control the distributive and consumer process. This applies Taylorism to the customer with an assortment of techniques for selling and advertising. Kevin Robins and Frank Webster refer to it as one aspect of 'Social Taylorism', which takes consumer capitalism further into the domestic sphere especially by means of (new modes of) television and other new information and communications technologies.[25]

⋅ Again, the use of the new technologies for the promotion of those new technologies can prove most effective. Direct 'personalized' mailings and the boardroom video for employees are two relevant examples. The aim is to orchestrate market responses by influencing choice. And it is clear that a degree of success is enjoyed by such advertisers. Parents have bought home computers in order that their children might 'keep up'; companies install computer systems for the sake of the 'image' and the prestige of being up-to-date. In the USA, cable television subscription carried high status in the 1970s. Such artifacts have acquired high symbolic significance.[26]

Typewriters are labelled old-fashioned; in one advertisement they are jettisoned from office windows to be replaced by Amstrad word processors. A Wang promotion offers technological convergence with the potential to reverse the effects of the biblical tower of Babel! 'A Wang sytem, installed alongside almost any combination of hardware, gets all your computers teamed up and working together to the full. . . . Before the Babel of computing confounds and scatters your business over the face of the earth, clip the coupon below.' And as for the home, virtually no gadget, implement or machine is now complete without some digital component, from cordless telephones to kettles.

Of course, it is true that 'consumerism' cannot exist without willing consumers and for many products there still appears to be no shortage of them. Sometimes – as in the case of British cable television's slow start – consumers have failed to respond to the marketing bait. But in many cases, consumers do just what the big companies want, and consume. Few consciously search for alternatives. This means that to an overwhelming extent the companies decide what will be marketed, and for what purposes. Development takes place in the laboratories of transnational corporations. The realm of choice is more and more severely restricted to acceptance or rejection. Yet IT is having a profound effect on lifestyles, not just existing products. Only consumer movements of a considerably more radical stamp than most of today's could hope to influence the development of IT in a meaningful fashion.[27]

The commercial factor is thus crucial to the shaping of IT, and in particular the activities of the big transnational corporations which can afford both to integrate their operations and to market their products on an international level. The kinds of convergence which take place are largely the outcome of corporate strategy, which often announces them in advance. One of the clearest examples of this kind of social shaping is the choice between OSI and SNA standards which is guided by much more than merely technical criteria. The whole point of the OSI is to allow interconnections between any make of computer and thus 'to preclude the total domination by IBM of data transmission networks would lock users into that company's computers'.[28]

The continuing importance of this factor at both the global and the local domestic level is assured by twin impulses: on the one hand, the perpetual quest within capitalism for profit and for market shares, and on the other, the activities of many governments in pursuing policies of deregulation and the return of once 'public' goods and services to the marketplace. When even the air-waves are up for sale in preparation for 'the coming explosion of radio communications',[29] it is clear that governments are also involved in stimulating competition. As we shall see, they are also involved in military and civilian R&D funding of IT and in the purchase and use of large IT systems.

The government factor

Although the mode of involvement varies from place to place, governments throughout the world are implicated in the research, development and marketing of IT. It is nothing new, of course, for states to intervene in economic life. In fact, no state in the modern era has not thus involved itself. But the combination of continuing Cold War, world recession and the priorities of national survival puts this major new technology in a peculiarly prominent position. IT offers an attractive means of attempting to guarantee the future on several fronts at once. That which could strengthen military defences might also rejuvenate ailing economies and at the same time help to consolidate the power of the state.

IT has become an important factor within some rather paradoxical contemporary political processes. They include these three. Several capitalist nations have for some years been attempting to 'de-regulate' (US) or 'privatize' (UK) industry. But this apparent 'drawing back' on the part of governments is intended to *secure* more overseas markets for national products. Similarly, the effort to 'roll back the state' in such countries is accompanied by increased (direct and indirect) state control of social life. And in state socialist societies tremendous tension is felt between the need on the one hand to keep in step technologically with the West, and on the other to prevent any potential weakening of the state's grip which might result from the diffusion of personal micro-computers.

IT equipment, bought by the state, serves to support the industry. Huge defence expenditure partly explains the leading position of the USA in several aspects of IT and, as we have seen, defence spending similarly accounts for much electronics R&D in other countries as well. Thus military procurement is a direct way in which many governments are stimulating IT industries. Governments also act as markets for computer-related products. Taxation, social security, and census bureaux are heavily computerized. The US federal government is easily the world's biggest computer customer.

But the main focus of what follows is state involvement in IT for national economic supremacy or (more modestly) survival, and the kinds of policies directed to this end. Although they are not ultimately separable from economic activity, in this section I shall comment only briefly on the military aspect of state involvement in IT (because I have already discussed it as a discrete topic), and on the significance of IT for state power (because I return to this theme in chapter 5).

One can discern at least four components of the rationale for govern-ment involvement in IT. Firstly, general agreement seems to exist that any country is better off with strength in IT than without it. The strategic importance of IT for developing new forms of industry, obtaining technological advantage, and thus building economic power and political leverage, is widely recognized. The Japanese with their relative lack of natural resources, feel this acutely. The Americans, who wish to lose none of their economic or political power, are equally clear about the national importance of IT. The Russians, who have for a while been ambivalent about developing microelectronics, now appear to be grasping eagerly at whatever new technology (Bulgarian computers for instance) they can lay hands on. And for smaller powers such as Britain, the threat of demotion to 'Third-World' or 'offshore-colony' status is a compelling one.

Secondly, it is believed that the haphazard commercial development of

IT requires some kind of coordination. Britain's Prime Minister Thatcher insisted, in 1982, that the propagation of IT depended upon 'the central role that government must play in promoting its development and application'.[30] While this managerial activity of the state may be seen clearly in the form of economic or industrial policy, it also extends simultaneously into several other areas of ecnomic and social life. Economic and industrial policy tends to be geared to compensating for a relative lack, on the one hand of technological expertise (practical 'state-of-the-art' knowledge), and on the other of adequate venture capital. But this inevitably spills over into educational policy and into industrial relations. Children must become 'computer literate'; employees must become flexible and adaptable.

Thirdly, government involvement in IT is viewed as a means of warding off specific threats, especially those represented by large trans-national corporations. It is the loss of national (economic and cultural) autonomy entailed in becoming an offshore technological colony which has to be avoided at all costs. Thus France has been prominently vociferous in its opposition to the incursions of IBM, and Canada generally anxious about the amount of sovereignty draining down data-processing channels into the USA. One response to this, particularly in Europe, is cooperation between several different countries (such as in the ESPRIT project) in order to try to compete in the world market. It must be said, however, that the threat of demotion to techno-colony status is more likely to be realized in some contexts, where political exigencies (such as high regional unemployment) have acted against the desire to remain independent, and where inducements have actually been given for foreign companies to establish their own plants with a domestic context.

Fourthly, the notion of government participation in high-tech develop-ment has been spurred by the example of the Japanese Ministry for Inter-national Trade and Industry (MITI). Much of the Japanese success in microelectronics and dynamism in exporting high tech has been attributed to the vision and coherence of MITI policies. Many nations (in the 'First' as well as the 'Third' World) look hopefully to the 'Japanese miracle' as a model of economic development or at least to get some clues about the routes to success. While none can either replicate a Confucian cultural his-tory, or pretend that it has no already existing legacy of 'cumbersome' econ-omic and industrial relations practices (which lack gave Japan the advantage of being able to create 'efficient' institutions from the start) many argue that the degree of state involvement is something which can be emulated.

What kinds of policies emerge from these varied attempts at state planning and intervention in the IT field? Beginning with MITI, one finds in Japan examples of the most far-reaching futurist visions. Japan's late development was of course an advantage in that lessons could be learned from the experience of other countries, and technology transferred from them. The drive to 'catch up' after the war was a powerful one, and was easily transposed into futurism once success came. By 1977 Prime Minister Fukuda had instigated a quest for 'national goals for the 21st century'. And when Prime Minister Nakasone was re-elected, he made a policy speech which spelled things out: 'a brighter future lies ahead. I can see in the distance a vision of Japan as a richly verdant Pacific archipelago . . . the home of a new culture integrating the best of East and West.'[31] MITI's grand designs took this into the realm of policy, closely aided by the Ministry of Posts and Telecommunications' announcement of the coming 'information society'.

Admirers of the Japanese approach see in the work of MITI a coherent and coordinated plan which is built on cooperation between bureaucrats and businessmen, which encourages with funding scientific and technological advance, and which has concrete expression in the designation of new 'technopolises' and soaring export figures. Those who are more sceptical argue that such futurism deflects attention from the problems of the present, ignores the massive disparities of income, wealth *and* access to the new information sources and technologies, and is blind to the social costs of modernization, seen in workaholism, reduced public amenities, isolation (especially of women) and so on. Apparently only a small proportion of the Japanese population (12 per cent according to a recent poll) actually believe that the future *will* resemble the bright one promised.[32]

Simon Nora and Alain Minc, who produced for the French government a rather more sober version of *l'informatisation* than those of the Japanese, correctly identified a number of tensions in policy. Above all, as they put it, 'a double contradiction remains between the need for state support and the need for a dynamic sector'.[33] This has been felt in practice. For example, should the state support a new information infrastructure by purchasing equipment for households (as in the French Minitel system) or by offering domestic users the opportunity to subscribe to cable TV (as in Britain)? Is the information society future better guaranteed by state-run or state-sponsored enterprises (such as the Inmos semiconductor company in Britain or the Fifth-Generation computer project in Japan), or by stimulating competition in the private commercial sphere (as in the deregulation of American telecommunications and privatizing of British Telecom?

One route followed by many countries and cities is to try to create an appropriate atmosphere for cloning 'Silicon Valley'. The USA already boasts 'Silicon Prairie', 'Silicon Valley East', 'Silicon Beach'; Scotland has its 'Silicon Glen', England, 'Silicon Fen', Germany 'Silicon Forest', and so on. Japan has its 'technopolises', similarly intending to bring together science and industry. More specifically, 'science parks' and 'technology parks' are located near universities in the hope of attracting business to enter mutually beneficial relationships with them. The aim here is that government (local or national) should *enable* free scientific and commercial enterprise to flourish, rather than controlling directly what goes on.

Even if such development-oriented ventures are moderately successful, however, governments still have very little control over the marketing aspects of IT. They may try to raise awareness on a national level, as in Japan's Tsukuba 'Expo '85' or Britain's 'Information Technology Year: 1982', but cannot create consumer demand *per se*. This is one reason for 'freeing' the market. As a British cable policy document puts it: 'Government policy is one of introducing and promoting competition so that both industry and the consumer can benefit'.[34] This assumes, among other things, that the public interest is indeed better served by the market than by 'public services' such as broadcasting and telecommunications.

It would be a mistake to give the impression that any other country has matched the coherence of Japan's IT policy, although France and Sweden have also followed a fairly clear path. Others frequently stumble at the early fence of definition. Although British policy apparently encompasses both computing and telecommunications within the 'information technology' concept, this is in fact subject to numerous different nuances of meaning. Most meanings depend upon an increasingly dated hardware-oriented definition, which had its origins in the emphasis of the Labour administration of 1974–9 on microprocessor production.[35] Similarly, cable television, being a 'new' medium in its computer-related form, is also subject to highly ambiguous policy definition which generates misunderstanding, delay and frustration among those involved in it.

The main reason why states are involved in economic life is because their continued existence depends upon it; they have an intense interest in maintaining a 'healthy economy'. The concern with IT has in recent years helped to accentuate trends towards increasing state activity in other areas as well. Educational initiatives have proliferated which are intended to supply appropriately trained and qualified personnel to the high-technology industries. This entails a higher degree of control over educational curricula, and a diversion of resources from liberal arts disciplines such as philosophy or modern languages to science and technology.

In the area of industrial relations, few countries have pursued paths which help labour unions to negotiate wages and control working conditions – in particular the introduction of new technology. Little regret is expressed over the ways that many IT developments, especially the introduction of labour-saving technologies, tend to erode the power of the unions. Add to this another aspect of government IT policy, to buy computer systems for administrative and surveillance purposes, and the benefits to the state in terms of augmented power come into clearer focus. In short, though this effect may be indirect and sometimes unintended, IT is valuable to states because it helps to increase effective influence and control over their citizens.

This reveals an apparent paradox. Governments which in recent years have trumpeted the 'rolling back of the state' simultaneously strengthen the state's role in monitoring and controlling social and economic life. 'Free market' policies are followed in tandem with 'strong state' policies. States are thus only 'rolled back' in rather specific domains. The ongoing presence and power of government, now intensified by IT in several significant ways, is an element to be reckoned with in any analysis of technological change. Whether coherent or confused, government policies have an important bearing on IT.

The shaping of IT

Information technology, the cluster of computing and communications technologies based on microelectronics, did not arrive from nowhere. While there is no doubt that its social impacts are profound, its social origins are also highly significant.[36] I have argued in this chapter that the technical history of IT is inseparable from its social context – military, commercial, government factors – and specific social shaping – as for instance in the case of battle between SNA and OSI standards.

Far from witnessing some ineluctable juggernaut of change whose motor is a microelectronic techno–logic, the evidence presented reveals no single historical tendency, no unique or overwhelming contribution from one factor. 'Autonomous technology' is indeed a mistaken notion.[37] Different social interests and values combine with other circumstances to produce different outcomes. If civil rather than military concerns had guided solid-state electronics in its early decades, for instance, the technical paths followed probably would have been quite different.[38]

In later chapters I will build on this view, claiming that just as social factors helped to fashion the kinds of technologies now available – and even their 'convergence' – so their 'impacts' may also be understood in terms of those factors. This calls in question the notion that new technologies *themselves* bring about new kinds of social relationships or a whole new 'information society' of a particular sort. Without doubt, social change is related to technological innovation. But the eventual outcomes are the result not of mere 'technological impacts' but of a subtle and complex interplay between technology and society.

3

A new economy: new classes?

> The men who brought about the Revolution ... have committed a great political mistake. They should have ... recognised the fact that the work of the scientists, artists and industrialists is that which, in discovery and application, contributes most to national prosperity ... they should be entrusted with administrative power.
>
> *Saint-Simon (c.1810)*[1]

> he was propped in the crutch of an oak tree – looking down – singing 'there's a man going round taking names' ... it couldnt've been more'n a few hours later when i happened to be passing by again – in the spot where the tree was, a lightbulb factory now stood – 'did there used to be a guy here in a tree?' i yelled up to one of the windows – 'are you looking for work?' was the reply ... it was then when i decided that marxism did not have all the answers
>
> *Bob Dylan (1972)*[2]

Central to the claim that we are entering an 'information society' is the belief that the economy is undergoing radical change. During the past century or so, a largely agrarian existence gradually gave way to life in industrial society. Today, it is said, another change is taking place. Information workers are replacing productive workers as the biggest sector in the economy. As steam engines extended the power of human muscle, now computers are extending the capacity of human minds. The processing and handling of information, often using new microelectronics-based technology, take on a highly significant economic role.

What does this mean for old economic and sociological categories such as labour and capital and social class? The prophets of the information society tell us that virtually everything is in flux, and that room must be made for new concepts. In particular, old ways of gauging the relative contribution of different sectors to the economy – traditionally thought of as agriculture, industry, and services – must go. This scheme also represents stages of economic development. England's 'green and pleasant land', once the context in which most English people lived, moved, and had their being, was transformed by the 'first industrial revolution'. Work was transferred, typically, from the fields to the factories. People lived, typically, in cities, not villages or hamlets. But later, while the urban drift continued, the range of occupational opportunities changed again, especially after the Second World War. 'Services' became more important as a major employer, a category which included nurses, garage mechanics, and telephone switchboard operators.

Today, it is urged, the emergence of the information sector amounts to another basic restructuring of economy and society. Two things are said to be happening. On the one hand, as modern economies have become more complex, more managers, accountants, researchers, bankers, advertisers and administrators are required. In short, there is an increased demand for 'information handling activities'.[3] On the other hand, information management is being transformed radically by the emergence of new information technologies.

New technology, it seems, has a more and more decisive effect upon both traditional production and information handling. How the sectors of the economy should be conceived has become a controversial matter. If the fundamental changes envisaged in the notion of a 'new economic sector' are correct, the consequences for social life in the coming century will surely be profound. If they lack substance, though, the whole 'information society' edifice is rendered rather fragile. This debate provides the focus for the first part of the chapter.

Criticial scrutiny of these same processes has also led to a reappraisal of social class relationships. Undoubtedly, major alterations in the occupational structure are occurring (even if their salience to the economy is not yet entirely clear). But what is their significnce for the ordering of social relationships? Is power falling into the hands of those who have access to information rather than those with property? Are the various groups of 'information handlers' forming themselves into a new dominant class of technocrats who manage, rationalize, and use novel techniques to control those without the information power required to answer back?

Karl Marx seemed to think that changing technology is a critical element in shifting relations of power: 'The handmill gives you a society with a feudal lord; the steam-mill, society with the industrial capitalist'.[4] Whether or not he was right, it is worth asking, what does the computer 'give you'? Do today's 'revolutionary' new technologies presage another epoch-making shift in which social classes are eroded or reconstituted along different lines? This is another controversial area of analysis in which at least three voices may be heard.

Some argue that the already waning relevance of a thoroughgoing Marxist analysis fades out altogether as information becomes a source of added value, perhaps even a new means of production. Others deny this, insisting that the 'information society' novelties are a blind. Old class divisions discerned by Marx are simply obscured by the dazzle of new electronic gadgetry. Yet others, while accepting that Marx may no longer have all the answers, if indeed he ever did, wonder whether the late twentieth century is witness to new axes of exploitation and alienation, in which education and technical skills form the main divisive factor (though even these are cut across by gender), and where information is power.

Technology and jobs, technology and class; crucially important and yet hotly contested topics which must be discussed in order to answer the question of whether indeed an 'information society' is emerging. Perhaps it is the case (as I shall argue) that the concepts of an information sector and of information workers pay too much attention to technology, and not enough to power. But do those theories which take power more seriously – in relation to questions of social class – succeed any better in illuminating the key trends of today's advanced societies?

Information workers and the information sector

Since the Second World War a steadily increasing proportion of the labour force has become involved in handling symbolic information. These people are often thought of as 'white-collar' workers. Government officials, school teachers, travel agents and telephone operators proliferate, while factory operatives and steel mill and shipyard workers steadily diminish in numbers. This is one face of the process explained as 'deindustrialization', an aspect of which is that a declining proportion of the labour force is engaged in industrial production.

As I noted above, two factors are relevant here. On the one hand, it is said that the proportion of primarily office-based workers, who handle information in one form or another, has increased from less than 20 per cent to over 50 per cent during this century,[5] at least in the USA. On the other hand, the kinds of technological inventiveness once applied to other economic activities (mining and agriculture as well as the manufacture of things like cars and sewing machines) have now been applied to 'information activities'. As traditional industries became more complex, more information handling was required to coordinate and manage multifarious individual tasks. But now information handling itself is subject to technological innovation. Word processors, computer-aided-design (CAD) and electronic mail are obvious examples.

The notion of an expanding information sector provides the economic cornerstone for the assertion that North America, Western Europe and Japan may be described as 'information societies'. The empirical economics of Fritz Machlup and Marc Porat,[6] which claims to demonstrate the existence and importance of the new information sector, leads the way. Theorists such as Peter Drucker, Daniel Bell, and Yoneji Masuda[7] quickly follow with their proposals that unprecedented social changes are occurring in the wake of the economic. The theme is taken up and elaborated by the mandarins of the global economy. The OECD (Organization for Economic Cooperation and Development), for instance, reports that Austria, France, Germany, Finland, Japan, Sweden, the USA and the UK are experiencing a 'profound change in their occupational structure'.[8] Indeed, they say, there is a 'fourth economic sector'. This is illustrated in figure 1.

Most studies of this kind waste no time coming to a series of conclusions, which are now well-rehearsed. The trend towards the information society is a natural development of the familiar process of industrial capitalism. The information sector will continue to grow more rapidly than any other. The application of IT will take over from advances in industrial efficiency as the main source of economic growth. Computer and telecommunications technologies increase in power and decrease in price all the time. So, as long as fear and ignorance which leads to resistance to the introduction of new technology can be reduced, and so long as vital information infrastructures are provided, long-term economic confidence is warranted.

A march through the sectors?

The idea that a new 'industrial sector' is appearing in the advanced societies echoes similar claims once made within 'postindustrialism'. It is also vulnerable to criticism along similar lines. The chief difficulties, as I

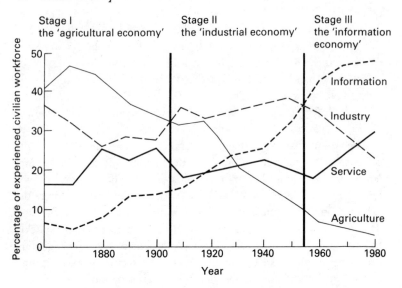

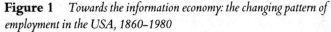

Figure 1   *Towards the information economy: the changing pattern of employment in the USA, 1860–1980*

The chart claims to show that almost half of America's civilian workforce are already employed in the information field. Things are said to be similar in Western Europe, where a considerable proportion of the service sector's work-force are also involved in generating, recording, processing and transmitting information in one form or another.

Source: Bureau of Labor Statistics, USA

noted in the introductory chapter, have to do with the way in which the sector is defined (and indeed, the fact that it is described as a 'sector' at all), and the frequent failure to make the clear implications for power and control of 'information activities'.

Postindustrialism posited the growth of an increasingly important technical and managerial occupational group, dependent upon an expanded educational system, greater general prosperity, and the dimini-shing significance of 'old-fashioned' political debates as power is diffused more evenly through society. It is also assumed that consumer choice is a crucial director of economic change. Informatics is now added as a key factor, on whose successful development hangs the hope of revived economic growth. IT also raises questions (discussed in subsequent chapters) of centralization, work experience, employment, leisure and state power.

Let me begin by questioning how the sectors are construed within postindustrialism. Krishan Kumar shows that the 'postindustrial' image of industrialism is flawed by its over-reliance on the English experience. For this case was unique, in that no other society ever had a preponderance of industrial workers within the labour force. Even in England the classic cloth-capped factory 'hand' was only briefly typical. In most countries the proportion of industrial workers has hovered around one-third during the twentieth century. And growth in the 'service' sector dates right from the beginnings of industrialism.[9] So the contrast between the different 'typical' workers of different eras is somewhat blurred when the evidence is more closely examined. In fact, American data show how industrial workers have remained a constant proportion of the labour force between 1900 (38%) and 1970 (35%), whereas agriculture has slipped from 38% to 4% and services have grown from 24% to 61%. The shift would appear to be from agriculture to services, rather than from manufacture to services.[10]

This progression from the economic predominance of one sector to that of another is dubbed the 'march of the sectors' by Ian Miles and Jonathan Gershuny,[11] who reject it as a profoundly misleading way of characterizing economic history. The advanced economies have simply not moved systematically and steadily from being predominantly agricultural to predominantly industrial and then predominantly service-oriented. The growth of services, for instance, *depends upon* growth in manufacturing. It is not an autonomous area of activity. Demand for goods has risen! Although it varies from country to country one can say that domestically, more is spent on cars, televisions and washing machines; less on trains, theatres and laundry services. Firms too use 'intermediate services'. All manner of IT-related consultancies have mushroomed in the last decade, for instance. Miles and Gershuny insist, therefore, that the classification of 'manufacturing' and 'services' is often inconsistent, in that many 'services' are clearly linked with 'manufacturing'.

The status of 'professionals' within postindustrialism is also queried. Although many occupational groups seek the rewards of professional status – and may even be classified as such – this in itself does not constitute evidence for a growing band of qualified personnel within the labour force. Not only is much work of a routine nature done by the new professionals but with the application of new technology skills may actually be evacuated from their jobs. Even doctors, architects and design engineers may be susceptible to such de-skilling.[12]

The postindustrialists' evidence of a new kind of society lies not only with professionalization, but in its link with the 'axial principle' of theoretical knowledge. They point to the growth of research and development, of higher education, and the political significance of science and technology. But Bell was looking in the wrong place. Charles Jonscher says Bell is mistaken to see the growth of scientific and technical occupations as a major cause of information workforce expansion. In the USA it accounts only for around 15 per cent, a proportion which is falling. The vast majority within the information workforce is concerned with the 'administration, coordination and organization of economic activity'.[13]

Despite the difficulties surrounding the postindustrialists' notion of a 'march through the sectors', in several accounts the rising importance of information-handling activities is portrayed as one more stage, one more sector. Popularizers of the information society thesis such as Tom Stonier rely heavily on the distinction between 'farm operatives, machine operatives and information operatives' in order to stress how clear is the line dividing one 'type' of society from another.[14] Thus the 'information sector' moves to a central position, displacing 'services'. Occupations concerned with the flow of information become the 'typical' jobs of the information society.

But the problem of identifying the information sector is similar to that of saying exactly what is the 'services sector'. 'Services' cover a diverse range of occupations, from social workers to bus drivers. And not all services are growing! Some, like personal services, have been declining since the Second World War. Fewer people are finding jobs in transport and distribution today than in the 1960s. These shifts relate to government policy and to industrial structure as well as consumer demand.

Any serious analysis of services reveals a high degree of complexity, both in their variety of types and in the way they came into being. This has implications for information activities. As Miles and Gershuny helpfully show, some services have been initiated by (among other things) public pressure, such as state welfare. Such are 'non-marketed' services, unlike 'marketed' services such as car maintenance. Some are 'final' services, such as hairdressing, and others, 'intermediate' services, such as computer consultancy. So the state, the market, and the household all play slightly different roles, and the modes of provision also vary. Some are benefits, some commodities, and some the self-service products of informal, unwaged labour, such as using a washing machine or making home videos. Distinctions like these also reveal gender differences in 'services'.

If the 'services sector' has a fuzzy image, then so does any 'information sector'. The welfare state (a product of political choice and public pressure) led to a growth in services in the post-war period. But deflationary and monetarist politics are shrinking the scope of state welfare and reducing its rate of expansion, thus cutting back employment in such services. What are the prospects for employment and growth in information activities in countries without the political will to create an appropriate electronic infrastructure? Many other contingent factors also play a part. For instance, in the mid-1980s it became clear that terrorist bombs could have a big impact on employment in tourist and leisure 'industries'.

Thus to superimpose the notions of 'information work' and an 'information sector' upon the postindustrial economy in which services are apparently paramount, and to suppose that this occurs in a process of steady evolutionary development, is simply misleading. So how may a better picture be obtained? On the one hand, broader contexts – national and international – have to be borne in mind. On the other, changes in industrial and occupational structure must be carefully specified.

The 'broader contexts' include the very important fact that the division of labour in the advanced societies is undergoing profound change. The growth of women's (often part-time) labour since the mid-century, and the rise of the 'informal economy' are key factors.[15] Equally, the modes of organization and the state of the infrastructure also affect the fortunes of industry and the occupational structure. The post-war boom, after all, depended in part upon mass-production methods and new communications networks.[16]

Another aspect of the 'broader context' is that the likely development pattern of one country cannot just be 'read-off' the experience of another. Japan, for instance, was able to 'leapfrog' several other industrial societies after the war by learning from their technical and organizational methods and thus avoiding bottlenecks and obstacles characteristic of others' practice.[17] Mexico, on the other hand, while it may appear from 'information sector' analysis to be on the road to an information economy, is in fact in a very different situation from others about which that claim is made. Agriculture still engages the biggest proportion of the labour force, and where computers and telecommunications systems are installed, they tend to be used not for production (as in the USA for instance) but in non-marketable areas like government employment. Mexico's 'information sector' could actually be at an economic *disadvantage* relative to other countries who use IT productively.[18]

As to the matter of specifying changes in occupation and industry, it is clear that the status of the 'information sector' is in some doubt. Exposing it to empirical analysis causes at least partial evaporation. Can one usefully mix, as for example OECD figures do, diverse categories of 'information work' from telecommunications researchers to television repairers? It is strikingly evident that information activities, including those using new technologies, are playing a more and more important role in all manner of occupations and within economic productivity in general. So the new Archimedes principle which sees information displacing other sectors as it expands is an illusion. The 'march through the sectors' must be jettisoned, and the concept of 'information intensivity' explored instead.[19]

Information activities: intensivity and power

An information sector, says Charles Jonscher, comprises 'the activities of all individuals whose primary function is to create, process and handle information' (the production sector does the same for physical goods).[20] The defining characteristic is the nature of each individual's *output*: 'information content' includes memoranda, reports, decisions, financial documents and lectures. Because industrial and organizational complexity has created a demand for information activities, and because these are being enhanced by IT, which is making strides in greater power and efficiency, information sector productivity will rise. IT will become the principal source of economic growth.

Similar assumptions underlie other attempts to make sense of economic and technological change in the later twentieth century. But their success is less than complete. The OECD, for instance, while trying to separate out the 'information sector', acknowledges that it 'cuts across' the traditional three sectors of agriculture, manufacture and services.[21] Earlier I placed CAD between electronic mail and word-processing, and this placing perfectly illustrates such 'cross-cutting'. Jonscher admits that the introduction of automated factory equipment blurs the conceptual division between information and production sectors (but he argues that this classification problem applies only to a minority of workers). Daniel Bell tries to get around the definitional difficulty by referring to 'extractive, fabrication and information activities'.[22]

Squeezing data into an 'information sector' concept is contrived. What seems to be happening is that all manner of activities are becoming more 'information-intensive', and this often includes their using IT. But this does not mean that 'information' should be tied to a particular technology. As Gershuny and Miles comment, 'Lumping together a variety of "new" activities under a common heading is a gesture of recognition to the problem, not a step toward solving it'.[23] But if the 'information sector' is rejected, what then?

For a start, as Trevor Jones indicates,[24] in attempting to gauge the significance of 'information activities' it is unsatisfactory to look at employment figures alone because they conceal big differences in productivity. Rather, occupations, reflecting similar content in terms of tasks, should be viewed in conjunction with industries, each with its common end-product. These in turn should be put in the contexts of supply, demand, and other constraints. Supply side-effects obviously include the desire to save labour, which with the application of IT may lead to a drop in the proportion of the labour force in 'information activities'. Demand side-effects have to take account of the desire of consumers to buy goods for private use (cars, not public transport; televisions, not cinema), although even this is far from straightforward. As for the 'constraints', these include 'free market' policies, labour practices, and the proportion of women in the labour force. The last is particularly significant as far as IT is concerned, as the steady automation of the office is eroding routine white-collar jobs.

Within such an analysis, 'information work' has a multitude of different meanings. Miles and Gershuny make distinctions between information work in production, processing, distribution and infrastructure (that is, a transmission network), and between 'activities that are intermediate inputs to producers, intermediate inputs to consumers, and final inputs to consumers, and between those that are marketed and non-marketed'.[25] They are, as a result, far more cautious about the future direction of information activities than most 'information sector' theorists.

They emphasize that political choice, not technological potential, will decide how information is used. They comment on possibilities for new forms of intermediate producer and consumer information services, and take seriously the idea that educational and entertainment uses of IT could expand, becoming compatible with a 'new socio-technical system' rather than merely the recuperation of the old. While they acknowledge the existence and realism of the darker and more dismal scenarios for a de-skilled or jobless workforce, social isolation (except for the company of 'wall-to-wall video games and computer nasties') and a surveillance state, they insist that turning the 'information society' concept into a forum for public debate could help swing things the other way.

The Miles/Gershuny dismissal of an 'information sector', and their careful and suggestive alternative analysis of information activities is highly commendable. A couple of problems are left outstanding, however. One has to do with relations of power. From a sociological point of view, not only is the content and distribution of work tasks significant, but so is the degree of control conferred by different forms of 'information work'. This latter concerns the hints about a 'new socio-technical system'. Such hints rest upon the revival of a theory about economic cycles, the 'Kondratiev wave' (see the next section).

First the problem of power. Within postindustrial theory, Bell suggested that the new axial principle was 'theroetical knowledge'. He implied that scientific and technical workers would have a key political-administrative role, especially in the universities. As I noted above, cuts in education expenditure and the politicizing of technology policy make this a sick joke. No direct relation betwen knowledge and power exists in this context at least, as Bell now admits: 'The fear that a knowledge elite could become the technocratic rulers of the society is quite far-fetched.'[26]

Julian Newman and Rhona Newman complain that other cavalier uses of the 'information work' concept have similarly vitiated 'information society' analysis. They remind us that Fritz Machlup was so keen to establish the importance of knowledge workers in the economy that he even included striptease dancers among them![27] The Newmans go on to propose some criteria whereby the common confusion of 'mechanism' and 'purpose' can be overcome. If information is 'that which destroys uncertainty', then its importance to the economy lies in its contribution to economic adaptation through decisions made by firms, governments, unions, consumers, and so on. And it must be seen in relation to organiza-tional processes which shape labour markets and work situations.

'Information operatives' such as draughtsmen or typists have little power compared with managers. So why not distinguish further between 'knowledge' and 'information'? 'Information is the answer to a question. Knowledge is the framework that enables the question to be asked'.[28] Seen in this light, workers tied to IT may well not have much power at all. A decision analyst (knowledge worker), while far above the word-processor operator in terms of knowledge and information intensity, is also much more likely to be near the centre of decision-making power than, say, a systems analyst, whose work is bound up with IT.

Such distinctions help to rescue the information society concept from trivialization, and to inject into it a fresh understanding of exploitation and power relations. The Newmans suggest that a new divorce is occurring, within the 'technocracy', between external intelligence (about threats and opportunities for the firm) and internal planning (with the latter firmly subordinate to the former). They also wonder whether rewards and prospects may not increasingly be related to this 'divorce'. Such paths lead to the discussion of class, and are taken up presently.

But class is not the only expression of such inequalities. 'Divorces' new and old are also evident, for instance, as technology mediates power along gender lines. Routine data entry and word processing are tasks frequently done by women. As 'information operatives' they have very little say over what they do or how they do it. Cynthia Cockburn points out that 'technological change doesn't of itself affect the long-lived pattern: men have technical skills and knowledge, women don't . . . In the electronics industry in Britain in 1984, 95 per cent of scientists and technologists, 94 per cent of the technicians, 98 per cent of craft workers and 97 per cent of managers were men'.[29] These differences, along with others, are all too often obscured within accounts of 'new technology and society'.

The information sector as slogan

So why is the 'information sector' idea so popular? Not so much because of its empirical credibility, I suggest, as because of its usefulness as a slogan. The felt connection between the service sector and information technology seems to make it irresistible to certain policy-makers and pundits. The burgeoning 'information sector' is hailed as the harbinger of the new age. A British government booklet entitled *Information technology: the age of electronic information*, for instance, asserts that 65 per cent of employed Britons earn their living in what may be broadly classified as information occupations.[30] The American Bureau of Labor Statistics comes to similar conclusions for the USA (see figure 1). The purpose of the pamphlet is to raise awareness of the commercial and industrial potential of IT. But the conviction behind it is clear: 'IT is going to transform our way of living.'

As a slogan, however, the idea of the information sector emerges from a typically Western faith in the transformative power of technology. At a time of recalcitrant economic recession and fragile international relations, IT is sought as a saviour. Hence the enthusiasm - and lack of critical inquiry - which too often surrounds the term.

Again, it is a problem of perspective. The focus is on amazing technical breakthroughs and the prognoses of confident computer tycoons or futurologists, which simply diverts attention from other matters. Examples of the latter occur both in the remainder of this, and in later chapters. They include these three. First, possible unemployment effects within information-related spheres are downplayed, alongside a refusal to integrate unemployment policy into a coherent industrial policy. Second, adjustments in power relations consequent on knowledge- and information-intensivity within occupations are often ignored. Third, shifts within the global division of labour, in which dirty, dangerous or boring manufacturing work is transferred to the Southern hemisphere, are minimized by talk of 'deindustrialization' in North America and Western Europe.

The 'information sector' idea is also bolstered by a theory known as the 'Kondratiev cycle'. In the 1920s, this Russian economist claimed to discern fifty- to sixty-year-long waves of economic activity. This appears plausible now, since the previous depression occurred in the 1930s; fifty years ago. But the contribution of Joseph Schumpeter to the theory has recently been revived by scholars such as Christopher Freeman. Schumpeter observed that Kondratiev's waves coincided with the dissemination of steam power in the eighteenth century, the railways in the mid-nineteenth, and the motor car and electricity in the early twentieth century.

Contemporary disciples of Kondratiev see in the development and diffusion of IT the potential for a further technologically induced wave of economic activity, bringing with it a new occupational and industrial structure based around the 'information sector'. Apart from the statistical difficulties involved in identifying the 'waves' (which are considerable[31]), as Tom Kitwood points out, a mere metaphor has been raised to the status of theory. All too easily, then, this substitutes for careful analysis both of actions of the *dramatis personae*, and of major social processes such as militarism and government policy.[32]

Having said that, Miles and Gershuny, whose work refers approvingly to Kondratiev, should not be associated with the kind of technological determinism which appears to lurk within (Schumpeter's version of) the 'wave' metaphor. They stress action and choice as well as socio-technological constraint. For myself, I prefer to distance discussions of information activities from any cyclic predictions emanating from economics.

In short, the 'information sector' idea is in trouble on several counts.

Within social theory, it compounds the misunderstanding of 'industrialization' which postindustrialism and 'information society' theories have in common. Information activities and services have grown within modern societies, but they are not new arrivals on the scene. The 'march through the sectors' from agriculture to industry to services never happened (and Kondratiev cannot make the information sector appear either). The whole picture is vastly more complex. So the prospects for a new 'information society' are correspondingly less easy to discern. The 'information sector', though it is used by serious analysts, is all too often a slogan used by those interested in precipitating us into the 'information society' of which it is, apparently, the vanguard.

New technology: new classes?

If the steam mill gave us a capitalist class, as Marx said, then what does the computer give us? What does the coming of IT mean for class and power in today's world? This is a pivotal question for any theory of 'information society'. Put this way, however, it is misleading. A form of agrarian capitalism preceded the steam mill; capitalism is not limited to *industrial* production. Hence there is no *a priori* reason why capitalism should not continue to help shape the development of the new technologies. The question before us is whether or not information technologies and their associated industrial and social processes actually help change the rules of the game. Daniel Bell, by putting his money on information as the key resource and central organizing concept, offers this as a clear alternative to Marx's equivalent treatment of capital.

For the sake of clarity, I identify three kinds of answers. One, new technology holds hope of abandoning 'class'; classlessness achieved by technical, not social revolution. As a conceptual casualty of change, this is 'class rejected'. Two, IT merely strengthens the hand of the already powerful capitalist class, giving it a wider (global) scope and the tools for tighter social control. This is 'class reasserted'. Three, Marx is now outdated, but not because classes are disappearing. The introduction of new technology tilts the balance of power in different ways, realigning classes and releasing new social movements. This is 'class reconceptualized'.

Class rejected

Many proponents of the information society give the impression that new social relationships appear all round. 'Old-fashioned' capitalism and socialism are frequently said to be doomed by the arrival of information technology. Not only has the 'white-collar' sector dwarfed the 'blue-collar' (which in itself has class implications) but today's industrial and political trends – according to Naisbitt – are leading the advanced societies away from hierarchy and domination to 'networking' and 'participation'.[33]

Japan showed the way for American companies, for example: 'Japanese workers, clustered into small, decentralised work-groups, made work decisions themselves, and the people on top received their word as something resembling gospel'.[34] The American experience, in turn, is instructive for Britons, writes Andrew Neil. Learn the lesson from Boulder, Colorado: 'The great joy of the information society is that it will be a liberating force in those in the lowest, most mundane jobs.' Why? Look at history: 'As Britain began the railway age, the Duke of Wellington complained that railways would "enable the working classes to move about". He was right . . .. The information revolution will take the liberation much further.'[35]

All in all, prospects are bright, wherever one is placed on the socio-economic scale. Daniel Bell is relieved to announce the end of that mechanized control of workers to the industrial tempo depicted in Charlie Chaplin's *Modern times*. 'The beat has been broken', he says.[36] (Why then, one might ask, the rather ominous re-appearance of Charlie Chaplin in IBM advertisements? Perhaps the digital beat is more benign.) At the other end of the scale are equally hopeful signs; a 'growing egalitarianism fostered in large measure by sectors of the knowledge elite'.[37] Unfortunately the only evidence which Bell cites for this is 'certain European universities' where 'even non-professional staffs are given a voice'.

Not that these authors are blind to current inequalities; each worries about the reappearance of 'Two Nations', North–South divisions, or about the social consequences of massive long-term unemployment levels. But, in a manner reminiscent of nineteenth-century sociologist of industrialism Èmile Durkheim, these appear as the temporary strains and frictions of transition to a new era. For Stonier, 'The major problem confronting Western governments in the 1980s is the need to devise . . . a smooth transition from an industrial to an information economy.'[38] The more popular or policy-oriented the account, the more the conclusion tends to be that the major task is to exploit the new technologies to the full. The resulting prosperity will benefit all.

Without disputing claims either that IT could be used in liberating and egalitarian ways, or that (potentially desirable) alterations are occurring within organizations and in other social relationships, it seems clear to me that these kinds of accounts are mistaken when they ignore or minimize questions of class and power. As is so frequently the case, the supposed technical promise is confused with social reality. IT is not a class-corrosive tool. The next two sections constitute critiques of this first position.

Class reasserted

Marxist analyses suggest that, while information technology does play a significant role within capitalist societies, it does not alter the fundamental relations of production which lie at their base. As David Albury and Joseph Schwartz put it: 'The so-called microprocessor revolution is part of the effort of capital to ensure its continued domination over social and economic development during a period of crisis and change. The myth of technological progress serves to disguise the class interest at work behind the introduction of these machines.'[39] Marxists' efforts are dedicated to exposing and countering that 'class interest'.

One could say that Marxism is a theory of *technological* societies. Nature is transformed by people, using tools. As Marx wrote, 'Nature builds no machines, no locomotives, railways, electric telegraphs, self-acting mules etc. These are products of human industry . . . the power of knowledge, objectified.'[40] So human activity is mediated through technology; but it is *class* activity; 'It would be possible to write a whole history of the inventions made since 1830, for the sole purpose of providing capital with weapons against working class revolts. We would mention, above all, the self-acting mule, because it opened up a new epoch in the automatic system'.[41] It is the view that new technology is *solely* bound up with class struggle – because it assists in the exploitative accumulation process – that characterizes Marxist accounts.

The use of machines ('machinofacture'), assembly lines, 'scientific management' and now automation and robotics is seen as an ongoing way of perpetuating the interests of capital, at the expense of labour. It may eat into new areas, expanding into consumption (especially the domestic sphere), culture, and previously unaffected parts of the globe, but it is essentially the same process at work. The continuing importance of the legal ownership of capital (whatever the changes in its composition) on the one hand, and the still considerable strength of the historical working-class movement on the other remain the key factors for Marxist analysis.[42]

Marxist discussions of IT take these items as read, although the internationalization of capital via the big global corporations is often described as the 'monopoly capital' stage. The primary rationale for technological change, then, is to 'restructure capitalism' so that nations and companies may be better placed to compete in the global market-place.[43] In the effort to accomplish this, it is argued, unions and the working class in general may expect to be threatened both by legislation aimed to curb their power, and by deskilling and job losses.

The issue of de-skilling has formed a dominant motif within the Marxist debate over IT. The work of Harry Braverman, which focuses on the effects of separating mental from manual labour, has been a huge stimulus to the class analysis of automation. Although his own conclusions are now widely regarded as badly flawed, the consequences of that 'divorce' continue to be researched (as we noted above in the work of Newman and Newman). As much of the next chapter is taken up with questions of jobs and skills, I shall not discuss those here. Suffice it to say that, once again, careful study of a variety of occupations and industries reveals no obvious general trends towards deskilling. At the same time, it is equally clear that in some contexts new technology does feature prominently in struggles between management and employees.

Other ways in which the ongoing relevance of class analysis to IT is stressed include the idea of cultural control. As well as the 'elite network' of corporations, foundations, universities, policy planning groups and government bodies which 'seeks to harmonize the interests of capital and filter out challenges to its hegemony',[44] the fact that IT is poised for a major expansion into the domestic sphere also bodes ill for consumers. Nicholas Garnham gloomily predicts that the new home communications set, far from introducing a rich range of fresh entertainment and services, will in fact simply extend the 'dull compulsion of economic relations to more and more spheres of social life'.[45] Monopoly capitalism stretches its tentacles into the area of consumption as well as production.

To the question, 'what does the computer mean for social class in today's world?' most Marxists would reply, 'more of the same'. 'A revolution of the fixed wheel' is an appropriate characterization, say Kevin Robins and Frank Webster.[46] So far from facilitating a new classless situation of open opportunities, the 'smashing of hierarchy' and freed time, IT reinforces the contradictions within capitalism originally identified by Marx. The relentless quest for accumulation pushes capital to penetrate new domains both on a global and a domestic level, as well as tightening the screw of exploitation within the productive workforce.

Discussion of Marx, IT and class continues below. But the focus changes. Because the nature of class is perceived to have altered by some who still use Marx as a kind of theoretical springboard, and because this also rings bells with others who would not begin with Marxian analysis at all, the next section is concerned with a rather different range of issues. The essential two-class model of classic Marxism is no longer in the foreground.

Class reconceptualized

Within the postindustrial society, according to Bell, workers in the predominant services (health, education, research and government) comprise the 'new intelligentsia'.[47] This professional and technical class does the typical work of information society; planning and forecasting, research and development. War-time emergencies stimulated such activities, and post-war technological and economic planning took them further. The goal, said Bell, is to 'realize a social alchemist's dream: the dream of "ordering" the mass society'.[48]

Like his nineteenth-century forebear Saint-Simon, Bell seemed to survey this 'technocratic' scene without qualm. Why should society not be organized more rationally? Having once referred to a 'knowledge class', however, Bell now denies both that it is a class on the model of the bourgeoisie, and that it could 'rule'.[49] Alvin Toffler agrees with him. 'Third Wave' advocates, including the mainstream of intellectuals, information-workers, and technicians are engaged in a struggle, but it is primarily a struggle for liberation from 'Second Wave' existence. Only by 'twisting the term' could one call them a 'class'.[50]

Other observers are not so sure. Knowledge work, and some information work, as we have seen, may well confer power on those engaged in it. It does appear that, as those with access to the decision-making machinery gain power, so others experience progressive powerlessness. Today's top manager can have more relevant information readily available at his fingertips, and may well be able to make executive decisions affecting subordinates without consulting them. Is access to and control of significant information replacing property as a new source of class division?

Let me put the debate in context. The concept of a 'new class' is inseparable from wider arguments over social classes and the potential of any one of them to transform industrial capitalism. Non-Marxist sociologists believe that social change has rendered irrelevant the Marxist account of class and class conflict. This includes the diffusion of capital by shareholding, the rise of 'managerial' power, the 'institutionalization of class conflict' within industrial relations and the growth of the 'welfare state'. Marxists, on the other hand, while admitting that social changes can occur, insist that their import does not fatally damage Marxist accounts.

The key problem, for our purposes, is that of the so-called middle classes. Marxism assumes a polarization of two fundamental conflicting social interests, labour and capital. But even Marx recognized the difficulty of placing intermediate strata within this scheme. Various 'revisionists' have attempted to cope with this difficulty during the twentieth century, but it was in the 1960s that several theories appeared which linked the middle-class problem with the new technology.

A number of French sociologists (Serge Mallet, André Gorz and others[51]) claimed that a new working-class segment could be observed within high-technology production. Higher educational and skills levels and more communal patterns of work organization within the 'new working class' enabled them to see more clearly the contradictions inherent within capitalism. Their inferior rewards and their lack of control became more visible. This insight can in fact be traced to Marx, who foresaw that the progress of technology meant that 'the human being comes to relate more as a watchman and a regulator of the production process',[52] the implication being that this would also create space for workers to see themselves in this light.

Such ideas have been countered in several ways, however. High-tech workers do not necessarily understand the processes in which they are involved. Within a semi-automated chemical plant, for instance, one study found the majority of workers still doing unskilled, dirty, and arduous 'donkey work'.[53] Big variations of responsibility and skill exist even within apparently homogeneous groups such as 'technicians'; there may be skilled and unskilled computer workers. And whatever the specific circumstances, no clear evidence exists of such a class trying to overthrow capitalism. For instance, higher degrees of militancy, as Duncan Gallie found when comparing French with British workers, relate more to the way they are treated by management. British managers, by more frequently seeking consent, contain potential strife.[54]

Still, debate over the 'new class' continues. Barbara and John Ehren-reichs, for instance, see in the USA a third force between the capitalist and working class of traditional Marxism: the 'professional-managerial class'. Many in this class for various reasons have anti-capitalist sentiments, but find themselves in a curious position vis-a-vis the working class. 'Both classes confront the capitalist class over the issue of ownership and control of the means of production. They confront each other over the issues of knowledge, skills, culture.'[55] These are also the issues that Nicholas Abercrombie and John Urry (more from the perspective of Max Weber) emphasize in a British context. They hint at the power of what they call the 'service class' to affect the future shape of society. However, they distinguish between this class, which performs functions relating to capital, and 'deskilled white collar workers' whose position is closer to the traditional proletariat.[56]

These discussions bear strong affinity with a seminal argument, in the early 1970s, of Alan Touraine. For him, educational credentials are becoming increasingly important for determining one's class position. The division between manual and mental labour is the basis for a new kind of class conflict. He did not hesitate to isolate technocrats as a new dominant class, whose decision-making power is crucial both to maintaining their position and to alienating those denied it. Thus 'in the programmed society, neither firms nor unions are today the chief actors in the struggle over social powers'.[57] By the 1980s, Touraine would assert that socialism is dead. So far from the bearer of a universal project of human emancipation, it is now a mere forum for sectional interests.[58]

So where is the new opposition? For Touraine, resistance comes from those excluded from participation in the decision-making process, who find themselves at the mercy of technocracy. They may include trades unionists, but also feminists, ecologists, members of peace movements, people involved in 'alternative' media and so on. Widespread support for the environmentalist group, 'Greenpeace', the 'alternative plan' for socially useful production drawn up by the Lucas Aerospace Combine, or the opposition of computer scientists to the SDI programme are examples of the kind of resistance Touraine has in mind.

Of course, counteracting the technocracy is not easy. As 'critical theorists' Herbert Marcuse and Jürgen Habermas have striven to show, modern societies are characterized by a pervasive 'technocratic consciousness'. That is to say, as more and more attempts are made to run society along 'rational' lines, space for resistance efforts based on a moral or normative critique becomes more and more restricted.[59] Jacques Ellul makes a similar point, in a different way: *la technique* excludes questions of purpose.[60] As informatization occurs, this process is likely to be carried further, thus adding urgency and contemporary relevance to Ellul's critique. As I indicate in chapter 8, understanding this appears to have galvanized at least some computer professionals and others into a quest for appropriate purposes and a socially-informed normative approach.

In the hands of a Touraine or a Habermas, the concept of class struggle is taken a long way beyond Marx. For Habermas in particular, the increased role of science and technology in the production process undermines Marx's reliance on the labour theory of value. Class conflict no longer has the potential to affect the central structures of society. Nevertheless, struggles will go on, in the hope of helping direct social change. New movements are appearing, according to Touraine, which do provide challenges to the status quo and resistance to the technocratic mentality.

But to return to the central question, is it appropriate to think of there being a new 'class' which holds power in any effective sense? The conclusion of John Goldthorpe is apposite. Whatever apparent divisions may exist within what he calls the 'service class', overall professional, administrative and managerial personnel tend to be basically conservative, and are unlikely to challenge the wider status quo.[61] Earlier in the chapter I commented on the relative impotence of universities to control their future, let alone that of wider society, in the later twentieth century. They are in general less central to 'knowledge production' today. Such work is commonly done in large corporations and government laboratories as well. Moreover, we have seen that involvement within high-tech industries does not necessarily confer power on individuals or groups. 'Information workers' may in fact be very routinized and have little access to decision-making.

'Knowledge is power' is a misleading slogan. Knowledge may well be important to the maintenance of power, but that does not mean that the knowledgeable are powerful. Any ruling elite (think of the USSR) may use the apparatus of science and technology to buttress their dominant position. Bell's 'knowledge elites' may even be indispensable to the running of society, but that indispensability does not in itself confer power upon them except in so far as they may be able to limit the activities of their paymasters. (Slaves, after all, were indispensable to Athenian life, but had no say in its direction.)

While the changing occupational-industrial structure does have implications for class and power, none of these seems at present to alter the fundamental shape of capitalist industrial societies. But – and here's the rub – 'capitalist/industrial' does not necessarily exhaust the possible ways of describing modern society. The growth of technocratic consciousness, and opposition to it, is a factor that cannot be ignored, especially as the whole process of rationalization is augmented by the introduction of information technology. As I shall argue, information certainly does spell power in another context, that of surveillance. So new social movements, while they might not have the potential to transform society single-handed (as Marxian theory requires of class), may yet point the way to alternative forms of social organization.

Conclusion

The cornerstone of the popular information society thesis is that a new 'information sector', comprising 'information workers' has become a dominant economic factor in the advanced societies. But the composition of this cornerstone is fatally crumbling. The evidence points, not to an information sector, but to the increase of a diverse range of information activities, whose social significance depends on a complex series of variables. Many kinds of work are likely to become information-intensive, but this does not add up to a new sector.

Similarly mistaken is the notion that the new classes may be accompanying the spread of information technology. Education and skills levels are becoming a more important criterion for determining social position, but this does not (yet at any rate) seem to have affected the basic social divisions based on property. Some technocrats may have more power, but do not rule. On the other hand, the simple Marxian view of class polarization is also open to serious question.

The matter cannot be left there, however. Consider Touraine once more. The value of his alternative view of the 'programmed society' is twofold. Firstly, he challenges those bland accounts of a smooth transition to an information society, and secondly, he dismisses the idea that class struggle is the only axis along which conflicts occur in modern societies.

Or to put it another way, new technology mediates other kinds of social relationships as well as class.

As I observed earlier, IT, often designed, developed, sold and used by men, may channel male power. Yet women are not meekly accepting such subordination. Nor are they accepting technology as defined by men. The slowly increasing strength of female participation in technology may open up new areas of contested terrain over fundamental issues. For example, Joan Rothschild comments that while women are challenging male predominance in high technology jobs, their involvement also leads to 'a refusal to make the sharp separation between work, family and personal life that is dictated by the male work–world.'[62]

Another major arena of power is this. Touraine sees control of and access to information as a crucial medium of domination. Although he overstates the newness of this phenomenon, its importance today is illustrated not only in the workplace – to which I turn in the next chapter – but also in the area of state administration. With greater computerization, new technologies both channel and help to generate this form of power as well.[63] Some implications of this are explored in chapter 5.

Clearly, class continues to be an important feature of contemporary societies characterized by growth in IT. But equally clearly, power has other axes as well. As long as human beings are depicted merely as 'labouring animals acting against nature in an alienating social fabric'[64] the full significance of IT for social relationships will be missed.

4

New technology, employment, work and skills

Can't you see the waste of it – waste of labour, skill, cunning, waste of life in short? ... I have spoken of machinery being used freely for releasing people from the more mechanical and repulsive part of necessary labour; ... It is the allowing machines to be our masters and not our servants that so injures the beauty of life nowadays.

William Morris (1888)[1]

Three popular images of working life in the 'information age' get to the heart of this chapter's concerns. The first is the robotic assembly line. Television advertisements bring us vividly memorable pictures of bleak but highly precise and efficient machines which assemble, weld, and spray-paint our cars: Nissan factories in Japan, Fiat factories in Italy. From the computer-simulated wind tunnel which gives the aerodynamic shape to the design, to the dealer's ordering process, new technology appears to have 'taken over'.

This image may be extended to include word-processor operators in the modern office, journalists bypassing typesetters as they compose tomorrow's headlines, or the automatic bank facilities in the high street. In each case it is apparent that 'work' has changed its character. But the nature of the change may be harder to discern. Some hear only the industrialists' impatient cry to make good the 'skills shortage'. From this, one concludes that the general skills level is rising. Others see only the job losses entailed in automation, or the skill losses from the jobs that remain.

The second image is that of new industrial relations. Glancing over their shoulders at what is happening in Japan or in 'Silicon Valley' the new technologists predict the shape of things to come. As one glossy publication puts it: 'One of Silicon Valley's most felicitous inventions may be the blurring of the boundaries between labor and management. An extra-ordinary egalitarian style of work prevails in which the boss listens to his associates as equals and where almost everyone shares the financial fruits of new technologies. . . . Status symbols and hierarchies are rare at Silicon Valley companies.'[2] But how far is it possible (or desirable) to transfer this kind of dream to other national and industrial contexts?

The European situation seems light years away from such halcyon conditions. Hierarchy, along with other traditional patterns of industrial relations, seems to be entrenched, with the result that introducing new technology is often fraught with potential conflict. The changing work and employment situation seems to engender fear and anxiety rather than providing challenge and opportunity.

Moving to a third image, we again find an implicit promise of 'restored relationships', in the 'electronic cottage'. This phrase, popularized by Alvin Toffler, points to a phenomenon which is indeed experiencing techno-logically encouraged growth, homeworking. Using computer terminals in their own homes, and connected to a central business or organization base by new telecommunications, these new homeworkers are viewed by many as the vanguard of the new era.

When ecological and practical advantages are added to the inevitable commercial ones, the attraction of the electronic cottage seems irresistible. But once again, serious analysis poses quetions: What proportion of the workforce is likely to be involved in such homeworking? How unambi-guous are the advantages? What are the actual trends (for example, are as many men as women likely to become involved)?

These three images provide a way into the themes of this chapter. The more clinical statistics of an 'information sector', or the broader brush strokes of 'new classes' are here translated into everyday human terms. In what follows we look in more detail at the debates over 'automatic unemployment' and 'de-skilling', and at the ways information technology is affecting industrial relations and women's work. All this puts us in a better position to assess claims that we are entering the 'information society'.

New technology and employment

The chips are down was the title of a discussion paper[3] and a television documentary which first alerted a wide cross-section of the British public to possible job consequences of developing the silicon chip. It had a visible impact on politicians and policy-makers, and thus played a role in the subsequent spread of microelectronics in the UK. For a number of years some American observers have referred to the new technology as a 'job-killer', and similar fears have been expressed elsewhere. But the underlying message is still a nettle to be grasped. The changes associated with the chip coincide with and contribute to changes in the very nature of employment.

Information technology affects employment at every level. The overall loss of jobs in the advanced economies, or at least the restructuring of employment opportunities, is intimately bound up with the 'chip'. Of course, present high unemployment cannot be blamed on new technology – it is part of a more general world recession – but neither can future job prospects be considered apart from that new technology.

For a start, it is clear that the chip makes possible a tremendous growth in labour-saving devices. Those car-factory robots do work previously requiring human dexterity and strength. And although the recession's effect of slowing investment rates may at present cushion the blow of 'automatic unemployment', it will eventually be felt in many other areas as well. For instance, when expert systems are installed in the construction industry – to gauge the strain on traffice-use on a bridge, or to analyse damp patches on ceilings – the eventual effect could be to halve the number of professionals in this field.[4]

Secondly, previous displacement of people from manufacturing was partly compensated for (during the 1960s and 1970s) by the growth of employment in the public sector, particularly in 'services'. Not only is the scale of this likely to be smaller now, given the contraction of public spending in many advanced economies, but automation is affecting this sphere as well. Local and national governments are setting up their own computerized systems for information gathering. And in offices, the steady spread of telecommunications networks and computer-based equipment heralds the labour-saving regime of electronic data processing. The French 'Nora and Minc Report' was among the first to make this plain. In a brief survey of banks, insurance, social security, postal and office work they warned: 'computerisation will result in considerable manpower reductions in the large service organizations'.[5]

In both these ways, then, new technology is implicated in the employment debate. Older manufacturing industries – 'smokestacks' as the Americans call them – are in decline as large-scale employers (at least in the Northern hemisphere). But the desire to 'have a job' within the traditional structure of employment has not declined in the same way. Indeed, the demand for jobs, which in the 1960s and 1970s was swelled especially by the growing proportion of married women in the labour market, is likely to increase further as the children of the sixties also enter that market. The gap between supply and demand for jobs is unemployment.

What will be the long-term effect of IT on employment? Plenty of opinions and forecasts are on offer,[6] but the range and complexity of factors involved make the question unanswerable. However we do know some of the significant factors on which the answer will depend. Colin Gill summarizes these as follows. One, the economic growth rate affects technologically induced unemployment. Japan, for instance, with a high growth rate, tends to lose less jobs than, say, Britain. Two, 'IT unemployment' is related to growth in the labour force. Where women and school-leavers are expanding the labour force, unemployment will be greater. Three, the emergence of new IT-related jobs may affect unemployment levels, but different skills are also needed, and they may not be required at all in areas of traditional industrial employment. Thus unemployment becomes unevenly distributed geographically, with areas like the British North-East or the American mid-West ending up much worse off.[7]

Most recent forecasts in Britain, for instance, predict that the greatest growth in jobs in the next few years will be concentrated in managerial, technical and healthcare occupations. Skills shortages will become more serious (and this is more true of Britain than some other countries, because salaries have not kept pace with the qualifications requirement). Some argue that the new managerial and supervisory jobs are likely to be more equally split between men and women, and in education and health the majority of jobs will go to women. Only half the number of women as men will fill engineering, scientific and technical positions.[8] But this obscures the depressing fact, noted by Heather Menzies in a Canadian context, that women displaced by clerical automation are themselves highly unlikely to fill positions in expanding technical echelons where men have the appropriate qualifications.

Older industries are first and hardest hit by automation. West German textile firms, for instance, have lost (by the mid-1980s) almost half the jobs which were available in 1970. At the same time, productivity has risen. But even in the older industries, big variations exist. Much depends upon the way in which new technology is applied. Some industries are slower to modernize than others, and for various reasons; lack of suitable machines or software, traditional management inertia or simply because they generate insufficient return. The combination of higher productivity but less available jobs is becoming a more common pattern, often referred to as 'jobless growth'.

Until recently, jobs have not been lost with great rapidity. For instance in 1961 Britain had 24.5 million people employed, a figure which rose to 25.2 million by 1980, and only since then has been falling.[9] It is the coincidence of this more recent fall with rising demand for jobs which makes unemployment so severe. Thus, even though unemployment which is directly attributable to new technology may not increase at an acute rate, the combination of factors noted strongly suggests that relatively high levels of unemployment will continue to be the lot of many advanced societies for several decades to come. Job-losses will continue to outnumber job-gains, more particularly in Western Europe than North America or Japan.[10]

However, not everyone agrees that 'unemployment' is the best angle from which to view these changes. Some see the displacing effect of new technology as a temporary phenomenon, an unfortunate but short-lived aspect of the transition to an information society. Once established, the new information-based economies will generate new jobs of their own, some with descriptions we would not even recognize today. Miles and Gershuny hint at the possibilities for a 'new socio-technical system' in which existing services might be transformed: and there could be the emergence of new information and advice services, and the growth of interactive informal use of telematics (to establish like-minded or like-needful groups for car-sharing, pressure groups, romantic liaisons, consumer advice, bartering of child-care and do-it-yourself (DIY) work . . .).[11] The 'might' and the 'could be' are not insignificant. Miles and Gershuny stress that no new socio-technical system will appear automatically. They are not to be numbered among the IT social alchemists. Novel career paths – particularly perhaps in information management – may well open up. But while no genuine rays of hope should be dismissed lightly, realism is also vital.

Apart from the fact that we simply do not and cannot know which IT-related fields will generate jobs, three other comments are pertinent. One, as mentioned above, the recession is currently inhibiting investment and thus innovation. This may mean that in a more 'healthy' (that is, according to the criterion of growth) economic climate wealth but not jobs will be created. And even if some jobs are created, in the context of today's world economy, the balance of jobs is likely to be tilted in favour of the Southern hemisphere.

Two, it is unlikely that many IT-based jobs will appear without the development of a suitable information infrastructure. This infrastructure, which involves above all a digital telecommunications network, would play an analogous role within the emerging society to that played by the expansion of roads, railways, and canals at the beginning of the industrial era. Thirdly, it is clear that a serious mismatch still obtains between the kinds of informatics-related jobs which might be created and the low skills levels typical among many of those currently seeking employment.

All such qualifications serve as reminders that information technology does not itself determine the future shape of society in general or of employment in particular. The appearance of jobs within an information intensive environment cannot be assumed in the absence of deliberate long-term policies for employment. Likewise, the information infrastructure is likely to develop more rapidly in countries where there is extensive state direction and involvement in it. The French commitment to videotex is a case in point. Their Teletel system has already dwarfed the British Prestel project which as an innovation once led the world. (Even in this case, however, in the later 1980s it is too early to tell whether IT investment fulfils long-term hopes.[12])

The other group who doubt the wisdom of seeing change simply as more unemployment are those who predict a 'leisure future'. In this view, the tremendous wealth created by the application of microelectronic technologies will free the growing proportion of the population to 'do what they wish' with their time. Clive Jenkins and Barrie Sherman toy with the idea of a 'leisure shock'.[13] Tom Stonier on the basis of his assertion that within twenty-five years we shall only require ten per cent of the labour force, sees scope for more of the 'happiness industry', which includes leisure but also aspects of health, education and social care.[14]

This group also includes some who perceive an irony in any socialist attempt to preserve jobs. André Gorz, for instance, wonders why, after spending a century complaining about the drudgery of some jobs, certain unions should now complain at their technological removal.[15] He has a point, of course. Microchip-related reductions in tedium and danger in jobs must surely be seen as a gain. For Gorz, new technology makes possible the 'abolition of work' and the 'liberation of time'. His is a radical critique of the present social division between an aristocracy of tenured workers on the one hand, the mass of unemployed on the other, with a smallish proletariat of unskilled temporary workers in between.

Questions must be placed against the leisure future view. Whatever the long-term consequences of information technology – and freeing (some) human beings from drudgery is undoubtedly one of them – the 'enforced leisure'[16] of the currently unemployed cannot simply be equated with Gorz's 'self-determined activity'. Within wealthy Western societies the unemployed are stigmatized, socially dislocated, economically disadvantaged and politically neglected. Even though Gorz sees the need for some kind of guaranteed income to make possible a society based on the free use of time (an economically feasible though as yet in most countries a politically unacceptable doctrine[17]), today's hardest hit unemployed – women, young people, ethnic minorities – could be forgiven for seeing that as pie in the sky.

Of course the hi-tech enthusiasts and utopians are easily dismissed. But the reason for their apparent magniloquence is quite sound. The social changes experienced at present are profound. Whatever one says about the 'information society' idea, the fact remains that Western – indeed global – economies are radically restructuring. Several old wineskins – whether social or conceptual – are stretched beyond their limit. And the 'new wine' has information technology as a vital ingredient.

One aspect of this restructuring is the growth of the 'informal economy', one of the newer divisions of labour mentioned in chapter 3. This residual economy itself contains important divisions; the 'black economy', which is undeclared and therefore illicit business, the so-called mauve economy which is personal services and home-based businesses on the margin of the formal economy, and the 'grey economy' of legal but uncounted domestic and voluntary work in which we are all engaged to some extent.'[18]

The growth in unemployment in the formal economy is no doubt part of the reason for the increase in 'informal' activity, although shorter working hours and higher living standards are far more important factors. The actual extent of the informal economy is far from clear. Again, new technology may well be implicated here, not so much in things like home wine-making, but in small household businesses assessing and penetrating markets more effectively, or offering information services. What must be remembered, however, is that the informal economy cannot exist without the formal. It cannot be an independent source of jobs.

For all our ignorance of the overall impact of IT on jobs, general agreement exists that the impact is real, pervasive and occurs at an increasing pace. This in itself puts a different complexion on the debate since the arrival of the 'chip'. New IT-related jobs are appearing, but it does seem doubtful that they could ever replace those lost (and they seldom replace specific jobs), let alone keep pace with rising demand. Another area of agreement is that whatever happens, appropriate education and training should be provided to enable all to prepare for changing circumstances. Social choice, as well as technological potential, is clearly crucial to whatever pattern eventually emerges. Right now, choices are short-term, and are largely based on a belief, dubious, as we have seen – that exploiting new technology as fully as possible will solve the unemployment crisis.

The de-skilling debate

The introduction to workplaces of computer-based aids profoundly affects work organization. New processes frequently mean new working relationships. This in turn has several aspects. It enhances the quality of some jobs; it also means new separations, of worker from product, and of worker from fellow-worker. In some cases it means new levels of coopera-tion between workers, in others, greater control by management of employees.

At a United Biscuits Scottish plant, computer-aided process controls were introduced at the mixing stage. Craftsmen ('doughmen') had previously done this, making ongoing adjustments according to tradi-tional skills, and working with a team of labourers. Now the doughmen's skills were translated into a computer medium, which then from a separate room controlled the mixing process. The skilled doughmen were left with fewer, and simpler tasks, saying when to start the machines, emptying the mixer and so on.[19]

The benefits of change included greater and more consistent product with less labour, but neither management nor doughmen were content. The latter complained of boredom, isolation, and a sense of deprivation as control shifted to the computer room. Management saw a deterioration in worker concentration, care, and willingness to take responsibility.

Looking back, all parties saw that things could have been arranged differently. The doughmen could have had more control-room respon-sibilities which used their skills, and there need not have been quite such a separation of tasks and people. The new technology would still have increased production (although overheads involved in setting up the separate control room could have been saved).

The debate over 'de-skilling' concerns situations just like this. It is nothing new, of course. The famous Luddites who resisted the spread of stocking frames in early-nineteenth-century Yorkshire and Nottingham-shire deliberately smashed certain specific machines which seemed to threaten their skills and their labour.[20] (Then as now most skilled workers were not anti-technology *as such*.) Machines have often been used to eliminate skills from work, and have sometimes simultaneously created a demand for new skills. Information technology gives this process a huge spurt. The question is, will its introduction tend to reduce the number of traditional apprenticeships and the knowledgeability of workers? Will management take tighter control of production, while workers' jobs are evacuated of their former skills?

The debate is focused around the controversial work of Harry Braverman.[21] He argues that capitalism has reached a monopoly stage, characterized by economic concentration and the domination of markets by a small number of large firms. Professional managers control the day-to-day administration of firms, and wish to maximize their control in order to remain competitive. Earlier this century the principles of (Frederick Taylor's) 'scientific management' aided the managers' cause by attempting systematically to eliminate all guesswork and rule of thumb from the production process. The 'conception' of a task was to be separated from its 'execution'. With the coming of IT, claim Braverman's followers, such 'Taylorism' is quickly extended into new areas, including the office. De-skilling becomes the dominant trend.

Braverman's enthusiastic reception was especially strong among those who saw his work as injecting a badly needed shot of real-life empirical study into a somewhat aridly theoretical Marxism. The malign forces of capitalism were clearly still evident in the workplace. The conflict between capital and labour seemed set to escalate as new technology was adopted. Braverman's work has stimulated an industry of de-skilling studies, which considerably modify his original claims. 'Bravermania' has thus been cooled.[22]

The main lines of criticism levelled against his work are these. He romanticizes the role of the traditional artisan in order to make a contrast with the de-skilled situation. He exaggerates the extent to which 'pure' Taylorism has been adopted both within firms and unilaterally across firms. In fact, many alternative strategies are evident. The boundary between 'conception' and 'execution' of tasks, which in reality is ever fuzzy, Braverman makes misleadingly distinct. He gratuitously assumes a cohesiveness within the dominant capitalist and managerial class, and at the same time seems to deny that workers understand what is going on, and minimizes their efforts at resistance.

That said, the connection between new technology and skills levels is still a crucially important area of debate and conflict. It takes further one of the key features of capitalist organization of the workplace in which wage-labour is monitored and controlled by management. Automation occurs pervasively, throughout a whole range of occupations, which means that de-skilling is much more than a mere product of neurotic anxiety. The well-known tendency for jobs to be made more routine and tasks to be taken over by machine is rapidly intensified as information technology is adopted. But this is by no means a uniform process. Experiences differ from industry to industry, firm to firm, and country to country. At the same time, demand for new skills expands, but unevenly in both place and pace.

One of the most frequently discussed cases is computer numerical control (CNC) machine tools. As in the example of the doughmen, operators of machine tools frequently feel that much of their traditional skill is drained out of their jobs as the tasks are computerized. Once up to their judgement, and careful hand-eye coordination, the shaping of metal components is now guided by computer program.

In one case cited by Barry Wilkinson a 'battle for control' resulted from the introduction of CNC machine tools: between the programmers (who believed they should have management-backed authority for all programming) and the machinists (who felt that, as their traditional skills were still embodied in the program, they should retain some say over it).[23] Under different management styles, of course, outcomes might be quite different. Wilkinson also points to *other* factors which take us well beyond the Braverman account.

For one thing, those workers who feel threatened by de-skilling are fully aware of what is going on (and may even use terms like 'de-skilling' to describe it!). They find ways of resisting the process. On the other hand, management intentions are not '*necessarily* to deskill or wrest control'.[24] They will, nevertheless, tend to use 'efficiency' as an ideological tool to legitimate technical – which are simultaneously social – choices.

Again, the notion of some technical or economic necessity is called in question. Choice is involved at every stage. David Noble, in a study of the development of CNC since the Second World War, shows how in an American context management desire for control was expressed in the choice of tools. An alternative to the automated system now preferred was 'record-playback', which allowed the machinist to begin each batch in the conventional manner, and it was then completed automatically. Apparently little economic advantage could be seen in either method. It seemed rather to be a political choice.[25]

In Britain, the work of Howard Rosenbrock at UMIST in particular indicates that alternatives to de-skilling are not necessarily 'uneconomic'.[26] He argues that despite the fact that the new technologies may well be used 'to extend the historical process of subordinating men and women to machine, and of eliminating their initiative and control in their work', actions based upon the belief that 'the full use of human abilities is a higher and more productive goal than the perfection of machine' could have deeply contrasting consequences.[27] His examples include computer-aided design (CAD), CNC machine tools, and expert systems, such as medical diagnosis.

From the evidence of the introduction of CNC, at any rate, it is unwarranted to posit a 'general tendency' towards de-skilling. As well as the varying motives of management, and the differing degrees of success at operator resistance to the new technology, it is often simply impossible for many tasks to be siphoned off to a control room.[28] Skills are more likely to be 'redistributed' than 'destroyed' with the coming of CNC.

Rather gloomier reports appear, however, about de-skilling within the office as IT is introduced. Although there are some hopeful signs that in this case the de-skilling trend will level off as the equipment becomes more sophisticated, at present it poses a real threat to white-collar workers. Needless to say, the threat affects women in particular, as they tend to be concentrated in the low-skilled routine jobs in the office. In Sweden, for instance, while 80 per cent of those in data processing *planning* are men, 97 per cent of those in routine data-entry positions are women.[29]

The principles of scientific management, applied within banking, insurance, and other office work, frequently lead to jobs being broken down to increase productivity and to save time. This holds obvious economic advantages, especially to big organizations in the public sector. The story is somewhat different for those using the new technologies. Machines which subordinate the clerk to the tempo of the machine, and remove the element of discretion, intensify the fragmentation and de-skilling of jobs. In this area again, however, Braverman is criticized for inadequately dealing with the evidence.

A British study, which focused in particular on a computerized treasurer's department, found that not only 'craft'-type skills (on which Braverman concentrates), but also 'control' functions had been significantly eroded.[30] In accountancy, insurance, and similar fields, clerks did once enjoy wider 'managerial' functions as a kind of intermediate stratum. But within a computerized batch system, where clerks are reduced to preparing material for the computer department, they (temporarily at least) forfeit control over the data.

The subdivision of labour increased as computers were introduced in the treasurer's department in question. While electronic data processing (EDP) means faster data handling, it also means a greater centralization of administrative resources. It also tends to curtail some middle-class 'careers'. The computer department takes over many tasks once performed by the clerk, who is left with residual tasks, such as checking payslips for dispatch. The only interest left in the job is dealing with the queries from payees. Thus knowledge and decision-making functions are digitally deleted from the clerk's job.

EDP makes the 'factory-office' a reality. Polarization – between predominantly male management and predominantly female, machine-paced clerks – may be acute. This is due to the loss of contact between the groups as the information once kept in the clerks' heads is now stored and retrieved from the computer. Thus clerks lose the overall view of the processes in which they are involved, and with it a sense of autonomy and control.

Some see hopeful signs, paradoxically, in the further development of new technology. For as the use of on-line distributed systems increases, and with it the possibility of direct entry, some clerks may recover some lost ground as they regain a measure of control over the whole process. Others argue that computerization may diminish the need for some 'middle management' functions (for instance, the data organization done by personnel officers), thus raising the status of other office workers (mainly secretaries and typists) who will have more direct contact with decision-making.[31]

This last item may not, of course, be such a 'hopeful sign' for some managers! Some recent research suggests that the biggest long-term impact of computerization upon the workplace is likely to be the erosion of hierarchy and the reduction in scale of organizations.[32] When British

Rail introduced a computerized system for controlling freight traffic, the old organizational hierarchy was found to be entirely inappropriate. Existing lines of authority and skills were simply bypassed by a new 'task-force' approach. In some cases, management did not 'know what was happening'. As workers and supervisors defined the new system, managers were sometimes its victims rather than its controllers.[33]

What all these reports and prognoses make clear, however, is that the de-skilling impact of IT depends above all on the way new machines and processes are introduced. The social impact is not determined by technical criteria alone. As labour unions and management have become more aware of this fact, new technology has been raised to a central position within industrial relations.

New technology and industrial relations

The mode of introducing new technology has emerged in recent years as one of the most striking developments within industrial relations. The issues are complex, and the situation rapidly changing. New technology is not only associated with specific alterations in the workplace or in employment, but is implicated within the restructuring of local and global economies. Older models of industrial relations become less appropriate as the traditional labour unions diminish in strength. But newer ones, including those influenced by Japanese examples, are insufficiently well-established to indicate the direction of long-term trends.

The pace of change is a crucial factor. At the beginning of the 1980s, for example, microelectronic devices in the office meant mainly word processors. By the mid-1980s, the impact of IT – the marriage of computers with new telecommunications – was being felt. EFT (electronic funds transfer) systems dispense with the use of paper in paying bills and salaries. Furniture showroom computer facilities allow customers to find out whether what they require is in stock. Old distinctions between office and warehouse are increasingly blurred. Similarly, in manufacturing, CAD blurs the distinction between design office and shopfloor work. And in the newspaper industry, simultaneous print runs in remote sites, and the direct entry of journalists' text into the typesetting process provide further illustration of the new situations facing workers and thus industrial relations.

Prediction is impossible. The industrial relations debate ranges from the optimism of those who see the future in the apparent egalitarianism of 'Silicon Valley' shirtsleeves and common canteen, to the sometimes bitter pessimism of those who regard every computerized working aid as a means to capitalist oppression and worker degradation. Questions of 'new technology and class' again appear, this time in more specific circumstances. The power relationship between labour and capital depends heavily upon the relative strength of each, which is in turn affected by new technology.

Claims concerning the changing nature of industrial relations should not be dismissed lightly. While the basic division between labour and capital may not itself be eroded by changes associated with the introduction of new technology, it is quite possible that the form of that relationship may alter. Within certain high-tech companies (where, significantly, technological and product change is structured into the very work process) this may already be discerned.

One study of a major American transnational computer company shows how the company philosophy of participation actually works for most employees: 'There was a seemingly satisfied and committed staff, an "enterprise consciousness", a lack of suspicion and conflictual opposition.'[34] Highly informal systems (which still maintain discipline, but by less overt means than traditionally) may well become more widespread, especially in certain industries, sidestepping conventional confrontation between unions and management. In different circumstances, however, new forms of control could well be emerging *within* such informal setups. The corporate culture of total loyalty and commitment to company goals, encouraged by some modern management techniques[35] may subtly exclude all alternatives and resistance.

Most unions have traditionally been concerned with wage levels, and only secondarily with working conditions. But the redefinition of skills and work tasks engendered by the coming of IT confuses the whole issue of wages, and helps set new agendas for industrial relations. Whether in making cornflakes or cars, popular media accounts portray unions as being slow to respond to the introduction of new technology. Insensitive management strategies and the sense of threat within such slow responses – especially those involving the newspaper and printing industries, where jobs and skills are intrinsically linked – have led in some cases to severe industrial conflict.

The arrival of new technology during recession has heightened both awareness and fears. During times of economic growth, new technology appears as less of a threat, and even as a welcome development. In recession, however, the introduction of new machines is sometimes treated with more suspicion. Much weight is given to the 'automate or liquidate' slogan, which seems to justify installing IT (sometimes to unions as well as management), *even though* it may mean 'temporary' hardship for some. Some openly expressed fears are sometimes thought to veil other, more deep-seated ones. They range from anxiety about adapting, and fear of job-loss, to concern about health hazards of working with VDUs.

Sometimes fears may be allayed by a sensitive and mutually agreed way of handling the arrival of new technology. In a CIBA-Geigy chemical plant, computer-aided process control equipment was installed in a manner which complemented the workers' skills. Men who once used to haul drums of powder, bottles of acid and barrows of ice around the plant were retrained as control-room operators and plant operators. They worked in rotation, in charge of the computer-aided pumping and mixing machines which had taken the heavy work – and much of the inaccuracy – out of the old process.

They found variety and satisfaction in the new arrangement, not least because their skills were complemented by the new machines. If something like a thermostat did go wrong, they had authority to over-ride the controls and thus prevent an expensive plant stoppage. This would not have been possible either with a more fully automated system or by using people insufficiently retrained.[36]

If, on the other hand, one recalls the history of new-technology disputes within the newspaper industry, a very different picture emerges. Of course, newsprint unions are in a particularly strong position, because newspaper owners can neither import substitutes nor afford to miss a day's production. Newspapers have to be local, in the right language, and contain 'news'. As early as 1973 the *Washington Post* introduced computer-ized typesetting without union agreement. Typesetters were taken by surprise by the speed of events. During the dispute which followed, 25 managers operated the computerized system, taking over 125 typesetters' jobs.[37] The typesetters' jobs, skills, and their union strength were all diminished by the outcome.

Typesetters and printers have also been involved in lengthy disputes in Britain, against the background of increasingly stringent laws restricting picketing. Unions received a crushing blow in the North of England when the *Messenger* newspaper adopted new technology. *The Times* newspaper did not appear for eleven months during 1984, for similar reasons. But the most celebrated dispute began in 1985, and continued throughout 1986, in which the key participants were the News International newspaper publishers and the unions Sogat '82 and the National Graphical Association.

In this dispute, not only was new technology installed, but a 'green field' site chosen (in Wapping, East London) quite separate from the traditional centre of London newspaper publishing, Fleet Street. The £100 million plant contains computerized editorial, composing and publishing departments, and is surrounded by massive security measures (not inaccurately dubbed 'fortress Wapping'). Rupert Murdoch, the News International boss, laid off no less than 5,000 workers, without offering them redundancy pay. By the end of the dispute, government intervention via industrial legislation, plus court rulings, resulted in Sogat '82 losing its £4.5 million funds and facing bankruptcy.

New and different skills are required at Wapping. One of the major questions posed is whether the already weakened unions can survive in the face of massive technological change, imposed 'from above' and with far from adequate consultation. The handling of the process of change has become a major industrial relations issue.

Are there any alternatives to such bitter and damaging disputes? In Sweden, where the print industry was in 1981 in a 'pre-Wapping' situation, a 'Utopia' project was set up: a team of social researchers and unions, working cooperatively. Its aims were to avoid massive job losses and de-skilling, based on the following principles: to adopt technology to enhance work-quality, not necessarily productivity, to encourage local decision-making rather than centralized control, to develop training in new skills *before* new technology was installed, and to produce technically feasible solutions. The Swedish state-owned printing and computer company Liber came to an agreement with the Nordic Graphical Workers Union to involve the Utopia team in discussions about work quality, training and 'man–machine interaction' relating to their text and image processing system (TIPS). Unfortunately, due to management reluctance to experiment beforehand, and demarcation disputes between journalists and graphics workers, that particular project was abandoned.[38]

That specific failure is not seen as fatal, however. Awareness of the issues has been raised, and Utopia was subsequently invited to advise local authorities intent on computerization of various departments. The British Trades Unions Congress explored similar possibilities within the report *Employment and technology*, which appeared in 1979. Guidelines were laid down for negotiating 'New Technology Agreements' which, initially at least, received widespread support. Similar kinds of agreement have been used within the rather different industrial relations contexts of other European (and especially Scandinavian) countries but no central labour union strategy has been developed in the USA. There things tend to be left up to individual unions.

Having said that about the USA, however, British practice also seems to be rather *ad hoc*. Informal and unofficial networks and relationships tend to determine what actually happens. This is due to a combination of factors: the newness of the technology, which means that it is an unfamiliar agenda item, and that past experience becomes the guide by default. The context of recession, in which traditional unions are weakened through loss of members. And thirdly, the fact that the (ideological) *grounds* for choices may well be concealed from the actual bargaining process[39]

New Technology Agreements which have been accepted tend to be limited in scope, covering physical environment and health and safety (particularly relating to VDUs) rather than job design and the quality of working life. Short-term, essentially defensive strategies have been the order of the day, in which job-holders, but not necessarily job positions, have been protected. The exception is Scandinavia, where the power-base of the unions, an awareness of their potential for influencing situations, and a knowledge about the developing technologies and their implications has given unions more scope for active involvement in the process of change.[40]

Most research on New Technology Agreements does indicate, however, that if industrial democracy is ever to become a reality the need for such negotiation is rapidly increasing. The idea that workers operate a kind of resistance reflex to technical change is quite mistaken. Evidence from British studies shows a high degree of positive acceptance of such change. W. W. Daniel found that by their own account managers often fail to communicate properly with the workforce over the introduction of new technology.[41] Unless more than the short-term is considered, and job-design explicitly included, the prospects are bleak for the harmonious and just adoption of IT. As Williams and Moseley observe, 'The longer-term consequences of a transition to an "information society" often seem remote in comparison with pressing day to day concerns – notably those relating to employment.'[42] They also emphasize that the present weakened union bargaining positions and relative slowness of techno-logical change are likely to be a significant part of the backdrop to more rapid change to come. Lessons from early efforts to influence the direction and control of new technology may acquire increasing importance.

The electronic cottage

A major theme within the 'information society' literature is that of work decentralization. The potential for this lies in the widespread diffusion of desk-top computer terminals with on-line links to a central computer. Alvin Toffler's special neologism for this is the 'electronic cottage'. It appears to hold advantages for the firm, the individual, for society at large, and also for the environment. Although it is hardly surprising that this should be one of the more attractive futorological promises, it is worth exploring exactly what are the prospects held out.

The state government of Baden-Württemberg in West Germany ran an experiment from 1982-5, using telecommunications technology to show how new technology may be able to create decentralized jobs. Part of the intention was to show how jobs could be created in areas of high unemployment. Both private companies and public authorities used the system, and half the decentralized work stations were in homes (the others being in local authority offices). Quite how successful the experiment proved to be remains to be seen. While in operation, however, the system met most of the difficulties experienced by similar projects.[43]

Use of IT as a tool of regional policy makes this project particularly interesting (although Sweden has also considered this[44]). The other reasons frequently produced in favour of such 'Teleworking' include the following. Workers' flexibility is an inducement especially attractive to women, who may prefer to combine homework with child-care responsibilities. Employers are supposed to be able to cut overheads involved in central (especially city) offices. Ecologically, the electronic cottage scores because travel to work, and thus energy use and pollution are reduced. Needless to say, the big reason, which may be obscured, is simply that computer-related homeworking has become a realizable technological - and economic - possibility.

In Britain, IT-related homeworking is increasing, but it is not yet possible to tell whether it will become a significant factor in long-term employment patterns. Homeworking in general accounts for seven per cent of the labour force, and of those, only 13 per cent are in manufacturing. So the vast majority of homeworkers, even before IT, were in white-collar and service work.[45]

Although in the 1970s some American futurologists were predicting that two-thirds of the workforce of the industrial societies would be homeworking by the year 2000, this should be taken with a pinch of salt. The take-up rate has been fairly slow, despite the belief in the early 1970s that homeworking would be an appealing solution to the energy crisis. American employers have found employees reluctant to work only at home, which creates difficulties in maintaining workers' spaces in the office. Such reluctance among women is understandable in terms of the isolation and double burden felt by those with both outside jobs and domestic responsibilities. Employers also argue that face-to-face relations are still required for efficient functioning, and that computer security is harder to monitor with remote terminals. Furthermore, labour unions have opposed homeworking on the grounds that minimum wages and other conditions are hard to enforce at home.[46]

What evidence does exist about the extent of IT homeworking suggests various likely trends. Firstly, more women than men are involved. The reason they give is that they prefer a situation where they have flexibility to arrange their own timetable around other homemaking and child-care functions. Secondly, a distinction must be made between the professional and the routine, for example data-entry, tasks of homeworkers.[47] The former tend to have greater security and autonomy, the latter, for example insurance company claim-form filers, lower pay and more monitoring.

This distinction actually highlights other factors which are often blurred by technophiliac effusions. In Britain much has been made of the celebrated case of the Rank-Xerox Xanadu project which cut staff numbers at a London site and allows professionals to work on a contract basis from home, using remote terminals. The employment trends towards big companies sub-contracting work and towards more self-employment may be more significant in the longer term than the modems and personal computers which allow such (suitably qualified) personnel to work from home.

As for those on the other side of the relative autonomy/more monitoring divide, Linda Thompson observes that 'cottage industry' 'suggests not only roses and thatch, but also long hours of toil by the dim light of rush candles for inadequate subsistence wages'. Will this be updated with 'backache and eyestrain of long hours keying-in at the visual display unit'?[48] This is already a reality for some routine workers at data-entry.

Added to this obstacle is that of the potential for isolation. Flexibility may be an advantage offset by the felt disadvantage (reported by both groups of homeworkers) of separation from work-mates and colleagues. On the other hand, many households find it difficult to accept the increased emotional strain of having family members together all day long. Certainly, evidence from the unemployed or early retired who spend major amounts of time at home indicates the potential for friction.

Generally speaking, labour unions have been unfavourable to the development of homeworking. Behind this is not simply the fear of 'sweated labour' or even the difficulty of monitoring wage-levels or working conditions, important issues though these are. As Carla Lipsig-Mumme argues, the larger context is the gradual break-up of the full-time unionized job. More fragmentary employment patterns enable employers to shift responsibility for costs back to the workers. Not only workers' rights, but unionism itself is threatened in the long term.[49]

The example of homeworking illustrates clearly the gap between futurology and social reality in the debate over the information society. Technological potential – in this case rather underdeveloped, given the lack of consistent standards for networking – is not social destiny. There is no good reason why the electronic cottage should not be a feature of a putative 'good society'. Some possibilities for remote work, developed along ecological, communal, and self-determining lines do contrast positively with many destructive, alienating, and oppressive aspects of work life in industrial capitalist societies. But the evidence suggests that without widespread awareness of, and the leverage to redirect the new technologies and their likely modes of adoption, the electronic cottage may fall short of its roses and thatch promise.

Restructuring and IT

It is easy to see how the social effects of the 'technological revolution' are overplayed in the area of work and employment. No massive fundamental change in the wake of IT's arrival is taking the advanced societies *beyond* industrial capitalism. No, many familiar features of that old system are still present, albeit with some new variations. The changes taking place are better thought of as a restructuring of industrial capitalism, against the backdrop of global recession, within which IT obviously plays a vital role. IT is an enabling technology, which simultaneously affects nearly every part of a given economy.

IT is helping dramatically to increase productivity in some sectors and, let it be said unequivocally, to enhance the quality of work experiences. It also contributes to alterations in both tasks performed and in their organization – often in unintended ways which have come as a surprise to their initiators. It is impossible to assess or predict the overall benefits of informatization, but it is foolish to deny that they are manifold.

The darker side, of course, has to do with the equally undeniable job losses, de-skilling, and divisions related to or perpetuated by IT. While some have made IT a scapegoat for unemployment, gratuitously attributing to it 'job-killer' status, the fact remains that much computerization by intent or by default is labour-saving in its effects. The implications of this vary in a complex manner from sector to sector and from firm to firm. Likewise de-skilling which, though not a 'general process' accompanying the adoption of IT, nevertheless occurs with dismal (because often needless) frequency. Social divisions, such as those of gender and race, are also apparent in situations affected by IT. I have referred throughout this chapter to ways in which women in particular continue to be relatively disadvantaged by the coming of IT.

All of this indicates once more that both existing relations of power and social choice, in conjunction with the potential of new technology, constrain and facilitate ways that the social impact of IT – whether blessing or curse – is felt by ordinary people in everyday existence. Some digital dreams of working (or non-working!) life in the 'information society' deserve to be dismissed. But it is equally irresponsible to imply that the outlook is uniformly bleak. While facing squarely the fact that in societies where the economic system encourages self-interest, new technologies may effectively displace or de-skill jobs and demean women and minorities, alternatives are available. Industrial relations at the American computer company, 'Comco', the Swedish 'Utopia' scheme and the British UMIST project to combine the 'full use of human ability' with automation – are all green shoots.

5

Information, democracy and the state

Computers, telephones, radio and satellites are technologies of freedom, as
much as was the printing press.

Ithiel de Sola Pool [1]

If you see the poor oppressed in a district, and justice and rights denied, do
not be surprised at such things; for one official is eyed by a higher one, and
over them both are others higher still.

Ecclesiastes, *c.350 BC* [2]

During the late 1970s a suburb of Columbus Ohio experienced what was
said to be a revolutionary technological breakthrough, the establishment
of an experimental two-way interactive cable television system called
'Qube'. Alvin Toffler (author of *The third wave*) gave the keynote address
at an 'historic event', the world's first 'electronic town hall'. Columbus
residents took part, via the electronic system, in a meeting of their local
planning commission. Seated in their armchairs, they registered push-
button votes for local zoning, housing codes, road construction and even
voted on when the chairperson should move to the next agenda item.

The information society pundits predict that the diffusion of IT will
have far-reaching political consequences. At their most optimistic, they
claim that new forms of participatory democracy will emerge as wired-up
citizens engage directly in voting, and contribute to the political process as
in Columbus. Experiment with television polling, using computers, is the
supposed shape of things to come.

Ironically, the Qube system had another dimension. When interactive,
two-way communication is used for polling, the information collected
(votes, opinions and so on) is stored in the computer memory. Political
views (notably concerning how Jimmy Carter was perceived to be

performing at the time), products selected from screen advertising, and preferences stated (about housing or whatever) are all storable data. Taken together with the demographic details (such as age, sex, occupation) complex profiles of individual citizens may be built up. (The issue of privacy was raised by several different parties in this context. It is unclear, however, whether any legal safeguards have yet been established.)

Thus the technological potential for push-button polling has more than one face. It promises on the one hand that (at least one, participatory, version of) the democratic dream of people governing themselves is realizable in the modern context. On the other hand, it holds the threat that personal information is being collated by some anonymous persons and organizations. Such may include state agencies, or simply commercial agencies who will sell the information to others. It escapes no one's attention that Orwell's 'Big Brother' used two-way television for surveillance. But the difference here is that the 'higher irrationality' (in C. Wright Mills's words) at work is the product of no evil conspiracy; simply the 'rationality' of the market and of profit.[4]

In fact, the Qube experiment – especially its potential for political involvement, which did not 'sell' well – is unlikely to be repeated in the near future. One important reason is that interactive cable television services are not being developed as rapidly as some commentators once imagined they would be. But its importance here lies in its symbolic value. For it flags a more general issue about the role of new technologies in promoting an informed electorate, and thus enhanced democratic participation.

Its other face is also significant within a wider context, that concerning 'surveillance', using IT, and its threat to personal 'privacy'. The process of collection and storage of information about individuals, whether by state agencies or private companies and organizations, becomes far easier and more efficient, using IT, than ever before. Credit card companies, drivers' licence offices or police forces did not wait for interactive cable television before computerizing their records.

I propose, quite deliberately, to discuss both these issues in the same chapter. One important reason for this is that what debate has taken place has tended to arise in different quarters; democratic participation relating to *telecommunications technologies*, and surveillance relating to *computing technologies*. IT, of course, brings them together. So, for instance, it is the computerized storage within the interactive cable system which yields its surveillance potential. And modern surveillance is augmented on a massive scale by the capacity of telecommunications to centralize data which once lay dispersed in geographically distant files.

Another reason for discussing both issues together is that they may be shown to inform each other. Advocacy of the 'democratic potential' of IT must be tempered by an appreciation of the 'surveillance potential'. But a common failing among those who feel the threat to privacy is precisely to underestimate the potential of democratic control of the new technologies.

Electronic power to the people?

The futurist world of the information society assumes progress towards participatory democracy. Yoneji Masuda, for instance, follows the post-industrialists' insistence that self-realization becomes more central to human existence, arguing this as his first reason why participatory democracy is the only way to make individual choices count. Only referenda could allow people to decide on matters which affect everyone, such as nuclear power and pollution, and which recognize no national boundaries. But the clinching point is that technical obstacles to full participation 'have now been solved by the revolution in computer-communications technology'.[5]

Two curious assumptions are evident here. The concern with *participatory* democracy could itself be read as a product of technological determinism. Current political debates in the advanced societies centre more frequently around notions of *representative* democracy; participatory democracy seems to arrive on the futurists' agenda more by virtue of the supposed capacity of technology to come to its aid. Following from that, secondly, 'participation' appears as something hitherto hindered by the lack of available technology, a case which is hard to substantiate.

Doubtless push-button polling, public access to new sources of information and the political use of systems like electronic mail are what Masuda has in mind. Western governments are already making limited use of the latter such systems, both to inform their members and their constituents. The Canadian parliament was first to install a central information system, which broadcasts press conferences and committee hearings over 104 television channels, gives MPs access to electronic mail and world data banks as well as to more mundane items like the parliamentary restaurant menus.[6] MPs hope that the system will increase mutual understanding between geographically remote provinces.

But at the grass-roots level also, new technology promises new opportunities for local participation in political activities, particularly by computer 'networking'.[7] The 'alternativist' wing of the ecology movement saw early on the potential of microelectronics as an 'appropriate technology'. The possibility of *full* involvement in decision-making is opened up by IT. John Garrett and Geoff Wright, for instance, look forward to a time when politics will be the 'occupation of the many rather than the personal gamesmanship of the few'.[8]

Optimism about the democratic potential of IT is shared by segments of both political left and right. Most, however, qualify their remarks in significant ways. Ithiel de Sola Pool[9] insists that policy decisions about how to treat the new communications technologies will be crucial to the future of democracy. He puts the new technologies in an (American) historical context, and warns that the consequences of regulating them heavily amount to a threat to free speech. The Federal Communications Commission (FCC) began to blot its copybook, as far as de Sola Pool is concerned, when regulating radio broadcasting. He believes the First Amendment will be denied further if electronic communications are not allowed to develop 'freely'.

As voice, text, numerical data, images and other forms of communication are increasingly merged, using electronic means, so previous distinctions between print, common carrier (such as the telephone) and broadcast models become blurred. De Sola Pool argues that the new media are misunderstood, and pleads that the conditions of democracy be not undermined by such failure to grasp the issues. If the founding fathers of America saw free speech as vital, how much more should today's citizens do so. 'In advanced societies about half the work force are information processors. It would be dire if the laws we make today governing the dominant mode of information-handling in such an information society were subversive of its freedom.'[10]

De Sola Pool's plea is that new communications technologies be allowed direction by market forces, with minimal government and legal controls. In a European context, by contrast, the view is more often expressed that in fact any notion of democratizing new technologies depends upon the existence of bodies which can use their powers effectively to monitor and discipline their use.[11] A third position, however, is that the new technologies oblige members of the advanced societies radically to rethink how they should be treated by law. IT renders old approaches obsolete. Electronic storage of data and text which permits alteration after storage presents almost insurmountable difficulties for those seeking democratic control.[12]

Several versions of electronic politics focus not so much on direct 'participatory' democracy, but on the use of new technologies for enhancing the awareness of the electorate. Ben Barber, for instance, aware of the potential difficulties of Qube-style electronic democracy – the tyranny of opinion, instant choices in areas where deep debate is required (for example abortion or the death penalty), and so on – advocates a 'multiple phase process'. He gives an example of how the state of California could come to a decision about Sunday retail trading, through the use of television and telephones for 'information, adversarial debate, and direct engagement' of citizens within their local communities'.[13]

While Barber is not sanguine about the chances of realizing such 'Jeffersonian' hopes in the present social and political climate, he presents them as preferable to the 'Panglossian' (technology will solve our problems) or 'Pandoran' (technology will produce a surveillance state) alternatives. In fact, several of his comments about the 'Pandora' alternative (on the technology facilitated private and state monopolies of information) are salutary for anyone enamoured of dreams of digital democracy. Barber's studies also raise fairly fundamental issues for the meaning of 'democracy' in a world increasingly suffused with IT.

Hopes for greater democratic participation, using new technology, are not limited to the USA. The Council of Europe, for example, produced a report on the subject in 1983. One participant in its deliberations was Stefano Rodatà, left-wing member of the Italian government, who believes that 'electronic democracies would offer more opportunities for direct involvement of all citizens in decision-making'. 'Effective public control of decisions' would follow.[14] Why? While traditional holders of power could augment their strength using new technology, new pressure groups are likely to appear as the technologies are diffused, to counter that threat. In general, however, it appears that scepticism about electronic democracy runs deeper in Europe than in North America.

Again, it is the fear of monitoring which is often prevalent in discussions of electronics for political participation. The ballot box remains an anonymous method of recording choices; the unscrupulous state could use electronic polling to discover facts about voters which they may prefer not to disclose. Switzerland, which makes frequent use of referenda, has resisted computerizing for this very reason.

Critique

Proponents of electronic democracy often strongly emphasize the technical potential but neglect present trends. Before turning to the key question – the potential for surveillance – two other factors must be mentioned.

The first has to do with the general levels of political participation in Western societies. There is no evidence that the opportunity for push-button polling would re-activate the increasingly apathetic and un-engaged citizens of modern 'democracies'. Television coverage of the House of Lords in Britain is already rated by many as dull and boring. Hardly an incentive to involvement unless it is believed that things could thus be changed! In the USA, however, TV coverage of the House of Representatives does have a small but interested audience. C-SPAN (the Cable-Satellite Public Affairs Network), though dismissed by operators early on, is now seen as a specialized selling point for cable.

Related to this is the actual use made by politicians and pressure groups of new technologies. The New Right in the USA, and the Conservative Party in Britain, have made extensive gains using computerized direct mail systems and television appeals. During the British General Election campaign of 1983 computerized monitoring of selected voters alerted Conservative marketing strategists to the need to deflect debate from unemployment to defence issues. It had a clear bearing on their eventual success. While Stefano Rodatà may be right about the potential for pressure groups, this applies to others of which he may not approve. In the USA, groups such as 'White American Resistance' and 'Aryan Nationals' are using computer bulletin boards to spread anti-Semitic and other racist ideas. Similar networks in Canada carry hate mail, thus circumventing restrictions which apply to the postal service.[15]

I am not arguing either that political use of IT is restricted to the Right – though they are usually most able to afford it – or that the potential misuse of new technology in politics is a reason for trying to exclude it. Rather, any hopes for the democratic use of new technology have to be measured against present social realities.

The second factor is the extent to which the reality of an informed public is actually being undermined by the development of IT. While it may be too early to make a judgement on this, Herbert Schiller pinpoints two processes already at work here. He describes a 'pincers movement against the public's knowledgeability'.[16] On the one hand, one-time 'public' information is put on the market as a commodity. On the other, private sources of information enjoy growing monopolies.

An obvious example of the former is the way in which government publications, such as social and economic statistics, are harder to obtain. Schiller gives the example of the US government 'library depository system' in which government publications are freely available to the public. In recent years this has been undermined by the practice of the 'National Technical Information Service' in selling its documents on a profit-making basis, including some of which would once have been included in the public depository.

The latter phenomenon is well illustrated in Britain, where some libraries are rapidly diversifying to become information brokers. London's British Museum, for instance, is busily transforming itself into a 'knowledge warehouse'. The decline of government subsidy has stimulated the search for ways of funding the maintenance and expansion of its 22 million volumes. Michael Hilton, the Museum's new corporate marketing manager, is quoted as saying: 'We've been hurried into this kind of thinking by the present political climate, in which all revenue must simply turn a profit. But now that we are actually thinking about making money, we are starting to see this new attitude as an advantage.'[17]

It is doubtful whether those who find they cannot afford the new 'services' will regard the demise of the public library as an unmixed blessing, especially if alternative sources of information are also privately owned. Schiller documents ways in which 'video cassettes, home recorders, video discs, cable TV, computers, and direct satellite broadcasting, are providing corporations whose main economic activities are not in media production with remarkable opportunities to reach mass audiences directly with their messages' (that is, in homes and workplaces).[18] In this view, nothing less than an 'informed democracy' is at stake. It represents the opposite pole from de Sola Pool. By dominating the audience with corporate messages, the market is now the threat to free speech.

Finally, it is worth noting that other, once-new technologies have been lauded for their democratic potential. In the USA, first the railroad ('An agent was at hand to bring everything into harmonious cooperation . . . to subdue prejudice and unite every part of our land.'[19]) and later the telephone ('Had the telephone system reached its present perfection prior to 1861, the Civil War would not have occurred'[20]) were seen as the midwife of continental democracy and unity. Whether or not information technology can succeed where these hopeful visions seem to have faltered remains to be seen.

Nothing I have said thus far should be taken as a denial that democracy may be served by an appropriate development of the new technologies. However, even the few isolated and short-lived experiments referred to provide little evidence to support the claims for electronic democracy. Current trends in political participation and the production of information do not augur well either. Added to which, political participation could continue to be the preserve of those with education and means (that is, those who could afford the right equipment and have the expertise to use it). But the biggest blind spot of the electronic democrats has yet to be explored, namely, the potential, using IT, for power to flow in precisely the opposite direction.

Electronic power to the state?

Sooner or later debates about the social impacts of IT come round to the question of 'Big Brother'. Orwell's fearful vision of totalitarian control via new communications technologies is received as a warning, a prediction about what could be, if citizens are not vigilant about the use of databanks and computer networks. All too frequently 'Big Brother' is invoked as a 'rhetorical device to dramatize a fantastic possibility, which is believed to be discontinuous with present political reality'.[21]

The fact that electronic means of potential totalitarian control are now installed in Western societies, and that 'Big Brother' is already watching, is thus neglected. Unfortunately, the 'Big Brother' image is also redolent of jack-boots and torture, so the point may also be missed that electronic totalitarianism is much more subtle. A better image would be that of Franz Kafka's *The castle* or *The trial*, where fear is engendered because someone knows about you, but you know neither what they know, nor what effect their knowing might have. In this scenario lives are absorbed into rather than brutalized by the system.

This section has three connected parts. Firstly, the extent of computerized surveillance is illustrated from a number of different societies. Secondly, this phenomenon must be put in an historical context; is such state surveillance really so novel? Thirdly, efforts to regulate and resist computerized surveillance – primarily by means of 'data protection laws' – are examined and evaluated.

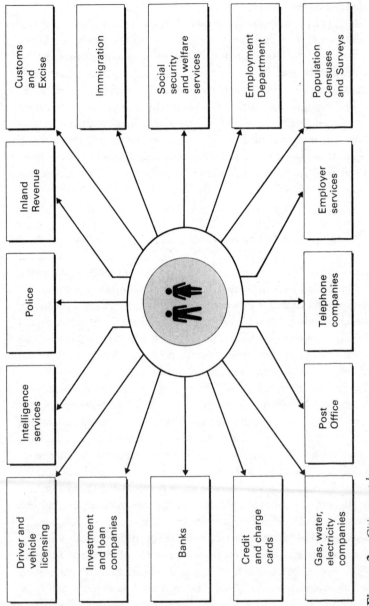

Figure 2 *Citizenwatch*

All sorts of government and private organizations have – or can get – information about individual citizens. Increasingly it is on computers; linked together, such data would provide an extremely detailed picture of each daily life. This diagram gives some examples. They vary from country to country

The heading for this section may be misleading in so far as it implies that the state may be the only agency storing information on individuals. This is not the case. In fact, surveillance activities are undertaken by numerous agencies, both directly administered by the state and independent of it. One major difference made by the advent of IT is the vastly increased capacity for different databases to be 'interfaced' with each other. This above all is perceived as a threat to personal privacy because essentially 'subject-friendly' systems may be linked with others in such a way as to increase dramatically the chances of their proving 'subject hostile'. This process is illustrated in figure 2.

Direct state monitoring of citizens takes a variety of forms. An extreme case is that of South Africa which from 1955, using IBM equipment, has had a computerized population register, the heart of the pass law system. The white minority government could not keep track of black employment and housing without the automated system. During the past thirty years it has been augmented by 'municipal administration systems' from Sperry, IBM and NCR, and an ICL-based National Police Criminal Investigation System.[22] But it is societies which would indignantly reject any association with 'police states' which are rather more interesting.

In April 1987 West Germans became the first citizens in Western Europe to be issued with computer-readable identity cards. Computer-readable European passports are due to follow in 1988. Sponsored by the Christian Democrats, and originally intended as a weapon against the 1970s spate of terrorism, the usefulness of the new system is even questioned by the police. Gunter Schroeder, chairman of the biggest police union, sees it as 'a secret police through the data door'.[23] Although it is said that the data collected once the cards are in use are for 'internal use only', Social Democratic and Green Party opponents are concerned that 'internal' already stretches from traffic wardens to the state intelligence agency and border police.[24] Already, passport or ID information on West German citizens is punched by hand into a central police computer.

In Britain no such ID system exists as yet (though there are plans for machine-readable passports), but widespread fears exist that similar personal profiles may easily be built up using the Police National Computer, and files of the Department of Health and Social Security (DHSS), Driver and Vehicle Licences, TV licences, blood groups, and Immigration Officials. Taken together, they total well over 113,141,000 individual files. Take one case. Drivers on the M1 motorway (and other routes) have their licence plates scanned by a computerized TV camera placed on a bridge. By the time they reach the next bridge, police have received sufficient information on specific vehicles to alert them as to which should be ignored, watched, or intercepted. (In Hong Kong, fears have been aroused by the installation of 'Electronic Road Pricing' which automatically charges motorists entering the city, using an electronic box in each car, and sensors under the streets. Who will record where people have been?)[25]

Used for tracing stolen vehicles or, more seriously, suspected murderers or terrorists, such computerized systems offer a welcome increase in efficiency. Officials from police or from different government departments routinely assure citizens that their systems are not porous. However, their critics remain unconvinced on at least two counts: one, decisions do not always appear to be consistent or coordinated concerning the conditions under which two systems may be interfaced with each other (and thus what access is available to whom); two, the checks on what occurs *unofficially* seem less than adequate.

The growth of police and other public agency information systems in the USA is seen variously as 'the rise of the computer state' (David Burnham) and the 'dossier society' (Kenneth Laudon).[26] Laudon traces the more recent expansion of the dossier society to the American national policy drive to reduce crime. He doubts its success in that quarter, arguing that its actual effect is twofold. It replaces interpersonal relationships between governors and governed with computer-mediated ones and simultaneously makes those relationships more centralized than dispersed.

Burnham argues that in the USA the National Security Agency (NSA) must be one of the most dangerous computer-driven organizations in the world. Unlike the CIA and FBI, it operates outside Senate or Congressional control. No one knows how many people work for NSA, how much it spends or what it does. Yet his investigations show that its computers break codes, make codes for sensitive phone messages, direct spy satellites, intercept telephone and other messages, and store, organize and index all its data ready for retrieval. It has been suggested that the British GCHQ 'spy centre' at Cheltenham, which does similar surveillance work, is linked to the NSA,[27] thus giving the USA great scope to observe Britons direct.

While all this may seem melodramatic, the mundane reality is that 'everyday' information becomes the basis of much 'surveillance'. Alongside the unprecedented growth of communication between computers is the increase in so-called 'transactional information'. Credit card companies, banks, stores, telephone and other utilities companies all use computerized records of a vast range of transactions. How could such data be used?

Companies such as Dun and Bradstreet in the USA and Infolink in the UK offer 'online credit information services'. Infolink has the whole of the British electoral register on its database, with details of bad debts linked to names and addresses. It also receives information not in the public domain, donated by subscribers. Providers of credit may well avoid bad debts, but the potential for abuse in such systems is enormous. One issue is the comprehensiveness of the database, which may give rise to cases of mistaken identity, for example after an address change. Another is the cheapness and ease of access for members, who would have few difficulties in misusing the system.[28]

Ways of collecting 'everyday' data increase each time a new 'home-based' service is offered, such as home banking, home shopping and so on. John Wicklein's book, *Electronic nightmare* rightly focuses on 'the *home* communications set and your freedom'.[29] Although in some ways the developments foreseen by Wicklein have not materialized as rapidly as he seemed (in 1979) to imagine they would, this probably has more to do with the pace of technological development than with the establishment of adequate controls. Wherever interactive communications systems exist the potential for surveillance is present.

The carceral computer?

Recognizing that their version of the information society might not come true in exactly the way they envisage, a number of social commentators warn against the threat of electronic totalitarianism as if it were a radically new departure. But as I have hinted already, a subtle mistake is obscured by this stance. Surveillance of citizens within nation states is no novel phenomenon. The collection and storage of personal data was a standard taken-for-granted feature of all advanced societies long before computer technology was introduced to augment its ease and efficiency.

As Anthony Giddens has observed, in many societies prior to the modern era, the writing of records was crucial for gathering taxes or tribute. But it is in the nineteenth-century European nation-state, where improving communications render obsolete older bases of power – the city, the local community – that this kind of surveillance develops its contemporary characteristics. The accumulation of relevant information on disparate and geographically dispersed people becomes an imperative aspect of any government's aim of holding such people together within one bounded territory, the nation state.[30]

Alongside its partner, increasing workplace supervision, the administrative monitoring of the modern state makes possible the coordination of persons who are not physically present with each other. Towards the end of the nineteenth century, European states started making extensive use of new statistical techniques for recording basic data – births, marriages, deaths – on their populations. Today, departments concerned with health or social security regulate in similar but vastly expanded ways the activities of numerous citizens, without either the citizens or the officials necessarily coming into any sustained contact with each other.[31] It is to this already existing aspect of surveillance in particular that computerization makes its peculiar contribution.

Interest in the phenomenon of state surveillance has been boosted in the 1980s by historical research into the prison system, and especially the debates surrounding the work of Michel Foucault. At the core of his argument is the claim that the modern prison represents not only a complete departure from punishment by public torture which preceded it, but also a form of social control which has social implications that extend as it were beyond the prison walls into the very texture of modern society.

Bentham's Panopticon, the prison architecture which permitted constant watching of all inmates, provided Foucault with his key image. The central inspection tower allowed warders full and unhindered opportunity to inspect all prisoners. 'Hence the major effect of the Panopticon: to induce in the inmate a sense of conscious and permanent visibility that assures the automatic functioning of power ... in the peripheric ring, one is totally seen, without ever seeing; in the central tower, one sees everything without ever being seen.'[32] (Today, the process is extended in direct ways such as the use of signal-emitting bracelets, anklets, or implants, to monitor the whereabouts of non-dangerous prisoners who are allowed home. The Albuquerque judge who pioneered the system is said to have been inspired by a 'Spiderman' comic!)

Foucault says that nineteenth-century prisons, as they were established, were related to other forms of supervision, including medicine and general education. He also sees the 'human sciences' as furthering this 'new type of supervision – both knowledge and power – over individuals who resisted disciplinary normalization'.[33] Thus not only did a new penitentiary technique emerge, but also administrative agencies (what Foucault calls the 'carceral archipelago') associated with the prison took that technique into society at large. Personal activities of a more innocent kind are supervised by various government departments. It gave capitalist society a vast new technology of control.

It is hardly surprising that some observers of social work or psychiatry today find Foucault's writings illuminating. But, as Mark Poster reminds us, the Panopticon antedates both the bureaucracy and the computer. Each considerably enlarges the ability to monitor behaviour. The watch tower is redundant. 'All that is needed are traces of behaviour; credit card activity, traffic tickets, telephone bills, loan applications, welfare files, fingerprints, income transactions, library records and so forth.' So the 'normalized individual' is not only the one in jail or the psychiatric hospital, but 'the individual in his or her home, at play, in all the mundane activities of everyday life'.[34]

So is it appropriate to speak of the 'carceral computer', given its major role in the enhancement of surveillance capacities both in the public sphere, such as the workplace, and the private, domestic, sphere? Is there indeed an emerging new 'mode of information', by whose social conduits members of the advanced societies are organized and controlled? Are today's citizens indeed becoming the hapless and unwittingly compliant victims of subtle and sophisticated IT-enabled technologies of power?

Privacy, persons and protection

The dangers of an electronic nightmare, the carceral computer, are real enough. The fact that in the modern Panopticon of fibre optics and remote terminals 'data subjects' often have no idea that their activities are being monitored gives it a singularly sinister mien. Little comfort may be derived from the knowledge that hi-tech enthusiasts tend to exaggerate the potential gains in efficiency, thus precipitating computerization. (In Britain the computerization of DHSS local offices was originally supposed to save £380 million over twenty years. It is now recalculated at £66 million saving.[35]) Add to this the patent desire of powerful agencies to retain their power, and a disturbing picture emerges.

Having said that, however, it is also necessary to examine the kinds of theories on which such pessimistic scenarios are based. David Burnham's celebrated work on the 'computer state' falls under the rubric of investigative reporting. Theoretically, he leans explicitly on Jacques Ellul's classic study of *The technological society* (which, incidentally, anticipates many Foucaldian themes, especially about the 'natural' appearance of modern surveillance).

Burnham quotes approvingly Ellul's comment that police techniques are not limited to 'criminal groups'. 'To be sure of apprehending the criminal, it is necessary that everyone be supervised. This does not imply a reign of terror or of arbitrary arrests . . . . But every citizen must be thoroughly known to the police and must live under conditions of discreet surveillance. All this results from the perfection of technical methods.'[36] As a pre-computer statement, it is indeed striking.

But the 'perfection of technical methods' is for Ellul a virtually autonomous process. The state's capacity to absorb the lives of its citizens is a 'result of the accumulation of techniques in the hands of the state'. He continues, 'Techniques are mutually engendered and hence interconnected, forming a system that tightly encloses all our activities. When the state takes hold of a single thread of this network of techniques, little by little it draws to itself all the matter and the method, *whether or not it consciously wishes to do so*.'[37] It is the words I have emphasized in italics which are most significant. Ellul insists that the most resolutely liberal and democratic states 'cannot do otherwise than become totalitarian'.[38]

Foucault, for quite different reasons, writes in similarly deterministic tones. (Recall that Braverman's work on 'de-skilling' was criticized earlier along much the same lines.) The Panopticon is described as if it had some mysterious force of its own. Against this it must be stressed that the establishment of new prisons did not occur, as Giddens says, 'behind people's backs'. In fact, the French prisoners subjected to these disciplinary regimes responded with a variety of resistance tactics. They rioted, refused to cooperate, developed their own language, and so on.[39]

Today, as with prison disturbances in nineteenth-century France, heightened public concern about computerized surveillance promotes efforts at resistance. Without minimizing the totalitarian *tendencies* of state (and private agency) computerization, Ellul's judgements about the state, like Foucault's about prisons, require critique. For judgements like these, with all others which betray traces of technological or social determinism, tend to neglect the role of knowledgeable human agents. Such people, in this case, are understandably reluctant to lose control over the processes whereby details of their personal lives are disclosed to others.

The Swedish Data Inspection Board was set up as early as 1972, to enforce the provisions of the Data Act. The aim is both to protect the integrity of the data held, and to prevent the linking of data from different sources. The board has recently had to deal with two relevant cases. In one, an industrial company planned to monitor by computer employees' phone calls, and to relate this to personal files. The plans were vetoed by the Inspection Board. In the other case, a major public controversy resulted from the discovery that a longitudinal sociological study – the 'Metropolit' Project – had for years been linking official personal data on subjects without their knowledge or consent. The resultant requirement of the researchers to seek consent led to the effective cessation of the project.[40]

In the American context, fears have been expressed about the complexity of proposed federal data banks, which might render them unaccountable. In the late 1970s, for example, the Inland Revenue Service Tax Administration System was withdrawn from active consideration after several years of scrutiny by Congress and concerned citizens.[41] A 1978 Datamation survey indicated that two-thirds of the public polled believed that more computer restrictions were required to protect privacy, over against only eight per cent of computer executives who thought so.[42] On the other hand, public concern has not yet succeeded in curbing the power of the NSA. One of the main difficulties with the Data Privacy Act (1974) lies in what it does not cover, and in what American governments have been unwilling to enforce.

This is a tricky question, which not all civil libertarians face head-on. Laudon's *Dossier Society*, for instance, focuses on the American Computerized Criminal History system, which, he warns, is only a few steps from a national information system. Not only is privacy threatened, but decisions about individuals are made on the basis of computer data rather than face-to-face impressions and interviews. This may adversely affect decisions because the data may be inaccurate, ambiguous or incomplete. However, Laudon fails fully to explain why Americans comply so meekly with such potential loss of privacy. As William Dutton observes, this has a lot to do with value-conflicts between privacy on the one hand and, for example, public health, safety or economic well-being on the other.[43]

It remains to be seen what will happen in Britain, but even in this case invasions of privacy do not occur entirely 'behind people's backs'. The 1984 Data Protection Act was passed after two decades of governmental heel-dragging, only appeared then to fall in line with other European countries and thus to avoid damaging British IT trading interests, and is in any case criticized for a number of glaring inadequacies.[44] Several important exemptions mean that, for instance, the police may hold unsupervised computer files relating to the 'prevention and detection of crime'. Further anomalies, concerning the relation of computer to manual files, are currently under review.

Perhaps the very weakness of the legislation will serve to alert more people to the dangers latent in computerized data. The rising general level of computer awareness should mean that the issues will be seen more clearly. It is one of the (admittedly few) 'social impacts' of computing touched on within IT education programmes. Moreover, several professional bodies whose members use computer files persistently voice their disquiet over the present law.

One prominent issue is whether data protection laws have any real concern for persons and their privacy. British social workers complain that the Data Protection Act only gives their clients the right to be informed about data held on them. No data holder is obliged to inform individuals of the existence of such files without a direct request. This seems to compromise the openness and honesty implied in the British Association of Social Workers' principle that 'clients are fellow-citizens'.[45] This point has clear implications for other agencies as well, including doctors and the police.

Unfortunately, the issues have yet to be clearly identified and recognized as possible infringements on individual civil liberties. At present the computerization of records proceeds far faster than either ethical discussion of precisely how human dignity and freedom are undermined by such use of computers, or public awareness of what exactly is going on. And this is just the problem. Geoffrey Brown argues that with the advent of the computerized database, the privacy debate is altered.

The common notion behind 'privacy protection' is along the lines of a public figure trying to conceal his private life from inquisitive press reporters. More worrying to people today is the fear of intrusion into one's personal life by a public figure (police, credit card company, government agency). Everyone knows and accepts that an inevitable feature of modern life is that personal records are held by doctors, employers and so on. But it seems that part of what is 'essential to the integrity of a person's social identity as seen "from the inside" is . . . that access to particular information about him is sytematically related in the appropriate way to the nexus of social roles which he occupies'.[46]

This occurs within a sort of 'moral vacuum' in which no 'mutually understood pattern of rights and obligations obtains'[47] and is compounded by the fact that technological development proceeds in an essentially unreflective manner. Thus for Brown personal integrity is threatened in novel ways by IT. Ellul seems to be proved right here in his judgement that 'technique has no place for the person'.[48] Even the legal language about people whose personal details are computerized refers to them as 'data-subjects'.

How the perceived threat by electronic surveillance to personal privacy will be challenged and mitigated is a matter of some debate. Groups concerned with civil liberties, some of which, like the French *Commission nationale de l'informatique et des libertés*, are expressly concerned with IT, are in the 1980s stepping up their campaigns against privacy invasion. Employees within organizations making extensive use of computer files for personal data – such as German police, British social workers – present an increasingly vocal 'challenge from within', directed against secrecy and closed-information policies.

It may turn out that such pressure from within becomes more marked, especially in relation to a wider awareness of environmental issues such as nuclear power, acid rain and the depletion of raw materials. Claus Offe argues, for example, that there is evidence of growing public perceptions of and disquiet about the 'blindness' to the results of modern technology, which gives strength to what the Americans call 'whistle-blowing'.[49]

Others maintain that the only way to curb bureaucratic and state surveillance is to reduce their size and scope. This of course flies in the face of the apparent benefits of such systems, granting greater efficiency for instance in processing welfare payments. The steady process towards the centralization of the means of social control, of which electronic surveillance is only the latest manifestation (though it currently accelerates the process) must be more radically countered than by mere legal restraint alone. Abbe Mowshowitz suggests how this could occur (and, incidentally recalls my earlier discussion of 'participatory democracy'). Social functions should be returned to local associations wherever feasible. 'If, for example, each level of government were to provide only those services requiring its jurisdictional spread, many services administered by large bureaucracies could be provided locally.'[50]

Similar arguments are put forward by Michael Goldhaber (of the Washington-based Institute for Policy Studies) and British Social Democrat Shirley Williams.[51] Each of them also foresees democratic potential as well as totalitarian threat within present IT developments. If this appears to bring the argument back to where it began, then it may serve as a reminder of the gap between present realities and even informed speculation about future trends.

Conclusion

Dreams of electronic democracy which appear in the more optimistic information society literature have to be tempered by a recognition of present technological and political realities. They are frequently ahistorical, forgetting that new technology by itself has never enhanced democracy, and also underestimate the anti-democratic tendencies associated with state surveillance. The democratic potential of IT cannot be realized without first confronting these social and political realities.

On the other hand, seeds have been sown which could sprout into electronic totalitarianism, though as yet they are not sufficiently recognized or resisted by citizens whose lives are monitored. The 'carceral computer' is a present reality, both in direct state administration and control, and in the potential for linkage with private data-bases. (It also serves as a reminder that power resides in other institutions than those of class or corporation.) But some predictions of total social control by computer are also ahistorical, in that past technological dystopias have not come into being, and may also be based on inadequate social theories.

Those 'inadequacies' have to do with the underestimation of both the knowledgeability and awareness of human agents, and the potential for democratic regulation and social redirection. Of course, the subtleties of electronic surveillance present new obstacles to precisely that human awareness at the same time as providing new means whereby the powerful may retain a hold of their position. Thus these issues are as much of a challenge to social theory as to political practice.

6

The global dimension

It's now possible to plan an economic quantum leap from village-based rural societies to the computer-based information society of the twenty-first century.

Edward Ayensu (1982)[1]

In the West we have come to think of the 2,500 communications satellites which presently circle the earth as distributors of information. For many societies they may become pipettes through which the data which confers sovereignty upon a society is extracted for processing in some remote place.

Anthony Smith (1980)[2]

The 'information society' is not only a 'First-World' phenomenon. The implications of developing IT extend far beyond the advanced societies. But, more importantly, the restructuring of those advanced societies cannot properly be understood without considering the global dimension. Although those who use the 'information society' concept often refer to its global aspects, frequently they fail to identify them in more than a superficial way.

Of course it is quite correct to say that we live in a highly interdependent, complex world, and that this 'closeness of contact' would be impossible without modern telecommunications. The problem is that those relations of interdependence are far from symmetrical. In the words of a recent book-title, the 'chips are stacked'[3] overwhelmingly in favour of those nations which are already 'advanced'.

When information society theorists speak of 'deindustrialization' in the advanced societies, this obscures the fact that assembly-line workers supplying their television sets or computers may now be found in the Southern hemisphere. When Western 'democrats' insist on the free flow of information, this may appear to the recipient of *Dallas* in the

Philippines or Ghana as a cloak for cultural domination. The erection of satellite dishes in the Third-World countries does not necessarily herald the arrival of the information age – at least as it is experienced in France or the USA. One has first to ask what they are used for, what language the messages are in, and who has access to them.

In what follows, I first examine various views of how the information society relates to the rest of the world, especially the so-called Third World, and suggest why they are often inadequate. This raises questions, secondly, about the longer-term relationships between industrial capitalist nations and other less-developed ones. Colonialism and its aftermath are significant here. Thirdly, since the Second World War, the picture has been modified dramatically by the emergence of transnational corporations. Their activities, fourthly, are closely bound up with IT, and often appear to present threats to national sovereignty in both North and South. Among less developed and thus weaker nations this felt threat has been resisted in recent years. A focal point of such resistance, fifthly, is UNESCO's proposal for a 'New World Information and Communication Order'.

Third Wave and Third World

The 'transnational economy' is one of the key features of the emerging order according to Tom Stonier's *The wealth of information*.[4] Whereas in Leeds, England, one once saw the steam locomotive being built from scratch, from local materials, today in other cities a jetliner is built with components from a dozen different countries. One cause of this is cheap transport and efficient communications, which has encouraged the shift of some labour-intensive industries to Third-World countries where labour costs are still cheap. Stonier says this has created jobs and also allowed countries like Korea, Taiwan and Singapore to move into 'developed countries status'.

For him, this is a goal to aim at. Indeed there are 'powerful moral, economic and imperative reasons' for advanced societies to 'bring about a massive increase in productivity to provide economic stability and pull the rest of the world into the next stage of social evolution'.[5] (I shall comment on the implicit agenda here in a moment.) He rightly identifies the obstacles to this as the 'information gap' between the advanced and the less developed countries.

Yoneji Masuda, Japanese theorist of the information society, already perceives a new spirit of globalism abroad in the world. Such a 'spaceship view', coupled with a sense of symbiosis (peaceful coexistence) and of 'global information space' (based on computers and telecommunications), is essential to the harmonious development of the information society.

But he too acknowledges the present information gap, and, recognizing that it is more significant than the earlier industrial gap, warns about the dangers of 'cultural discontinuity' and 'serious anarchical antagonisms' consequent on the widening of the gap.[6] His solution is to establish a system of government-led technical assistance which is both environmentally responsible and also sensitive to the cultural diversity of poorer countries.

Others make similar proposals, notably Jacques Servan-Schrieber[7] and Alvin Toffler. Each of these argues that a sort of leapfrogging could take place, whereby, in Toffler's terms, First- and Third-Wave civilizations could meet. This is 'appropriate technology'; IT adapted for the needs of the Third World; 'Gandhi with satellites'.[8] Why replicate the foolish experiments to impose 'Second-Wave' industrial civilizations on essentially 'First-Wave' agrarian societies? Toffler sees tomorrow's development strategies being home-grown in Africa, Asia, and Latin America, based on decentralized, appopriate scale activities, courtesy of IT.

Lastly, Daniel Bell, whose theory of postindustrial society has now given way to predicting the coming of the information society, also recognizes the international implications of IT. He discusses the new international division of labour which puts 'routinised manufacturing such as textile, shipbuilding, steel, shoe, and small consumer appliance industries' in countries such as Brazil, Mexico, South Korea, Taiwan, Singapore, Algeria and Nigeria, and keeps 'electronic and advanced technological and science-based industries' in the advanced societies.

Bell warns that the way this occurs is a major economic and social policy issue for all nations involved. In particular he notes that one issue with which the advanced nations will have to grapple is the dominance of Western - and especially American - telecommunications. He cites Intelsat, the international commercial satellite organization, as a case in point. Although it has over 90 member countries, and buys, for example, from British Aerospace, it is dependent on the (American) Hughes Aircraft Company, and is under effective financial control of other American companies.[9]

Let me make two things quite clear before I suggest some shortcomings of such Third-Wave/Third-World opinions. One, the above writers do not ignore the issues of IT and the Southern hemisphere. Rather, despite their (no doubt genuine) concern on behalf of the Third World, they tend to underestimate the extent of the difficulties facing the South, precisely *because of* the historical and present activities of the advanced societies.

Two, mere cynicism about their sometimes utopian aspirations for Third-World countries is misplaced. Nothing I say should be read as doubting the potential of IT for world development. Increasing crop yields, remote sensing of mineral deposits, computer-aided diagnosis of disease, improved administrative efficiency; all of these are areas (and there are more) in which gains could be made. Indeed, it is just because of this potential that it is necessary to be realistic about the obstacles to its realization.

The optimism of information society theorists which foresees the establishment of some IT-based 'global village' is vulnerable at several points. For a start, they say little about the forms of nineteenth-century imperialism which were crucial to the development of modern industrial economies. New technologies – especially those of communication – were already implicated within the empires of European nations.[10] Does this mean that the activities of today's transnational corporations somehow extend a kind of imperialism into the present? Although this is a moot point, it is certainly true that the 'information gap' is actually maintained and widened by the way such corporations operate.

This is seen most obviously in the area of new telecommunications, especially those using satellites, whether for remote sensing or for beaming television pictures into the Third World. Time was when the main issue here was that of imposing alien cultural images and standards on more traditional societies. While that is still important, its significance now extends further. For the new communications technologies carry all manner of data, particularly those which are crucial to industrial and educational development. This is not always highlighted by IT optimists.

However laudable the emphasis on 'appropriate technology' approaches to IT in the Third World, there are problems here too. In some cases it may simply be inappropriate to consider the application of yet more technology. The 'technological fix' is an outcome of a distinctively Western rationality. In others, whatever the proposed method, the belief that the criteria of success should be a higher material standard of living, measured by the possession of commodities (a belief encouraged, of course, by many transnational corporations) is equally suspect.

Beyond this, the authors quoted above who believe in the possibility of a 'quantum leap' of village economies into the 'information society' are due for disappointment. For as Juan Rada has shown, 'informatisation' is the *consequence* of development, not its *cause*. Informatics, by and large, is applied to *already existing* manufacturing plants, offices and services. Because of this, plus the already mentioned fact of unequal distribution of resources and knowledge, the idea that less developed nations can 'leapfrog' industrial development is thus mistaken.[11]

Views connecting 'Third Wave' with 'Third World', then, frequently display ethnocentric Western bias, adopt an ahistorical approach which conveniently forgets the connection between imperialism and techno-logical development, ignore some significant characteristics of IT, and thus underestimate the difficulties of 'closing the information gap'. As in other areas of 'information society' discourse, confidence about techno-logical potential takes precedence over social and political awareness.

IT in the world economic system

Information technology, while it represents a striking technological advance, and while it presents new or at least intensified global implica-tions, must also be placed in a longer-term historical context. The intricate complexity of today's world-wide web of economic and technological relations should not be allowed to obscure the fact that some of its major strands were woven over a hundred years ago.

The economic links between different societies on a global scale were a creation of the capitalist industrial system. Britain was briefly the centre of this system, and as Eric Hobsbawm explains, 'An entire world economy was thus built on, or rather around, Britain, and this country therefore temporarily rose to a position of global influence and power unparalleled by any state of its relative size before or since.'[12] Free flows of capital and commodities passed largely through British hands, and when challenged by other economies, Britain used her indispensability to underdeveloped regions to evade the challenge to maintain her economic (though not technological) superiority.

The phrase 'passed through British hands' should not be glossed over without comment. The means of transport and communication – canals, railways, roads, shipping and later the telegraph – were crucial to the circulation of raw materials, commodities and information about sources of goods and markets for selling them. If European naval power was used to open up 'new' territories for economic activities, then the telegraph took on the task of keeping contact with them. The cable link between London and India was completed by 1864 (Paul Julius Reuter used pigeons and horses to join the ends of as-yet-unlinked cables) and was a vital conduit for the rapidly growing traffic in commercial information. So resilient were those early networks that American press agencies were unable to compete with Reuters and Havas (a French operator) until before the Second World War. Even today it is sometimes easier to telephone or travel between African countries via London rather than direct.[13]

Mention of the USA, however, calls for comment about its peculiar situation. Until the American Revolution communication patterns were imperial, on an East-West axis between London and the American Colonies. While this pattern persisted for some time, it was gradually replaced after 1812 by an internal variant on the theme, with New York succeeding London as the central element. New York, because of the Hudson River and the Erie Canal, won out in the vigorous competition with other Eastern cities to become the new geographic centre of trade and communications. It could control the continent westwards while simultaneously isolating other Eastern cities and the South. Nevertheless, it was the British connection which facilitated the slavery on which part of the burgeoning American economy rested.[14]

Two other points must be noted before proceeding. Firstly, the system of capitalist industry was not only marked by being global in reach. It also contained an internal dynamic which constantly stimulated technological innovation. For capitalism is an economic system involving a drive towards chronic accumulation. Capitalism introduced throughout society a system of paying wages in exchange for labour expended by workers. But commodities produced by those workers are sold at a higher price than the wages paid, such that after plant overheads, raw materials, transport and so on have been paid for, profit is still made. Because workers resist being treated like 'commodities', and because the enterprise is always in competition with others, constant pressure is exerted to find ways of increasing *productivity*. Improvements in technology – the spinning jenny, the assembly line, the robot – are the result.

Secondly, as Anthony Giddens has observed, capitalism emerged in nineteenth-century Europe, where the modern nation state was coming to birth. Again, the development of communications made it possible for large-scale territories to come under single administrative systems, as they did in Europe and the United States from the late eighteenth century. The nation state was conducive to the growth of capitalism within its boundaries. But at the same time, maintaining those boundaries between states became a more sharply contentious issue (bitter wars had always characterized a previously more fragmented Europe). Thus 'Capitalism developed within a military "cockpit" in which the expansion of industrial production very soon came to be seen by all ruling groups as the *sine qua non* of national survival'.[15]

The colonial system, on which the development of both European and North American capitalism depended, was maintained more or less intact until the Second World War. The political ties which had bound the destinies of many - particularly African - countries together with Europe were formally dissolved. Nevertheless, the Europeans left a legacy of 'nation state' forms of political practice which, as Anthony Smith observes, made it hard for people such as Ashantis and Ibos to come to terms with being Ghanaians or Nigerians.[16] Less obvious at first, however, within these 'newly independent nations' were the complex *economic* ties which remained. Those ties may be expressed as the doctrine of 'development', based on Western notions of economic growth, which in early days was accepted with enthusiasm by aspiring ex-colonies.

The doctrine of development, or of 'modernization', assumed that the politically independent ex-colonies would, along with other 'traditional societies', 'follow in the footsteps' of the industrial societies. Daniel Lerner, for instance, described a Turkish 'grocer of Balgat', who became a central figure within the drama of development. Access to the city (Ankara) and to communications media (the radio) were crucial to the 'passing of traditional society'. The grocer was typical of those whose urban contact was contributing to raised literacy levels, a quest for a higher standard of living, and a desire for democratic citizenship.[17]

Today, traditional social or economic patterns of life have certainly been eroded substantially. And many of today's 'Third-World' cities exhibit evidence of their contact with the West; streets crowded with motor vehicles, brightly lit shopping areas, and satellite TV dishes on the roofs of high-rise hotels. But what has happened, as Smith says, is that

> Western economic models have been introduced, tying the receiving
> country ever closer (but in a condition of dependence) to Western
> companies; then came the introduction of a technology of a kind which

has rendered the society helplessly expectant of Western cultural content, which in turn has 'softened up' the local elites for the further spread of Western economic patterns.[18]

The hydro-electric dams which power the bright lights, computers, and televisions of city-dwellers also push subsistence farmers off the land, driving them as migrants to live off the garbage in the shanty towns surrounding the same big cities.

Many 'receiving societies' in the Third World, realizing the real nature of this new form of *economic* colonialism, have resisted its spread. Some, such as Tanzania, have attempted to forge their own forms of development, appropriate to local conditions. Others, notably the 'Gulf States' have been able to use their possession of oil resources to form an economic cartel (OPEC) against the West. Yet others, such as Taiwan, Korea, Brazil, and Nigeria pursue paths of entrepreneurial and industrial expansion which challenge the West at its own game.

Needless to say, even this last option is a difficult one. Local investors, dubious about the chances of success in domestic companies, often put their money into the bigger, 'safer', transnational corporations (TNCs). So only relatively backward sectors of the economy depend on local capital. Some governments, realizing this, may try to control the situation in order to ward off dependence on the TNCs. But even if they succeed, they still frequently lack access to appropriate technology, which is virtually monopolized by the TNCs. Whether or not the technology is locally appropriate, it is needed if the Third-World countries are to compete on the world market. Payment for the technology deepens their debts to the West. And the technology thus obtained is increasingly likely to be labour-displacing – or at least not labour-intensive – which exacerbates the unemployment crisis.[19]

At a global level, using the United Nations, the case for resisting and finding alternatives to such Western economic domination has been increasingly vociferous during the past decades. Calls for a new international economic order (and its expression in well-known documents such as the 'Brandt Report'[20]) have more recently been followed by the demand for a New World Information and Communication Order (NWICO). This follows the growing realization that new information and communications technologies, central to the operations of many companies operating in the Third World, are powerful means of extending both cultural and industrial dominance.

The significance of the NWICO demand is discussed below. But to put it in context, two other factors deserve mention. One is that, despite criticisms of the weakness of the UN, and the allegedly compromising effect of involvement in it of bodies like the World Bank, Western governments have, in the main, not responded at all favourably to calls for economic and cultural decolonization. The motives of Third-World leaders are often doubted. The American withdrawal from UNESCO is no surprise move.

The other factor is that not only industrial, but military power is at stake. For many newer nation states have indeed followed in Western footsteps – by importing military technology, to which IT is again vital. Argentina, Brazil, China, India and Israel have significant defence industries and participate in the global arms trade.[21] North and South Korea, the Philippines, Taiwan and Pakistan produce military aircraft, and several Third-World countries also make missiles. But the cost of this military security, once more, is dependence upon the superpowers for technological know-how.

IT and the transnationals

In the late twentieth century, the international character of economic, political and cultural life is intensified. The main agencies of this process are the transnational corporations (TNCs), whose strength has grown tremendously since the Second World War. They influence employment patterns and political alignments, and control the global flow of information and cultural 'commodities' such as television and video. Recession in parts of the world economy may have slowed their growth rates but not their capacity to control increasingly wide commercial and industrial domains.

The TNCs include such giants as Exxon, General Motors (GM), and IBM – whose chief executive, John F. Akers, is probably right to claim that the computer business will soon be the 'biggest industry in the world'.[22] Realizing the accuracy of this, GM bought Electronic Data Systems and Hughes Aircraft. IBM, knowing that computing alone is not the way forward, have obtained telecommunications companies, such as Rolm. Although Akers's prediction that IBM will see sales of $200 billion by 1992 is likely to be way out, a 1986 third-quarter *fall* to $1.08 billion profit gives some idea of its size.[23]

Economic aspects

The TNCs are largely responsible for the flexibility of the international division of labour. The so-called deindustrialization process, in which a decreasing proportion of workers in the advanced societies are directly involved in production, is an important aspect of this. It comes about as companies headquartered in New York or in Silicon Valley have 'offshore' manufacturing plants elsewhere, often in the Third World. Hewlett–Packard, a case in point, has major facilities in Mexico, Singapore, Scotland and other countries.[24]

'Deindustrialization' does not mean, however, that the advanced countries are any less concerned to make or to buy 'industrial' products. This is an important point, sometimes overlooked by those who believe that the Southern hemisphere may be able to bypass any 'industrial' phase of development, moving directly into an information-intensive economy. Rather, it means that more jobs are either automated or done elsewhere. Such 'exported' jobs are typically less skilled. The technical and marketing expertise of the high-tech companies remains in the advanced societies.

A *Datamation* article puts its finger on the implication of this: 'At a time when many US high-technology firms have taken to waving the flag and sounding the cry "buy American" to counter the threat of growing competition from Japanese and foreign rivals, a number of these firms are "buying foreign" when it comes to the labour market.' The piece continues by observing that the American corporations offer jobs 'to non-US workers in countries where wages are often a fraction of those paid here and corporate taxes minimal or non-existent'.[25] Especially during times of recession, less-well-off countries offer tax concessions and other inducements to companies willing to contribute to local employment.

Daniel Bell was certainly right to foresee the deindustrialization process as a point of tension. However, some of the difficulties appear to be more intractable than he anticipated. Whereas some countries are able to benefit from their comparative advantages such as cheaper, readily available labour, and do so in ways which allow some genuine local development, in many ways this situation seems less benign. In the short term, where assembly work on microelectronic products has not been automated, Asian women often bear the brunt of poor working conditions and health risks. Eyesight is often strained if not permanently impaired, and dipping components in acids may also cause burns and sickness.[26]

In the longer term, however, the effect of retaining the technical expertise in the Northern hemisphere (among the main competitors for leadership, the USA, Japan and Europe) is to prevent the Southern nations from developing their own modern industrial base. This is why the gap between North and South is widening at an accelerating rate. And the more the advanced countries develop IT, the faster the gap widens. This is poignantly illustrated in the case of a Third-World electronics producer like Malaysia. Stephen Maxwell observes that 'it supplies the cheap labour to make the electronics components which when put to work in manufacturing and the new information industries confirm its dependence and increase its vulnerability to exploitation.'[27]

There are two main reasons for the widening gap which relate directly to IT. One is that the advantage of having cheap labour is easily undermined by the increasing automation of assembly jobs. If only an assembly plant is located in the South, it is easy to shut down, and relocate back in the North. The other is that the advanced nations are increasingly investing in telecommunications equipment. An optimistic estimate of the worldwide telecommunications equipment market in 1990 gives 86 per cent to the developed countries, and only 11 per cent to the developing countries. It is 'optimistic', because the deepening debt problems of countries like Mexico and Nigeria, which have large telecom and informatics projects, will serve to retard them further.[28]

Improved telecommunications largely determine the 'multiplier effect' of IT, in every area. Manufacturing, office and service productivity increases at a faster rate as communications infrastructures are enhanced. Thus as their development is more rapid in the advanced nations, so the gap grows, faster, between them and the South. Capital saving is also facilitated by better telecommunications. The SWIFT (Society for World-wide International Financial Telecommunications) system, for instance, makes it possible for finance houses to buy or sell at any time. A kind of stateless currency thus circulates around the globe, twenty-four hours a day, again to the advantage of developing nations.

Political and cultural aspects

The TNCs also wield considerable political power, therefore, because they do much of their business beyond the reach of national governments. This works two ways. On the one hand, they can avoid regulations within their country of origin (for instance those which protect members of labour unions, or others which demand taxes) through the judicious location of their operations. On the other, they are able to erode the national sovereignty, not only of the less developed countries, but of advanced societies as well.

France was one country to recognize the import of this early on. The 'Nora and Minc' report on *l'informatisation* warned explicitly about the dangers posed to domestic industries by IBM.[29] IBM's commercial success, and its sensitivity to the market, give it an apparently unassailable world lead today, holding over 60 per cent of the market. Not only in data processing, but now increasingly in telecommunications as well, IBM is very powerful.

The issue here is known as 'trans-border data flow'. Canada, not a 'Third-World' but an industrially advanced nation, has had an increasingly acute experience of what this means for national sovereignty. The use of advanced telecommunications, particularly those using satellites, makes possible the processing and storing of commercial and even administrative data at a distance from where it is collected or from those it affects. Canadian data drains easily over the American border. In 1979 the Canadian government responded to the perceived threats this poses. They include decreased national control over privacy protection, interruption of services, human and technical resource development, foreign companies and data banks and a potential for undermining national telecommunications networks by the use of satellites.[30]

In the same year Brazil also justified protective policies directed against TNCs involved in microelectronics. No company may use foreign data banks without permission from the authorities. In Venezuela and Colombia controversies have arisen over the use of ultramodern transnational medical networks. Those wishing to be up-to-date scientifically press for its benefits. Others, aware of the disjunction between foreign high-tech medicine and national medical infrastructures, argue that cotton wool, surgical spirit and bandages are more urgently required than computer terminals.[31]

As for the 'cultural effects', with about 80 corporations controlling 75 per cent of the international communications market,[32] it is no exaggeration to say that Western ideas and images appear to dominate the world. On one national Philippine TV channel, nine of ten largest sponsors are TNCs such as Pepsi-Cola, Colgate and Nestlé.[33] Indeed by the mid-1970s over four-fifths of Latin American TV programmes – such as *Route 66*, and *The Flintstones* – came from the USA.[34]

In view of the other processes to which reference has been made already, particularly the trend towards concentration and integration of ownership and control within TNCs, we can expect this 'internationalization of culture' to continue. Combined with technological breakthroughs, notably those associated with direct broadcasting by satellite (DBS), the TNCs are a cultural force of growing power. Their position is further strengthened by two factors. One is the connection between communications media and flows of information, whether of a financial or scientific kind. As IT is developed, more and more diverse kinds of data use the same electronic 'highways'. The other factor is that this cultural power helps create the conditions for the further spread of 'Western' values of materialism, competition, individualism and so on.

Earlier the question was raised whether or not there is a direct line of descent from nineteenth- to twentieth-century linkages between the advanced societies and those which are 'less developed', 'developing', or 'underdeveloped'. Are we discussing new forms of 'imperialism' or 'colonialism', of an economic or cultural kind? The question is not easily answered, although it must be said that some write as if it were a foregone conclusion.[35]

Clearly, the new 'post-colonial' nations of the 1950s were anything but 'post-colonial' economically. This fact is the starting point for viewing the activities of TNCs as a new form of colonialism. When Tom McPhail describes 'electronic colonialism', therefore, he refers to the 'dependency relationship established by the importation of communications hardware, foreign-produced software, along with engineers, technicians,'[36] which together help foster foreign values and expectations within domestic cultures. In some situations it is evident that 'imperialism' also describes this relationship well. By controlling access to information sources and channels, and by siphoning off local capital while simultaneously selling 'cultural' and other commodities, TNCs may for their own profit effectively dominate local economies to the latters' long-term detriment.[37]

But this is not always and everywhere the effect of TNC operations. Cees Hamelink argues that 'cultural synchronization' is a better term than cultural imperialism.[38] He freely acknowledges that colonial and imperial relationships persist, and are perpetuated by the TNCs. But the situation in which more and more societies are drawn into a sort of 'universal culture' (elsewhere dubbed 'wall-to-wall Dallas') need not necessarily be imperialistic. Whatever position one takes in this complex debate, the crucial factors are twofold.

Firstly, the dominance in IT of the USA, Japan, and, to a lesser degree, Western Europe, puts all other would-be advanced nations in a dependent relationship to them. Secondly, often following patterns reminiscent of earlier empires, though now modified by the *transnational* nature of corporations, such dependency means that the poorer, peripheral countries face severe threats to their cultural autonomy and are thus vulnerable to exploitation by the richer, better developed countries.

Prospects for decolonizing IT

Given the heavy imbalance of power and influence between North and South it is hardly surprising that the noise of fierce competition to obtain and control new telecommunications – television satellites being an obvious example – drowns out pleas for a more equitable global order. Yet the mid-1980s witnessed significant events – the withdrawal of the USA and Britain from UNESCO (The United Nations Educational Scientific and Cultural Organization) – which arose in part from precisely such pleas.

In 1976, African countries represented at UNESCO proposed the establishment of a 'New World Information and Communication Order'. Having begun in an effort to redress the North–South balance in areas such as journalism, advertising, and television, during the 1980s its remit was widened considerably. The rapid development of new technologies for the transmission, storage and retrieval of information, with their accompanying ramifications for economic and cultural influence, coincided with growing interest in the 'new order'.

Electronic colonialism has not occurred behind the backs of the Third-World countries. Many Latin Americans, Asians and Africans are acutely aware of the effects on their own development both of the TNCs and the local elites who collude with them. Many aspire to using the technologies of the advanced nations for their own indigenous development, and recognize their need to cooperate with them in the development process.

But major obstacles lie in their path. One is the difficulty of achieving a genuinely local consciousness of each unique situation. Many countries can only afford to buy news from the international agencies rather than gathering and disseminating their own. In such situations it is easy to see how having a degree of control over the means of communication becomes a vital issue. As Frank Ugboajah puts it 'In the developing – or, to be more precise, the deteriorating – nations, communication has been a weapon in the struggle for independence and in efforts to transform social structures and solve economic problems.'[39]

This relates not only to news and TV films, however. Industrial and technological self-reliance also depends upon such 'cultural decolonizing'. As Nigerian Ikoku explains, this is a 'battle for the mind'. He advocates a 'direct struggle against cultural imperialism which sought and seeks to subdue the entire cultural traits of former colonized areas through direct infiltration of the educational systems, the arts, technological ambitions and other value systems'.[40]

The so-called 'MacBride Commission', set up by UNESCO in 1977, produced its findings in a much-debated document entitled *Many voices, one world*.[41] The fundamental issue running through the debate is this. Western governments share a belief that the powers of press and government should be separate. But this is simultaneously an *economic* doctrine, part of the ostensible commitment to *laissez-faire*. Many Third-World countries protest that in their contexts, where governments are frequently frail, a free press could lead to unnecessary and undesirable political and social instability.[42]

Within the document, however, is a parallel concern, whose long-term import, though only dimly perceived, is already clear enough to warrant extensive and urgent attention. As the report puts it, 'in all industrialized countries and in a growing number of developing countries interest is focussed on the extraordinary new opportunities being opened up by technological innovations.' Unfortunately, they are out of reach of some, for they are often 'initiated, and may be controlled for a long time to come, by a small number of countries and a few transnational firms.'[43] IT is viewed as a key to development; its accompanying transnational companies, an obstacle.

The debate over NWICO has spurred some local initiatives in Third-World countries aimed at promoting grass-roots forms of 'alternative communication'. These take various forms. Examples include a video experiment in Manila, where street vendors of cigarettes 'story-told' their experience of struggles at the migrant margins of society,[44] and church-based production of 'magic lanterns' in Calcutta.[45] Beyond this, debate continues within international fora as to how to curb the power of the TNCs, and how to harness their technological expertise in ways appropriate to local situations in the South.

In the Northern hemisphere, however, the NWICO debate has

apparently helped to accelerate the departure of some nations from UNESCO altogether. By 1981 a US House subcommittee said that by 'regulating the flow of news and information around the world' NWICO would violate First Amendment principles. A co-sponsor of the eventual House resolution argued that it would 'support tyranny and thought control'. A dissenter from such views was Hamid Mowlana, who pointed out that NWICO's efforts were analogous to those of the American Associated Press to break the domination of world news reportage by Reuters and Havas sixty-five years before.[46]

The debate oversimplified the issues. The tyranny referred to was that of Eastern Europe. Third-World demands for national sovereignty, supported by state socialist countries, were seen as steps in that direction, despite Third-World denunciation of government information control in those countries. Meanwhile American amnesia about her previous championing of decolonization continues to be an irony not lost on her former dependents who themselves now seek to define their own interests, needs and values.

Because UNESCO failed to heed Western warnings over this and other issues, the USA withdrew in 1984, followed by Britain and Singapore in 1985. However worried they were by the 'shrill demands'[47] of Tunisian Mustapha Masmoudi, and whatever the truth in allegations about autocracy and inefficiency in the person of Senegalese Director-General of UNESCO Amadou Mahtar M'Bow, it seems likely that withdrawal will retard progress towards agreement about information flows.[48] This in turn cannot help to foster the kinds of technical cooperation in informatics which Third-World countries seek.

To some, the idea of a world information and communication order may appear to be unrealistically utopian, and the politics of UNESCO a mere ripple in the sea of international relations. But it does serve to draw attention to the dependent plight of Third-World countries, and to stimulate within them eforts to counter transnational power with indigenous alternatives. In the advanced nations, however, withdrawal of support for UNESCO reduces the chances of having genuine dialogue on informatics development, and also providing a means of accountability for TNCs. At a time when informatization widens the gap between North and South at ever faster rates, this is bad news for all who seek for greater justice on a global level.

Summary and conclusions

Any concept of the information society must be global in scope; informatization is nowhere a merely local process. The notion of a 'global village', however, should be treated with caution. The international telecommunications web of satellites, cables, and broadcasting frequencies seems far from producing the 'one world' hinted at by that phrase. Indeed, given the inter-connections between states, TNCs and military interests involved in IT, the 'global village' is a pathetically hollow concept. Recognition of the technological potential for world-wide development too frequently ignores or glosses over the deep-seated divisions and conflicts between countries possessing IT capabilities and others which do not.

The forces which created these divisions are found in the legacy of colonialism which, though formally abandoned on a large scale after the Second World War, is perpetuated by economic ties of dependence. While some countries – such as India, Singapore, and Nigeria – have managed to take advantage of their relationships with former colonial powers, and have begun building the informatics infrastructures which are crucial to future development, others find themselves rapidly falling behind.

The main reason for this is found in the way transnational corporations operate. However well-intentioned their policies, they tend to have a negative effect on the indigenous development of Third-World countries. Their presence all too often benefits only metropolitan elites rather than rural subsistence farmers or migrant shanty town dwellers. They offer manufacturing assembly jobs, and Western-style clothes and television shows, but do little to transfer technical expertise which would enable receiving countries to develop their own industries and culture.

Operating outside the jurisdiction of either their own governments, or those of the less developed nations, they exploit to the full the new communications technologies. They may move capital with ever-increasing ease to where labour is cheapest, advertise wares and sell cultural commodities directly to consumers, and remotely monitor by satellite crops, minerals or fish and animals to the advantage of Western commodity markets.

Recognition of this process has prompted efforts at resistance and local development on the part of Third-World countries. The UNESCO-sponsored call for a New World Information and Communication Order, alongside pressures for an International Economic Order and for 'Technical Cooperation among Developing Countries' symbolizes this. American and British withdrawal from UNESCO equally symbolizes Western unwillingness to confront responsibly the realities of electronic colonialism.

Despite this, evidence from different sources is not overwhelmingly negative from the viewpoint of the developing countries. In 1982 a joint communiqué signed by Mexican and French government officials pledged to protect each others' national identity, especially where communication languages in information systems are concerned. They also noted that major data-bases and -banks used criteria not always appropriate to the needs of developing nations.[49] Another example is the way in which transnational corporations have been successfully established in the Third World. 'Brazil's Petrobras and Kuwait Petroleum already rank among the world's top manufacturing companies, while Hyundai (Republic of Korea) has grown bigger than France's Michelin and Britain's Rio Tinto-Zinc'.[50] Admittedly, they do not yet offer much by way of technology, and are far less sophisticated than their Western counterparts.

Within some Third-World countries renewed energy is directed towards providing alternative forms of communication and information flows at a local grass-roots level.[51] While this may appear to be a puny response to the might of the TNCs, the long-term effects may not be negligible. Indeed the efficacy of such projects could well be enhanced if combined with efforts in the North to restrict the steamrollering of cultures which is a current effect of TNC operation. Despite US attempts to shift the balance of communication more in its favour (while simultaneously upholding 'free-flow' principles) the UN General Assembly passed a resolution in 1982 which obliges satellite owners to obtain 'prior consent' before broadcasting messages over others' borders.[52] How this can be enforced is another question.

The growth of informatics on a global scale means that what were once issues of 'communication and cultural autonomy' (and highly significant in their own right) now also crucially affect the chances of economic and political as well as cultural development in the nations of the Southern hemisphere. Analytical problems of this new and unfolding situation are chronically intertwined with ethical and policy issues of great complexity and urgency. Given the current debt crises, alongside famine and hardship for millions, and increased military capabilities of the South as well as East and West, ignoring the issues or withdrawing from the debate are options which are neither safe nor responsible.

7

Information, meaning and culture

The vast material displacements the machine has made in our physical environment are perhaps in the long run less important than its spiritual contributions to our culture.

Lewis Mumford (1930)[1]

We wear a dangerous set of blinkers if we do not appreciate and further explore how computers can become the carriers of culture and of a challenge to our way of thinking about ourselves.

Sherry Turkle (1980)[2]

In an information society, it is said, a majority of people spend their time doing tasks which relate to information – expressing, gathering, storing, retrieving and disseminating it. People manipulate information for the purposes of travel, entertainment, instruction, control and so on. From disc-jockeys to designers and from the police to programmers, the daily routine involves data-processing of one sort or another. The data processed are forms of symbolic information.

In the past, the kinds of technologies used for handling information have often affected its quality and nature. The emergence of writing made possible contact with others over both time (laws, for example, encoded in written form, apply across generations) and space (the newspaper links together those within a given geographical area). It has been suggested that literate people, by scrutinizing their thoughts in written form, become more self-aware, and think of themselves more as 'individuals'.[3] Will the diffusion of information technology bring similar changes?

IT undoubtedly contributes to the breakdown of categories of information. The same electronic medium may carry voice, video, financial or technical data, photographic images or written text. Old distinctions thus get blurred, as for instance in the phenomenon of 'desktop publishing', where functions of writer, publisher and printer are rolled into one. Similarly, IT appears to have an impact on social and cultural categories. Whereas it was once possible to distinguish between 'home', 'work' and 'public' culture, IT helps erode the boundaries. Homeworking (using remote terminals), movable work (using portable computers and cellular radio-telephones), and the increasing invasion of the domestic sphere by the public market-place via advertising and home entertainment all illustrate this trend.

But do changes such as these hold out a promise – or threat – of deeper cultural transformations? Three aspects of this question are worth considering. One, what is the impact of new technologies on entertainment and leisure activities? Computer and video games, cable and satellite television, and the use of video cassette recorders all raise questions about traditional forms of broadcasting, about *where* leisure time is spent, and about the actual range of choices opening up to consumers. Two, what are the effects of increased personal interaction with computerized machines? Not only the leisure activities just mentioned, but also workplace tasks, increasingly involve keyboard and screen. Do 'user-friendliness' and 'artificial intelligence' mean human beings and computers are entering into new kinds of meaningful relationship? Three, what evidence is there that new outlooks or lifestyles are emerging, associated with the 'information revolution'? Is the caring, personal society, with its emphasis on education and the 'life ethic' a reality or an illusion?

Unless one is committed to the dogma that human beings are essentially little more than tool-making animals, or that human life is decisively defined by labour, then these cultural questions are crucially important. This does not mean that other issues are insignificant. De-skilling, surveillance, or the persisting local and global inequalities between (information) rich and poor are still pressing matters. But if people do not live by bread alone, then the world of the symbolic, of culture, must be viewed in dynamic relation to the material.

In fact, this could be taken further. If today's society is characterized by the transformation of symbols – language, image, information – rather than material goods, then this has implications for power. Political problems may be related as much to the cultural as to the economic sphere.[4] If this is so, then the cultural questions raised by the diffusion of IT take on a new complexion. The 'information society' theme, all too often the cue for fanciful fantasies about the peace and prosperity available

courtesy of clever machines, clearly deserves to become the focus of much
more serious attention than it has been accorded to date.

Electronic culture

Without doubt, IT makes inroads into traditional forms of entertainment
and leisure activities, especially those based 'at home'. Video cassette films
and computer games, satellite TV received either direct or via a cable
station, compact and laser discs, information services such as travel and
weather news – all these augment older one-way radio and TV transmis-
sions. In a growing proportion of Western homes the television screen is a
medium for many different kinds of information; as well as the traditional
sports, news, films and comedy from TV stations, the same screen may be
used to show the state of one's bank account, to move through 'pages' of a
clothing catalogue, or as a monitor for word-processing, programming, or
computer games.

The pundits claim that the huge new array of cultural commodities
means much more choice for everyone. The conventional patterns of
control in TV programming will be overturned, giving rise to an unprecedented diversity to suit every individual preference. As British journalist
Andrew Neil enthuses, 'Satellite and cable and all manner of new
technology is going to put the power in the hands of the consumer, and
we'll move from a producer-dominated system to a consumer-led
system.'[5]

But on what are such predictions based? Although they sound
egalitarian – more choice for all; the end of paternalist broadcasting – what
is the evidence? Social divisions have always been present within 'free-
time' activities. Are they not likely to reappear in use of and access to new
sources of leisure and entertainment activities? For all the complaints
against 'public service broadcasting', is it not fatally threatened by the new
potential diversity? And if free enterprise and self-help are the order of the
day (in many Western societies), why do 'grass-roots' movements such as
community radio fare so badly?

In what follows, the promise of 'extended choice' is examined,
particularly in leisure activities affected by IT. The promise is issued, for
instance, by the advocates of cable and satellite television, who argue that
'more channels mean more choice', and by high-tech researchers who say
it is only a matter of time before one is able to select preferred tracks to be

'customized' onto each compact disc. Of course, the long-term trends are impossible to predict, and the outcome of technological developments may be affected by numerous different factors. In most would-be information societies, for example, cable television is only slowly being established, and is in danger of being overtaken by broadcasting by satellite (DBS). However, the promise is closely related to a trend which *is* identifiable, and which yields some clues as to the likelihood of its realization, namely, commodification. The issue here is the marketplace for cultural commodities.

The chances of 'greater choice' becoming a reality are well illustrated by the case of cable TV. In Britain, cable TV is seen by government as a means of establishing an information infrastructure, the grid of electronic highways required to carry the digital traffic of the future. Rather than paying for such a network out of public funds, however, the British devised a scheme whereby domestic users, lured by the dangling carrot of multiple channel television, would themselves underwrite its costs. By this curious logic, *The Muppet Show* and *Rambo* would lead the way to the information society.

Since the granting of a number of franchises in the mid-1980s, however, the promise of choice seems a little tarnished. Apart from the fact that only urban areas are cabled and that some would-be subscribers find that they cannot afford the new services (which immediately restricts 'choice'), it is not clear that competition actually extends choice either. For in fact, only the big international companies can afford to make programmes of a commercial kind. Added to which, once new distribution channels are opened up, national operators are faced with a lack of local software (films, news, and so on), which means they will draw upon already existing – and thus often American – sources.

In Italy, the deregulation of television has flooded screens with dubbed American soap operas, short-lived amateurish (and often pornographic) low-budget programmes, and undisguised advertising channels, devoted to selling anything from fur coats to furniture. And in the USA, where cable television was effectively born, choice often means numerous re-runs of old movies – *Close Encounters*, *Superman*, and the *Muppet Movie*.[6] But this is not always or necessarily the case. In some American cable areas, such as San Diego, a qualitative move towards genuine diversity has taken place. So while Richard Collins is correct to observe that, 'Any provision of new services – any extension of choice – fragments the audience for existing services and diminishes the revenue base of all services'[7], this may only be a partial picture, limited by technical or social circumstances.

As telecommunications – new and old – become the site of ever fiercer commercial competition, the range of available programmes for television viewers is progressively restricted. Audiences are 'sold' to advertisers, using whatever programmes will keep them in front of the box. The ratings are an index not so much of audience enjoyment as of profitability.

In times of recession and economic restructuring, not only the 'attraction' of the flickering screen but also the lack of alternatives open to particular social groups keeps audience numbers high. In Britain poorer segments of the population cannot afford increasingly expensive forms of 'public' leisure activity, and are obliged to remain at home, where the television is the focus for 'relaxation'.[8] In the USA this has been described as the '50 per cent have, 50 per cent have not problem'. Communications 'services' such as cable TV are either unaffordable or unavailable to roughly half the population. Rural areas, ethnic minorities and inner cities suffer.[9] Similar cleavage lines are appearing with other new technologies as well.

Video cassette recorder (VCR) sales received an immense boost in Britain with the Royal Wedding in 1981, although at that time their price kept low income earners out of the market. Subsequently the practice of renting VCRs with TV sets has brought them to many more homes. But one survey[10] shows that groups in the occupational scale tend to use them for pre-recorded films, whereas those higher on the scale use them more for catching up with programmes missed because of clashing schedules.

Use of new domestic technologies is also related to educational career patterns. Penetration of VCRs is lower in homes where more time has been spent in full-time education, but the converse is true of home computers. Since the early 1980s, when Sir Clive Sinclair and the BBC introduced relatively cheap machines, many households have acquired them, both for playing games and because of the belief that their children's education would be enhanced thereby. Rather more than 13 per cent of British households had computers in the mid-1980s, but this hides the fact that they are six times more likely to be found in the homes of professional and managerial groups than those of the unskilled or unemployed. Choice again appears to run along tracks defined by income and occupational factors.

The threat of commercialized culture is probably most strongly felt among supporters of 'public service broadcasting' (PSB) traditions. Whether seen as 'deregulation' (USA) or 'privatization' (UK), providing further diversity in information and communication channels seems likely to erode the position of all PSB networks. Various worries are expressed in this connection, but they centre around the belief that contenders such as cable and satellite television tend to promote cultural sameness, a relatively unvaried diet of commercially oriented programming.

PSB (in both radio and television) has aimed to reach all within a given geographical area, and to provide for specialist programming for educational, ethnic or aesthetic interests. But the newer technologies, by challenging this privileged position, could well irreversibly alter such traditional patterns. PSB's position is likely to be weakened by competition, which would put its revenues at risk, and could be swamped by American-originated material. Under previous arrangements, for example, French state radio has attempted to keep below 50 per cent the amount of American popular music broadcast. In Britain, TV networks could carry only 14 per cent of non-EEC material.[11] Sections of both political right and left deplore such a scenario. The former fear a further decline of elite and traditional values, the latter protest against both the decline of the public sphere and the continued invasion of the home by capital.[12]

Related to this is a more general concern about the effects of what might be termed cultural commodification; a broader diffusion of 'garbage information', socially undesirable products and electronic trivia. Computer and video games have always had close associations with violence and war, not to mention sex. (Those who can deal coolly with megadeaths in the games arcade have even been offered jobs in the armed services.[13]) The inventor of the original computer games, Nolan Bushnell, has now graduated to producing 'petsters', computerized cuddly toys which he hopes will soon replace messy and exercise-seeking domestic animals. As for the novel world of 'information services', French jurists have become alarmed by the use of the successful *Minitel* system for commercial sex message systems.[14]

While some dismiss all such electronic artifacts as innocent toys or pastimes, others raise deeper questions about what interests are served, what attitudes encourage and what human needs are met by such items. Discontent with the direction of electronic culture has also spurred efforts designed to offer alternatives.

Not surprisingly, the desire to forge alternatives to dominant commercial forms of electronic culture is frequently frustrated. Cable TV 'arts channels' find it hard to remain viable, or (in the USA) have to charge higher rates. Cooperative, peaceful and ecological computer games have appeared in recent years, but it is too early to gauge their success. Making cable TV channels open to 'public access', despite an initial euphoria about the technological potential for such 'community television', has run up against major obstacles again relating to economic viability.

The 'alternatives' just mentioned are, of course, alternatives only in the sense that they operate at the margins of the mainstream. Resistance to what is perceived as dominant cultural expression may take more radical forms. In the USA the Coalition for Better Broadcasting, which objects to televised sex-and-violence, has resorted to the 'media strike' (refusing to watch programmes or buy products from sponsors) in an attempt to change the content of programming.[15] In several countries community radio is considered to be a better (because cheaper to run) means of trying to ensure that minority voices are heard and interests catered for. The British experience is salutory, however. Government (in)action has led to the failure of numerous applications to run legally franchised community radio stations, and frequent raids on illegally operating 'pirate' stations, most often ones owned by ethnic minorities.[16]

It seems that the expanding diversity of channels and commodities within the 'electronic culture' is leading, paradoxically, to less rather than more choice. That is to say, choice is increasingly circumscribed by commercial criteria. On the one hand this means that the large corporate interests which control the fields of publishing, broadcasting, and software (from films to games) will make their decisions about content according to profitability rather than, say, the ethic of PSB. On the other, ability to pay will determine more and more who has access to what kinds of information and cultural product.

Within this debate, old and new cultural questions are intertwined. Traditional concerns about the social divisions of culture are given a new edge as problems relating to the media, information and communication begin to eclipse traditional 'social' issues as a central arena of politics. Other dimensions of the 'newer' questions, to which we turn next, have to do with the personal and psychological effects of human contact with and use of electronic media of information and communication. The telephone, television and now the computer have taken us progressively further away from both oral and written symbols. Do today's 'intelligent' machines threaten our personhood even more deeply than Marx and the Romantics once argued that 'energy' machines do?

In the computer image

As more and more people within the advanced societies not only 'play' but also work with the keyboards and screens of computerized information handling, what effects does this have on their awareness of themselves and the world? Does the appearance of 'user-friendly' machines signal new relationships and a new rapprochement with technological artifacts? Or does it mean, as Mark Poster suggests, that 'The reversal of priorities Marx saw in the factory whereby the dead (machines) dominate the living (workers) is extended by the computer into the realm of knowledge'?[17]

High-tech hopes are certainly high. It is no longer the 'high frontier' of space which captures the imagination, but the 'inner frontier' of conceptual space. Computer games addicts and hackers perceive the screen as a window opening onto a multidimensional world which can be navigated by keyboard, joystick or mouse. Link this alternative world by telecommunications, and it may become a shared world already seen embryonically in computer bulletin boards and networking.[18] More than one commentator sees in this conceptual space the promise of a more ecological outlook and emphasis. Plenitude replaces scarcity as the fundamental reality of human existence. While at the same time computer simulation clearly delineates the limits on certain real resources.[19]

For artificial intelligence researchers, the frontier lies well beyond human capacities. One envisages a time when 'together, man and machines . . . may be able to subdue many, perhaps in time most, of the world's afflictions'.[20] The resources available to such researchers are huge, given that, both in Western Europe and the USA, vast sums are being channelled into meeting the challenge of Japanese 'Fifth Generation' computers. Artificial intelligence (AI) is a vital part of those research programmes. But equally awesome are the kinds of questions posed by AI. They range from 'should robots have civil rights?', a topic already covered in a University of California course,[21] through the connections between AI and military research (of which the controversy over the 'Star Wars' Strategic Defence Initiative is but one example) to queries about the ethics of 'artificial' decision-making.

On a more mundane level is the matter of metaphors. Is there any special significance in the increasingly pervasive use in everyday talk of terms such as 'programmed', 'debugged', 'hacker', 'on-line', 'interface' and so on? What kinds of human image do people work with, and what are the important metaphors for organizing experience? Do computer users think of themselves (or others) as 'information processors'? (If so, what is so 'artificial' about computer 'intelligence'?) And with regard to gender, if high tech in general has an aura of *machismo* about it, does IT in particular have some peculiarly 'masculine' qualities – algorithmic over against (more 'feminine') analogical thought-patterns?

The best place to begin is with artificial intelligence, because this area represents computer research's highest aspiration, to create machines that 'think'. The literature of AI enthusiasts constantly gives the impression that it is 'only a matter of time' before computers will understand natural languages and perform other tasks that up until now have usually been thought of as the exclusive province of human intelligence. So-called expert systems are the most familiar aspect of AI, computer 'consultants' used in medical diagnosis, chemical identification, structural analysis and, of course, anti-ballistic missile defence systems.[22]

Already, in order to describe AI, I have used typically 'human' terms: 'intelligence', 'thinking', 'understand', 'expert' and 'consultant'. At this point controversy starts. In the 1930s British mathematician Alan Turing described a 'universal computing machine' which by the year 2000 would be able to imitate human intelligence perfectly. Today's software-makers find their roots in his pioneering work. Only now, with the microelectronic hardware to go with the programs, they also anticipate the fulfilment of his dream. Needless to say, the prizes would also be great, as the range of IT applications would expand astronomically.

Reference has already been made to the seemingly extravagant claims of some AI scientists. However, there is evidence that certain AI claims may be taken very seriously by defence personnel, cognitive psychologists, and even sociologists. One of the latter, who enquires, 'why not a sociology of machines?', also reverses the usual query by asking 'in what sense can we continue to presume that human intelligence is not artificial?'[23] But wherever the 'strong AI' – thinking machines – case is put, one also finds robust and also scathing objections and rebuttals.

The leading (self-styled) heretic works inside the world of AI research at the Massachusetts Institute of Technology; he is Joseph Weizenbaum. For him, the crucial error is to suppose that the thinking processes underlying human thinking are essentially the same as the computer's information processes. He insists that while 'computers may perform impressive feats of calculating . . . they cannot make judgements, because judgements depend on more than information extracted from the real world; they depend on meanings'. And meaning, he avers, emerges from the thinker's active participation in the world.[24]

Weizenbaum excoriates AI research for other reasons as well; most prominently its complicity in the arms race and its debasing of education. He is not alone in his scepticism. Hubert Dreyfus has for years provided a counter-balance to high-tech hype by stressing 'what computers can't do'.[25] And Terry Winograd, another AI researcher, admits that in natural language research 'We are setting ways of understanding . . . that create a forgetfulness about responsibility and accountability.'[26]

Yet many AI researchers share a common aim of inventing a mechanical super-brain with 'intelligence' superior to any human expert, the responses of which are comparable to those of a person. Success in this, according to one judgement, will be 'more by virtue of reconceptualising what it is to be human than by capturing some essence of human intelligence in a program design'.[27] Such an inversion of the AI question – not, will computers become like people? but, will people become like computers? – also forms the focus of serious debate today.

The contention of David Bolter's book *Turing's man* is that 'men and women of the electronic age . . . are indeed remaking themselves in the image of their technology'.[28] That is to say, computers are becoming what he calls a 'defining technology'. Leaning on Lewis Mumford's assertion that the clock is the typical symbol of industrialism, contributing pervasively both to precise measurement of time and thus also to the organization of daily life,[29] Bolter suggests that the computer may now be supplanting the clock. If the clock defines humanity in terms of a 'clockwork image', the computer alters this such that people view themselves as 'information processors'.

Now, Bolter's argument is couched within the history of ideas (the implications of which are examined below), and he brings little empirical evidence to support his case. Indeed there is at present not much to go on, although the scientific and commercial question for user-friendly machines is stimulating research in this area.[30] Sherry Turkle's much-quoted work is one important exception. She argues from her studies of computer experts, students, and children that the machine may be thought of as a 'second self'. Children in particular, she says, often define themselves 'not with respect to their differences from animals, but by how they differ from computers'.[31]

Turkle takes very seriously the filtering into everyday speech of computer terms such as 'debugging' or 'stuck in a loop'. But she takes equally seriously references to computers constraining choices (elevators which only stop at floors designated by the badge worn by employees), encouraging violence (Space War players wanting more points for killing than surviving) or atrophying minds (through children not using their heads for calculating).[32] To her, computers are 'Rorschach'. Like this famous inkblot test (in which psychologists ask subjects what they 'see' in a splash of ink), computers may be 'projective devices', providing metaphors for thinking about people and social organization.

Others' studies of hackers (obsessive computer enthusiasts), hobbyists, computer professionals and children learning with computers complement Turkle's work,[33] although it is probably too early to draw any firm conclusions. But Turkle's work does have some interesting parallels with Bolter's. Both refer to the aesthetic as well as the calculating aspects of computing, and both see tremendous potential for cultural transformation as experience with computers is more widely diffused in society.

However, another reason it may be 'too early to tell' is that as computers are developed, awareness of how they operate may diminish. I have no need to know *how* the word processor on which I am writing this works. But it does not follow from this objection that computers will not become a 'defining technology'. In order to make this point, however, we have to go beyond Bolter. It is not just that Bolter, entranced by the magic which enables users to 'work at one level without understanding the details of operation at levels below him',[34] fails to note that those levels might include exploitation of assembly workers who made the machine, or the obsessive absorption which designed it. Rather, it is that Bolter has paid insufficient attention to how the clock might be a 'defining technology'.

The clock became a 'defining technology' both culturally, by providing a metaphor for mind, and also socially, by helping to define the parameters of human existence. With industrialism, accurately quantified time gradually came to predominate over traditional rhythms of seasons and night and day. But simultaneously, as 'time spent' was bought and sold as 'labour' within capitalism, this came to be distinguished from 'free time' or leisure. Similarly, the 'home' and 'workplace' division expresses this spatially.[35]

So, is the computer today performing a role which in some significant respects is analogous to the clock, culturally *and* socially? As it happens, a strong case may be made for just that. Computerization is undertaken as a key means of control over processes and people. The notion of 'surveillance' expresses this well. In Giddens's work it incorporates both the monitoring of populations by the agencies of commerce and the state, and the direct supervision of employees within the workplace. The installation of IT simply strengthens both kinds of surveillance. Linking telecommunications with databanks facilitates monitoring, while computerized machines pace and 'program' the worker, whether he or she is in the factory, the office or for that matter working from home.

Could it be that in the 'civilizing process', ably described by Norbert Elias, a further stage is becoming apparent? He argues that over time the power of the wider community to restrain behaviour has given way to more 'self-control'. At the same time, greater specialization in the division of labour and tasks has led to greater interdependence. But as machines were used to reduce the unreliability of the 'human factor', self-discipline itself underwent change.[36]

Helga Nowotny makes the connection between Elias and new technology by pointing out that new technical systems, if they are to interact successfully with human beings, must have built-in assumptions about how human beings operate. The automatic bank teller in Main Street is installed on the assumption that people prefer the convenience of unlimited access to personal contact with a bank employee. The automation of production tasks often assumes that people only contribute their dexterity or eye for detail to the process. Nowotny pessimistically concludes that 'Eventually, this reified image of the human being acquires the compelling force of a new social norm, to which actual social beings will have to learn to adapt in an approximation process.'[37]

Indirect forms of computer regulation may emerge as exchanges take place almost entirely without human mediation. As computers 'converse' with each other – for instance about one's welfare benefits, creditworthiness, or health – such exchanges could have decisive effects upon individuals' lives. As Mark Poster asks: 'Machine conversations are part of our linguistic community: they constitute an increasing portion of our social interactions. As members of our linguistic world, what is their relation to a democratic community?'[38]

Furthermore, the cultural divisions associated with the clock may also become blurred with computerization. Practices such as remote work via 'homework' terminals or portable computers and telephones, and the extension of the public sphere into the home via new telecommunications and information services all illustrate this possible trend.

In short, Bolter may be partially correct in seeing the computer as a new kind of 'defining technology'. His analysis is not so much wrong as inadequate. It is commendably historical in sweep, but lamentably asocial in depth. The cultural implications of IT, and their intrinsic connections with the conditions of social life, form a promising vein, which calls for investigation and mining.

A computer culture?

Beyond questions about the production of cultural commodities and about computer-related human images lies the wider issue of 'civilization'. If Silicon Valley really is the new 'Fertile Crescent' as its admirers and emulators claim, what does this mean for 'Western civilization'? Differences of opinion run deep on the shape of the cultural landscape in the 'information society', running the gamut from peaceful and humane to conflict-riven, impersonal and alienated scenarios.

Alvin Toffler's Third Wave puts the accent on individuality, diversity and cooperation, all of which are facilitated by the development of IT. Similarly, John Naisbitt's *Megatrends* lead to a 'hi-tech, hi-touch' society: 'The more technology we introduce into society, the more people will aggregate, will want to be with other people: movies, rock concerts, shopping.'[39] Each focuses on the new – attitudes, tastes, moralities, lifestyles – contrasting these with the old.

A British survey concludes that the 'outer-directed' values of the industrial era are already on the wane. People holding them tend to be 'status-conscious materialists, orthodoxly ambitious, traditional, and pro-authority'. The 'new people' reject all this, moving beyond the 'work ethic' to a 'life ethic', in which educational opportunity provides the base at any age to switch jobs, and a national wage replaces unemployment benefits, allowing people to use their energies either in employment or community service. Thirty-six per cent of Britain's adult population are already 'new people', a figure only exceeded by The Netherlands' forty-seven per cent.[40]

Generally, the optimists foresee a more relaxed outlook on life, a greater devotion to leisure pursuits, and a long-awaited chance to promote the general welfare of society – the rise of a 'communal ethic' as Daniel Bell once termed it.[41] But this vision finds itself rather sharply contradicted by another, darker dream. Two of its features connect with the preceding discussion of 'cultural commodification' and of the effects of increased human–machine relationships.

Firstly, despite the burgeoning diversity of choice apparently presented by the growth of IT, greater choice may not necessarily be reflected in what is actually available in the area of information sources, entertainment and leisure activities. Communication could become an even more 'top down' process, as fewer people and companies control the means of broad- and narrow-casting and transmission. The information 'haves' may be able to afford a wider selection of programming, while the 'have-nots' are limited to a narrower range of choices.

The resulting trivialization of the media can also be related to the general creation of 'artificial needs' within modern societies. Ask, 'what is IT *for?*', and the sceptic could answer that it has no clear justification as previous tools such as spades or steam engines did. As Hans Jonas observes, 'communication engineering answers to the needs of information and control solely created by civilization itself which made this technology possible, and, once started, imperative'.[42]

But to return to the issue of placing information and communication in the marketplace, it is hard to see how this will not lead to a decline in 'general welfare'. Making entertainment and information available only at a price, rather than as public services (like water or roads) seems to betray the opposite of a 'communal ethic'. Link this with the amnesia about responsibility which is said to accompany the appearance of 'thinking machines' and a more dismal picture indeed emerges.

A glance at life in Silicon Valley today raises further questions about the 'communal ethic'. While it may be objected that Silicon Valley could never be cloned elsewhere, the fact remains that some hold it up as a 'guide to the future'. Judith Larsen and Everett Rogers describe the Valley as 'a vigorous knees-and-elbows kind of industrial development that ignored public benefits', comparing it with the 'tragedy' of common grazing lands in medieval England: 'Each man is locked into a system that compels him to increase his herd without limit – in a world that is limited.'[43]

Secondly, I turn to the issue of human–machine relations. A survey of research on this finds that 'computing use tends to isolate individuals, reducing their interaction with other people in both work and leisure settings'. The same survey notes that computer users at work are seldom 'liberated' from routine for more 'discretionary' time, and in fact often choose to spend more time with machines than people. On balance, say its authors, the broadest social impacts might be characterized as 'antisocial'.[44] The evidence of 'hackers' is simply the extreme end of the continuum.

Any form of computer-mediated communications – electronic mail, teleconferencing, (computer) bulletin boards and so on – illustrates this. While it may eventually transpire that hierarchy is undermined and differences of status eroded by the use of impersonal computer messages, concern is expressed at present about the effects of anonymity and reduced self- and other-awareness. The historical, contextual and non-verbal clues we are used to in everyday conversation, and that are already muffled by the telephone, are missing altogether in electronic signals. Such 'do not efficiently communicate nuances of meaning and frame of mind, organizational loyalties, symbolic procedural variations, and, especially, individuating details about people that might be embodied in their dress, location, demeanor and expressiveness'.[45]

James Carey argues that this simply extends a process already visible in other modern communications. Extending language over space 'drains it of its capacity to serve as an instrument for emotive meaning' and thereby weakens significant social bonds. At the same time, that distance-stretching of language creates new power relations and also produces 'special classes of readers, listeners, viewers, computer freaks with little prospect of communication among them'.[46]

Of course, it could be objected that such despondent expectations are unfounded. One common response is that the development of information technology is at too early a phase for any serious predictions to be made; over time new computer cultures will evolve to overcome the problems raised by the present impersonality of systems. Or again, it could be said that reliance on traffic signals and parking meters has not atrophied all sense of moral responsibility, so why should computerized library check-outs or personal identification numbers at the bank do so?

The main difficulty with such objections is that, as is so often the case, technological change is seen as being somehow distinct from social and cultural processes, and acting upon them. But social and cultural transformation is misunderstood if seen as a kind of reflex of technological or material change. In fact neither makes sense without the other; they should be thought of as interacting with each other. Human beings do not 'need' Nolan Bushnell's petsters or the Strategic Defence Initiative; their manufacture only becomes a plausible possibility because of their symbolic meaning – be it status, security, or whatever. At the same time, the existence of (and legitimating arguments for) petsters or SDI may encourage the belief that more technology sweetens or sustains human life. New technologies may both express and channel symbolic meaning.

Western culture is marked by its supposed dependence on rational forms of thought; a dependence which today is intensified by reliance upon that acme of logical operations, the computer. Early-twentieth-century fears of Max Weber are now deepened. He felt that Western societies were steadily constructing for themselves an 'iron cage' of instrumental rationality, expressed in capitalism and in bureaucracy, from which there was little chance of escape. In the late twentieth century Joseph Weizenbaum is perturbed by the 'imperialism of instrumental reason' embodied in the computerization of society.[47]

Like Weber, Weizenbaum is apprehensive for the future of a society which fails to focus on proper purposes, goals, or ends, and is rather concerned only with the technical question of means. Putting computers in schools is a case in point. But, he says,

> once the characterisation of the educational process in informational-theoretical-technological terms is ripped from in front of one's eyes, once the reality of what is happening in, for example, US secondary schools is exposed, then it becomes absolutely clear that the problems facing schools and educators everywhere are personal, political, financial and spiritual. These will not be solved merely by putting more terminals and video screens into the classroom.[48]

Of course, the critique of technique-centredness and technocracy is nothing new. Herbert Marcuse, from a neo-Marxist viewpoint, and Theodore Roszak, from a more mystical perspective, expressed their versions of it in the 1960s (Roszak updates it in *The cult of information*).[49] And so did Jacques Ellul, with his devastatingly prescient (and prophetic) warnings about encroaching *technique*.[50] However Ellul adds another dimension, which is to argue that 'technicism' is a sacred phenomenon of the modern world. In the words of Michael Shallis, who extends Ellul's argument to encompass IT, Western society, in its very commitment to a calculating – and now computerized – rationality has actually created a 'silicon idol'.[51]

The silicon idol, according to Shallis, has two key features. On the one hand, human beings are redefined in an inhuman way, such that their humanness is diminished. Increasing belief in computers, which is encouraged by their power to 'take over' and to simulate aspects of human activity, simply exacerbates the problem. Yet, on the other hand, 'it is a technology that springs to mind from motives of power from a military/

industrial base with intentions to pervert truth and to subjugate the population'.[52]

One might add to this some other symbolic connotations associated with IT. Reference has already been made, for example, to the 'machismo' of high-tech, which is especially apparent in the 'workaholic, eccentric entrepreneurs' of Silicon Valley.[53] This aspect of IT symbolism also connects closely with actual social relations; women are under-represented in the industry, particularly in research and design, and are frequently vulnerable to computerized regulation in the workplace by means of keystroke counting and so on. Girls in school find it hard to get close to the computer facilities when they want to, dominated as they are by the boys.

Behind the efforts made in Western cultures to convey the impression of consistent adherence to the canons of calculating rationality lie constraining beliefs, and commitment to symbols. Applied to IT, Shallis thinks of this as 'silicon idolatry'. As Marshall Sahlins points out, whereas Marx thought that so-called primitive society could not exist without diguising the real basis of social existence in religion, this is in fact a hallmark of modern (capitalist) society! For behind the growing Gross National Product (which may be quantified) is the mode of symbolic production (which may not).[54] The very saleability of such things, that is, depends upon their symbolic value. I have already illustrated this with the examples of petsters and SDI.

Sahlins mainly discusses the symbolic nature of the production processes involving material things. He regards the institutionalization of the symbolic process as dangerous not only because it is hidden, but because of the implications of its being elaborated within a single social order. That is, in the interests of growth it does not hesitate to destroy 'other forms of humanity whose difference from us consists in having discovered not merely other codes of existence but ways of achieving an end that still eludes us: the mastery by society of society's mastery over nature'.[55]

How much more dangerous, potentially, is the emerging system in which economy and society become increasingly information-intensive, where more and more symbols are manipulated by fewer people by virtue of their definition and control of the means of communication? The kind of social order based on electronic interaction could well introduce novel dimensions into human social and cultural existence, though not necessarily of the salubrious variety more usually coupled with the popular 'information society' thesis. The conjunction of the continued quest of growth, now focused in the new technologies, with technicism – or silicon idolatry – does not augur well.

Ethos and ethics

A tragic sense of hopelessness is understandable among those who spend time with the latter-day critics of computerized rationalization. For their insight is that, with the advent of IT, Western culture (including of course that which is exported) reaches a new phase of technicism. Ellul, for instance, says that 'the computer ensemble plays the part of a nervous system in the technological order'.[56] The convergence of computers with telecommunications presages a social-cultural transformation of awesome dimensions – a new *electronic* cage.

Or does it? This is not the view of all discussed in our survey of the computer ethos. Turkle, after all, sees the computer as Rorschach, capable of cultural interpretation in a variety of ways. It is the meanings socially bestowed upon information technology, not the development of microelectronics *per se*, which are crucial. At the same time, the consequences of machine contact and machine dependence could well be extensive and possibly inhumane.

But the very existence of a robust critique of the prevailing computer ethos, alongside constructive proposals for alternatives to it, is an antidote to that sense of the tragic. Shallis, Weizenbaum, Dreyfus and others write from within the very departments and institutions committed to high-level computer research. And it is from the same ranks that warnings about the vulnerability or unworkability of large systems (such as SDI) also come. This is the kind of cultural conflict predicted by several social theorists including Habermas and Touraine.

Beyond this level, it is also premature to underestimate the efficacy of the broader political process, through which changes are made (albeit slowly, and often for the 'wrong' reasons). The protection of privacy and the impact of technological change upon work and skills, are items already on the political agendas of the advanced societies. Still, that societal control of society's mastery over nature, of which Sahlins speaks, also depends upon another level of discourse: the ethical.[57]

The field of 'computer ethics', though expanding, is as yet hardly adequate to the task.[58] Cees Hamelink suggests a way forward, however. His critique of the 'myth of the information revolution' carries over into a 'counter-myth' with strong 'normative implications'. These 'raise the issue of moral restraint when the world thought it had liberated itself from moral demands and was able to conduct its own business'.[59] He proposes a programme of 'heretical ethics'. This includes a 'judo strategy' for confronting the power of technical social institutions, and a demand for limitations on the direction and extent of technological development.

Tasks ahead

I am aware that this chapter could be characterized as observations in search of a theory. I have only hinted at what sort of theory is appropriate, but some of its components are these. My quest is for a third way between the errors of what for want of better terms are 'optimistic' and 'pessimistic' views. Optimistic versions of social-cultural trends (such as Bolter's) lack the realism which (in part anyway) social analysis can supply. Pessimistic accounts, on the other hand, tend to be locked into some version of determinism (technological or social) and thus miss both the significance of reflexive human action for countering threats posed, and the crucial observation that those threats come not from one source or system, but from several.

Social theory dare not slip either into proposing that cultural issues do not belong to the 'real' arena of social processes, or into suggesting that understanding of and approaches to new technology will be essentially similar in all contexts. Having said that, it may well be that the kinds of issues raised by the social-cultural analysis of IT revive interest in the concept of 'alienation'[60] in more than one sphere. 'Machine-pacing' at work or the sense experienced by subjects of computer databases of being 'bureaucratic accessories' are likely to stimulate this. Another common item for debate must be the task of promoting an awareness of the distinctions between data, information, knowledge, and wisdom, a task already begun by Weizenbaum, Shallis and others. I touch on this again in the final chapter.

Social theory and analysis along these lines is inseparable both from the ethical task of determining the nature of, and appropriate responses to, the challenge of IT, and from forms of political activity aimed at limiting, yes, but also at *re-directing* technology. But what is the 'good society' towards which 're-directed technology' might aim? Are there genuine alternatives to dominant modes of 'doing technology'? These questions form a *leitmotif* of the next chapter.

8

Information, ideology and utopia

At the present moment a discussion is raging as to the future of a civilization in the novel circumstances of rapid scientific and technological advance.

A. N. Whitehead (1925)[1]

In my Eden we have a few beam-engines, saddle-tank locomotives, overshot waterwheels and other beautiful pieces of obsolete machinery to play with: In his New Jerusalem even chefs will be cucumber-cool machine-minders.

W. H. Auden (1955)[2]

The 'information society' expresses the idea of a novel phase in the historical development of the advanced societies. Not just a 'post-industrial' society, but the advent of new social patterns is predicted, consequent upon a 'second industrial revolution' based above all on microelectronic technologies. A growing proportion of people, it is claimed, is involved in an unprecedented variety of information-related jobs. Scientific and technical workers gather and produce information, managers and supervisors process it, teachers and communications workers distribute it. From domestic life to international relations, and from leisure activities to industrial relations, no sphere of social activity is left untouched by this 'informatizing' process.

Notions such as Alvin Toffler's *Third wave* – virtually synonymous with 'information society' – have entered popular imagination. A television film has been made of the *Third wave*, and in the UK, the 'Third Wave' is the slogan for a British Telecom advertising campaign. The 'information society' is increasingly used as a handy catch-all for focusing discussions of 'the future' as we approach the third millennium. Government policy also draws upon this concept, particularly with regard to education. The

British are assured, for instance, that 'Our educational system will be a major, perhaps the dominant factor in ensuring the economic prosperity of the UK in a world-wide information society.'[3]

However, certain questions are too frequently left unanswered or treated only to oblique or opaque responses. What are the connections between new technology and society? To what extent and under what circumstances does technological potential become social destiny? Is it warranted to see an epochal social transformation in the kinds of economic and social restructuring currently taking place? And whether or not we are witnessing the emergence of a 'new kind of society', are its advocates correct to assume, as they often tend to, that the social effects of information technology are generally benign?

Much of this book has been taken up with just such questions. Not necessarily to determine what the 'answers' might be, but to suggest some possible lines of investigation. In particular, I have tried to do this by drawing together themes otherwise treated separately, in an effort to reach balanced but yet tentative conclusions. For example, the convergence between computing and telecommunications, often treated as a separate 'technical' moment, prior to the social 'impact' of information technology, is shown (in chapter 2) to have some important *social* dimensions itself. Again, in chapter 5, optimistic predictions about the democratic potential of IT are brought face-to-face with darker diagnoses about the potential for IT to undermine democracy.

But at the end of the day, the question remains as to whether the information society concept should be consigned to the wastebin of redundant ideas, or retained as a tool for social analysis. Might it have a future as an illuminating concept, as it points up one of the most significant aspects of contemporary social change, namely that associated with the diffusion of information technology? Or should it be abandoned precisely because it gains credibility more through the daily appearance of yet another 'microchip' gadget than because of its power to explain social realities?

There is another aspect to this question. The information society concept sounds a hopeful note in the midst of recessionary gloom. In Japan it has found ready acceptance among certain groups as a rallying cry for mobilizing research and entrepreneurial energies. While many social prognoses are pessimistic, seeing only decline (economic) or disaster (nuclear) ahead, the information society sounds positive and apparently provides some sense of purpose and social goals. Just when intellectuals bemoan the death of progress or the dearth of utopias,[4] an older vision is revived, of a good society growing out of the present. So not only the usefulness of the concept for social analysis, but its social role within present national and global contexts deserves examination.

In what follows I take this latter question a little further. My first concern is to comment on the long connection between politics and technology, in the light of which it would not be surprising to find that the 'information society' has ideological aspects. That is, its use may help buttress the *status quo*. Secondly, exposing the ideological uses of the information society concept leads in turn to another task, the discussion of resistance to the new technologies and to alternative proposals and strategies. Lastly, I return to the major issue; an agenda for social analysis – which in turn suggests some options for political action and public policy – which arises from the constructive critique of the 'information society'.

The politics of technology

New technologies have been infused with a potent symbolism at least since Francis Bacon's time. He proposed that science and technology be viewed as a means of overcoming the malign effects of the human 'fall' from God's grace. In fact his utopia, *New Atlantis* (1627), straddles the 'theological' and the 'natural' interpretation of human affairs. While he continues to use biblical language, the spirit of his writing underpins a dominant theme of Western culture following him, that human progress is assured through the scientific and technological exploitation of nature.

This Janus-faced character of Bacon's writings is caught in these contrasting interpretations: Arnold Pacey quotes him approvingly (and I would concur) for his emphasis on science and technology motivated by a 'love of God's creation' which issues in using the 'fruits of knowledge' not for 'profit, or fame or power . . . but for the benefit and use of life'.[5] But in Bacon's attempt to establish a 'chaste and lawful marriage between Mind and Nature', Evelyn Fox-Keller finds a rather different spirit. Nature, almost always 'she', is brought to obedience by the (male) scientist. Though Bacon indeed admits a caring aspect to science and technology, today it is largely lost. Fox-Keller connects this loss with the move towards a more 'self-contained' science in which 'the explicit role of God has disappeared'. The modern scientist's 'kinship with Bacon survives in his simultaneous appropriation and denial of the feminine'.[6]

Considerable debate arises over the relative contributions of religion and politics to the origins of modern technology.[7] While Max Weber is often imputed with the view that the religious – and particularly the Protestant – origins were decisive, others have challenged this. Weber stressed the contribution of Christian theology to justifications of technological activity. It is part of a God-given task of sharing his supervisory and transformative work, and is given added impetus in the context of a suffering world, cut off from immediate access to the Creator.

But for others the more decisive influence is that represented by Machiavelli. He succeeded in lowering the ultimate goals of political life while at the same time increasing the possibility of their worldly realization.[8] For him, technology, when harnessed to the production of unlimited wealth, is justified by its contribution to the common good. Technological activity is thus uncoupled from religious or ethical concerns – to do with the stewardship of nature or justice in economic relations – which might otherwise serve to curb or redirect it. Attention is rather focused on appropriate techniques for attaining this-worldly ends.

By the eighteenth and particularly the nineteenth century, technology was strongly linked with belief in progress. Its close associations with burgeoning capitalism, which increasingly required new technology as a means of maintaining and boosting profit levels, assured a dominant place to the Baconian or Machiavellian doctrine. Progress, for many Victorians, was at once a political aspiration, to be achieved via the application of science and technology to all areas of life, and also a means of explaining social change. It undergirded early sociology.[9]

Progress, industry, science and technology were immortalized in the Great Exhibition in the Crystal Palace, London in 1851. But although widespread British faith in technological advancement was not to wane for many decades, it could be argued that the centre of gravity of 'technological progress' shifted across the Atlantic. In the USA, as nowhere in Europe, technological progress was made by some into a panacea. Technological utopians – as Howard Segal calls them[10] – provided detailed blueprints for the good society. Edward Bellamy, the best known, envisioned in *Looking backward* an America criss-crossed with electrical and telegraphic communications, and in which everything from music to food was piped into homes from central sources.

The possibilities of such social and material engineering were seized upon eagerly by numerous Bellamy Clubs, for whom *Looking backward* expressed a common belief in the inevitability of technological progress.

The desired future represented no break with the present (the heyday of technological utopianism was 1883–1933), but would grow steadily out of it. Moreover, in Segal's words,

> The utopians were not oblivious to the problems technological advance might cause, such as unemployment or boredom. They simply were confident that those problems were temporary and that, furthermore, advanced technology held the solution to mankind's chronic problems, which they took to be material – scarcity, hunger, disease, war, and so forth.[11]

It scarcely seems necessary to bring the account up to date, given the patent connections between these earlier technological utopias, the 1960s celebrations of the 'electrical sublime' in Buckminster Fuller or Marshall McLuhan,[12] and the 'wired societies' and 'silicon civilizations' of today. But the connections and continuities are significant. The technological utopia grows progressively from present conditions and will in the long term ensure the peace and prosperity of all. It is possible to rectify the less desirable consequences of technological innovation by further applications of technology. Today more stress is laid upon the effort required to bring about the new society (socialist versions emphasize the issues of justice and equality alongside technical development). And the USA is not held up unequivocally as the 'leading' society. Japan is felt to be threatening its supremacy.

Until now I have gone along with Segal's designation of these 'possible futures' as 'technological utopias'. But is this entirely appropriate? Let me sow some seeds of doubt. While 'utopia' may refer to an ideal, hoped-for and maybe even worked-for society, it often has other features as well. Thomas More's original *Utopia*, which gave its name to the genre, was a cutting critique of monarchical and clerical tyranny in sixteenth-century England. True, it traced the outlines of a good society, but this was a radical alternative to present conditions, not a continuation of them. More himself was eventually to lose his head for his temerity (in objecting to the wishes of Henry VIII).

The 'information society' shares utopian aspects with some previous technological 'good societies'. But as we have seen, the ways in which IT is developed and adopted frequently widens the gaps between already divided social groups and nations, extends the capacity of the state and other agencies to monitor and control people's lives and augments the power of ever-growing economic interests. In the light of this, the 'information society' also appears to have some highly charged ideological aspects as well.

Such 'ideological aspects' may be teased out to show how the information society concept connects politics and technology in a peculiarly modern way; it often obscures the vested interests involved in IT, it deflects attention from some embarrassing contradictions, while at the same time giving to the coming of the information society the appearance of an entirely natural and logical social progression.[13]

In the 1960s, a full decade before informatics entered public discussion, Jürgen Habermas argued that expanding forms of 'technocratic reason' present a serious threat to human freedom. Public communication and decision-making are distorted so that most of the population are kept in the dark about the real distribution of power and control in a given society. Habermas said that political debate is systematically reduced to a purely technical level (the language of 'controlling the economy' being a good example), and at the same time technology becomes almost a rival force to politics.[14]

Reducing political debate to the technical means that people are denied the chance to participate freely at the level of morality and justice, and thus also to affect outcomes by means of political action. Today, IT developments illustrate this well. Slogans such as 'a computer in every school' or 'automate or liquidate' narrow any discussion to the question of means, rather than ends. 'Why do children need exposure to keyboards and screens?' and 'Who will benefit from automation?' are the unasked questions which lead logically to a consideration of valuing and purposes. Moreover political decisions are frequently presented to the public as a *fait accompli*. Few British people are privy to the reasons why a new cable infrastructure rather than an upgraded telephone network became public policy.

The further aspect of Habermas' contention, that technology becomes a rival force to politics, is also evident today. He quotes Herman Kahn's 'cybernetic dream' about the use of new techniques for surveillance and mass education, direct electronic communication with human brains and so on. The upshot would be 'planned alienation'. But IT has indeed made possible many things once dismissed as 'science fiction'. The theoretical possibility of the 1960s that political decisions could be computerized became in the 1980s sober fact. Anti-ballistic missile warning systems are a case in point.

What, then, of the 'ideological aspects' of the information society concept? First, inequalities and relations of power are very much in the background. For instance, while it is not inappropriate to hope that the diffusion of IT would have a similar positive role for democratic participation as the diffusion of print media once had, it is irresponsible to declare that this is likely to happen. The fact that more people buy ever-cheaper home computers does not add up to an 'information revolution'. Cees Hamelink concludes that

> control over and access to advances in information technology are very unevenly distributed in the world, and the fact that millions of people can fiddle with their home computers does not change this. The management structure of the information industry is not affected by the proliferation of electronic gadgets. If anything, it is considerably strengthened by the widespread use of its products.[15]

All manner of vested interests are involved in IT, but the concept of the information society is all too often used in ways that obscure their role. Sometimes those interests are intertwined in ways that have yet to be carefully explored. The coincidence that defence funding supports so much research in IT *and* that the world of IT frequently excludes women deserves just such exploration. Technology in general is undoubtedly associated with maleness, socially and culturally; IT no less so.

Secondly, the information society concept papers over not only the cracks but also opposing movements in society. Underlying contradictions are even less likely to be exposed than inequalities and conflicts on the surface. Opposing movements may be seen, for instance, in the IT context, along the fault-line of information as public good versus saleable commodity. The real threats of current IT development to public service broadcasting and to public libraries are manifestations of deeper dynamics of opposition.

Thirdly, the coming of the information society is viewed (by its popular proponents at least) as an entirely natural occurrence. It is the obvious way forward. The future lies with IT. The new technologies must be 'whole-heartedly embraced', declare the captains of industry. This is why educational systems have to be re-oriented, the market unshackled, and high technology research and trading deals engineered. It is also why Luddism has to be stamped out.

This particular ideological aspect – information society as a natural and logical social advance – is further buttressed by the typically Western belief in progress via unlimited economic accumulation. What Shallis calls 'silicon idolatry' resonates with this still-strong belief. As Bob Goudzwaard observes, if indeed this faith is a driving force within economic and technological expansion then two things follow. One, the 'overdevelopment' of both spheres comes as no surprise, and two, it is 'accompanied by an expectation of happiness that relativises anything that might raise objections against them.[16]

Having made such comments about ideological aspects I ought to repeat and extend the qualifiers made in the introduction. I am not arguing that a 'dominant ideology' exists to hoodwink large segments of the populations of advanced societies. Nor is there a conspiracy to deceive such publics. Rather, I am warning that the danger of using the information society concept uncritically is to disguise or gloss over the reality of domination by powerful interests.

I should also stress that the point of exposing such relations of power is not simply to replace them with others, but to open the door for a properly normative approach. Fe/male partnership in new technology will not eliminate war, but as a way of recognizing co-humanity could begin to reorder technological priorities. Revealing contradictions of IT development is rather futile unless it leads to a questioning of economic life itself: is it about producing things, or is it fundamentally relational?[17]

Resistance and alternatives

Anyone worried about the encroaching tyranny of technocratic power embodied in IT should not ignore countervailing movements also present in contemporary societies. True, the information society idea is strong and popular, but there are many for whom it is remote and unreal, and yet others who regard it with suspicion and hostility. For them, the critique of ideology may itself appear as a less than central task; more urgent is actual resistance to the adoption of new technology. Examining forms of resistance – particularly the 'Luddism' scathingly referred to above – is one thing, however; joining the quest for alternatives is another. I shall argue that both strategies are required if the information society as depicted here is not to become a self-fulfilling prophecy.

The intrusion of IT into numerous areas of life – only this week I discovered that my plastic card could buy a train ticket at the local station and that my office is soon due to be connected with a central IBM computer – has revived interest in Luddism as a mode of opposing technology. While some use it as an epithet to be directed at all 'anti-progressives' who quite irrationally wish to 'put the clock back' by refusing to adapt to new technology, others – both conservative and radical – willingly accept the label as correctly portraying their stance. 'If Luddite means the preservation of all that is good from the past and the rejection of things that destroy good', says Michael Shallis, 'then I would welcome the term.'[18]

It seems that most of those who are credited today with 'threatening our future' are members of labour unions who resist the unchecked spread of new technologies within the workplace. (In fact, plenty of anti-Luddism exists within unions. A Calderdale components factory union is on record with the following: 'You cannot hold back progress.' 'We don't want any latter-day Luddites here.'[19] The first Luddites were strong in Calderdale.) The charge of Luddism is heard most frequently in celebrated cases, such as the newspaper and print workers' disputes discussed earlier in this book. But it occurs in other contexts as well, in mining and manufacturing (automated and robotic assembly lines, CNC machine tools) and also in offices and schools where serious doubts are expressed about installing computerized machines.

Of course the original Luddites, who attacked factories and broke new machinery in early-nineteenth-century Yorkshire, Lancashire, Cheshire and the Midlands of England, made their protest against industrialism in the days before labour unions were established. Evidence shows the hallmarks of carefully planned night-time raids, in which only specific machines thought to threaten the livelihoods and skills were destroyed.[20] Clearly, fear of the new was involved.[21] But it is helpful to put Luddism in a much broader context. Those machines were symbolic of a whole new way of life which accompanied the spread of *laissez-faire* economic doctrines, the growing scale of factory enterprises, new divisions between home and work, and the loss of older patterns of mutual responsibility between employer and employee.

Among those who deliberately adopt a Luddite stance *vis a vis* today's technology, Kevin Robins and Frank Webster spell out the connections most clearly. They argue that contemporary Luddism demands on the one hand a refusal to submit to the dictates of *laissez-faire* political economy in which economic interests ride roughshod over customary lifestyles, jobs and skills. On the other, recalling the Luddite resistance not to machines *per se*, but to the social relationships represented by them, they insist that

Luddism is a way of seeing, a '*critique* of developments which because they are presented as mere matters of technical change, appear unstopable and unobjectionable.'[22]

Appropriately enough, for a critique of developments within capitalist societies, those 'social relations' represented by information technology are seen mainly as *class* relations. Relationships of men to women, of ethnic majorities and minorities, of individuals to the state (and so on) thus tend to be interpreted in class terms also. Clearly, such analysts recognize that in modern societies labour movements have not simply been displaced by others – such as peace movements or feminism – and that, furthermore, labour movements may well act as 'carriers' for wider concerns. Added to which, it is patent that many key social issues raised by IT have to do with the world of work and employment. But there are limits to reviving Luddism as a class-based critique alone.

For a start, the labour movement is not 'inevitably the prime source of opposition in capitalist societies'.[23] Opposition may originate elsewhere. (Media coverage contributed to the ending of the Vietnam war; mobilizing local opinion blocked Sunday trading in Britain.) Moreover, the labour movement may be unwilling seriously to take new technology issues on board. Cynthia Cockburn, assailing male dominance in technological change, pleads that labour unions be willing to question the direction and content of IT development. But she ruefully acknowledges that unions too often see the main challenge as ensuring that 'the benefits of change are distributed equally', and that the 'ideology of technological progress' is contested not by them, but by ecology and peace movements.[24]

Placing too much stress on class relations and the labour movement may also deflect attention from other issues. In IT, transnational corporations predominate, but the attempt similarly to internationalize labour movements is negligible. But apart from this, if it is correct to argue that IT facilitates the massive strengthening of state powers of surveillance, then why does so little critical and adversarial activity take place in this arena? Civil liberties groups have yet to make serious dents in government complacency about the protection of citizens from unwanted and unnecessary prying and control. Questions like this (which may be extended to the cultural area in general) will not be answered satisfactorily if class is retained as a key mode of explanation and line of battle.

Lastly, Luddism as a class critique is limited by its negative and often pessimistic stance. Herbert Schiller's devastating account of global capitalism's IT interests finds its most hopeful moment in a forecast of 'social conflict in the core of the transnational corporate system'. It is unclear how this conflict will arise. But if it fails to materialize, one may be able to fall back on other 'powerful sources of potential breakdown in the overall [American] economy'.[25] In fact, a similar negativism is found in non-Marxist Luddism. Michael Shallis concludes that IT is 'an invention of the devil . . . born destructive . . .' which 'enchants people into false belief in a false god. . . . We need to be informed about the machines that "think" but we should become ashamed to use them.'[26]

Latter-day Luddism represents resistance to new technology, and is essentially negative. As such, it is an understandable reaction in the face of apparently antagonistic forces. Nevertheless, as Robins and Webster point out, the kernel of an *ethical* response is also discernible in Luddism. This again broadens the question from being merely one of class relations. It hints at the potential for positive alternative strategies.

Return for a moment to an earlier theme. Edward Bellamy's utopia *Looking backward*, while it attracted widespread acclaim in the USA, horrified at least one English reader, William Morris. *Looking backward* seemed more like a *dystopia* to him, and his response was to pen his own famous satirical utopia: *News from nowhere* (1890). His utopia, though informed by Marxism, is anti-industrial as well as anti-capitalist. In his dream he looks back from a world of meaningful and artistic craft-work to a time when 'they forced themselves to stagger along under this horrible burden of unnecessary production'. In this system, little care was spent on making things, but ceaseless energy spent on turning out as much as possible, to which project 'everything was sacrificed'.[27]

Morris offers an authentically utopian alternative to the oppressive vision of a centralized production-and-consumption-oriented world. Whether or not one agrees with the rather romantic nostalgia that appears in the details of Morris's alternative, it is undeniable that human freedom and fulfilment is a high priority. Attention to the features of the 'good society' is as significant as resistance to alienation, domination and dehumanization.

What form should be taken by 'alternative visions' to the 'information society' idea? At least two criteria should be satisfied. One, the normative basis of the alternative(s) must be made clear. Two, the different levels on which intervention might take place, and modes whereby policies may be implemented, must be indicated. This involves offering practical examples of altered practice and of the potential for choice in techno-logical innovation.

Technocratic thought, especially that embodied in today's computer logic, tends to minimize or exclude debate about ethics. Discussion of 'alternatives' brings this into the foreground. Unfortunately, as Hans Jonas observes, an ethic suited to the global and long-term aspects of today's technology is largely lacking.[28] The ethics of the personal is far better developed. That said, once it is recognized that the 'information society' gives the false impression that we are entering an *entirely* novel social situation, then certain long-trodden ethical paths become pertinent.

A further problem here is the relative lack of contexts within which such moral debate may take place. Professions, for instance, have always provided such opportunities (even though they have sometimes been self-interestedly abused). Medicine, involving 'technologies of the body' has traditionally been hedged by moral qualification, dating back to the Hippocratic Oath. Today's computer professionals evidence a very low level of membership or interest in any comparable organizations.

It may be that IT raises new moral problems. The ease with which data can be permanently and untraceably erased may be one, the way in which privacy is invaded by computers, another.[29] But among the most pressing issues is that of the status of information itself. This raises old questions about the proper relation between data, information, knowledge and a fourth category, which has a low profile today, wisdom. But IT gives their ethical consideration a new urgency, and also connects them with another cluster of problems to do with property: information as a commodity. 'Information' is produced for sale in the marketplace. But what should rightly be defended as 'public information', as a 'resource'? What should be the limits to commodification?

The second criterion is that of realism about strategies. It is all very well for 'processed' (read 'alienated') San Francisco office-workers to parade the streets wearing cardboard visual display terminals over their heads, but such demonstrations do not exhaust the possibilities of strategic action relating to IT. The kind of realism required is that which connects possibilities for alternative action with actual conditions in a given social context. Despite the apparent cohesiveness of the 'information society' vision, it is unlikely that alternatives to it will be similarly homogeneous.

Although it may be possible theoretically to show how modern societies are increasingly divided between classes of people with and without control over and access to information,[30] in real life their struggles are on numerous and often unconnected fronts. The labour process and industrial relations offer some obvious examples of appropriate strategies. New Technology Agreements, for whatever reason they are introduced, may be used to monitor and control the process of adapting to new technologies. Demonstrations of automation and robotics whose introduction does not de-skill or displace labour are vital here.[31]

Other strategies run through a spectrum including formal political activity within existing parties, involvement in the political process by social movements, attempts to influence communications or educational policy, and local grass-roots action. Legislative change, such as data protection, clearly requires activity of the former sort. But concern for IT alternatives may also be expressed in conjunction with other movements. In Britain, the 'Microsyster' organization attempts to redress the gender imbalance within IT, while 'Microelectronics for Peace' encourages the fostering of alternatives to military developments, mainly within the big IT transnationals. Similar organizations, such as the American 'Computer Professionals for Social Responsibility' exist elsewhere.

As information and communication become increasingly important categories both at a global and a local level, so groups and movements emerge whose aims are to re-channel such developments or to broaden participation within them. Some such strategies have an egalitarian impulse, in which access and control are key issues, whereas others go beyond this to inquire as to whether in certain contexts proposed or established new technologies are appropriate at all. On the international level, the debate over the New World Information and Communication Order laudably considers both sorts of question, although legitimate doubts have been expressed both about the viability and efficacy of the UNESCO forum and about the intentions of some participants.

On the more local level the twin concerns of justice and appropriateness may be confronted again. On the one hand are the attempts to found a decentralized communications system to which public access is guaranteed. Examples range from the Homa Bay radio experiment in Kenya[32] to community television pilot schemes in Western Europe or North America.[33] On the other are projects which explicitly aim to reverse the common pattern of technological development, starting with research on social and personal 'needs'. These relate in particular to disadvantaged groups, such as the disabled, single-parent families, isolated elderly people, and so on. The German study *Sozialpolitische Chancen der Informationstechnik* is one example, Elisabeth Gerver's *Humanizing technology* is another.[34]

The information society problem

The 'information society', paradoxically, has both ideological and utopian aspects. It should not be abandoned on either count. By way of conclusion let me offer four important reasons for saying this, with accompanying qualifications.

Firstly, the 'information society' raises questions about new social circumstances, but not always for the reasons its better-known protagonists think. As I have shown, expectations for this 'new society' are frequently based on highly dubious economic arguments about the predominance of a new 'information sector'. Its adjuncts, the widening dependence on microelectronics, computing and telecommunications, and the growing cadre of 'information workers' provide the supposed social dimension which justifies talk of an 'information revolution' and an 'information society'.

It is not at all clear that the information society is emerging in any of its dimensions. The centralism, monopolies and inequalities of capitalism are not disappearing, and services continue to expand (as ever) *alongside* industrial production (though some of the latter is displaced into the Southern hemisphere). Participatory democracy, with immediate access of all to information sources, does not appear to be just around the corner either. And what is absent in the political realm is also missing in the cultural. Where exactly are these promised new choices in diverse and individualized cultural experience and activity to fill the widely augmented leisure time offered by automation?

That said, it does appear that the process of 'informatizing' social, economic and cultural life raises significant sociological questions. While it is perfectly true that, for instance, surveillance by state agencies and by employers has a long history prior to the introduction of informatics, the impact of the new technologies at a time of general economic restructuring may turn out to have long-term (and unforeseen) consequences.

At economic, political and cultural levels the effects of informatics appear to be profound. Its influence within industrial relations, both direct and indirect, is far from negligible. The rising awareness of the (often unwelcome) monitoring of personal lives by computerized agencies may stimulate new kinds of social movement in response. And, judging by past history, the media through which information passes and the kinds of human image enshrined within 'smart machines' may be expected to contribute to alterations in our cultural experience.

Secondly, the technological convergence expressed in the term 'information technology' is socially as well as technically significant. The once-clear categories now blurred by the diffusion of IT have important social ramifications. Concepts like 'journalism' or 'middle management' acquire new connotations with the arrival of direct entry text and the computerized marshalling of data. More widely, I have indicated that surveillance, though made more efficient by mere computerization, is massively strengthened by computerization *with* telecommunications. Furthermore, it is in precisely this area that rapid changes are now taking place.[35] Again, in the global context, the debate about communication and cultural dominance of North over South takes on a quite different complexion as IT makes those same communications the conduits of economic power.

The 'convergence factor' also has policy implications, as William Melody explains with this example. In a situation where industrial policy promotes rapid expansion of telecommunications networks, including cable television, direct broadcast satellite and integrated services digital networks, imports of equipment could expand drastically. The new networks could open the country to further imports of data-processing and information-related services, 'displacing domestic production and services ranging from databases to television production. This in turn could bring about a serious balance of payments problem and result in more jobs lost than created, and undercut domestic cultural policy.'[36]

As indicated above, the same issue bristles with ethical problems, above all those associated with the plethora of uses of 'information'. Questions of social, personal, public, private, commercial and cultural information are all pertinent here. Each requires appropriate ethical analysis in the context of their revised technical and social usage.

Thirdly, in all 'information society' discourse it must be remembered that technological potential is not social destiny. The easy slide from discussing the technical breakthrough to proclaiming its social benefits is simply unwarranted. (Even the technical breakthrough is a social construction. Research, experiment and planning take place for a long time before an innovation is launched as an *economically* viable product.) This is not to say, however, that IT has inevitable socially malign or sinister aspects.

Without doubt, there are many innovations based on microelectronics for which we have cause to be grateful. Writers like myself are not the only ones to be glad of the increased efficiency gained through word-processing. Robotics and other forms of automation within factories and offices often reduce the level of soul-destroying drudgery. Computerized irrigation and crop-production systems, and satellite sensing of natural and animal resources make possible huge strides in conservation. Computerized medical diagnosis increases the likelihood of correct and speedy detection of disease.

But in so far as the information society idea depends upon versions of technological determinism it should be resisted. Such determinism is demonstrably false. Technological development does not have pre-set social effects which are predictable, universal or, for that matter, just or beneficial. It can be shown to be the outcome of social shaping itself, including certain deliberate political, economic and cultural choices. Although the pattern of technical advance does sometimes appear to be 'self-augmenting' (in Jacques Ellul's terms), even that process could not continue without the recursive involvement of human agents.

Equally, the spectre of social determinism should be exorcised. This may take more than one form. Theorists such as Harry Braverman and Michel Foucault, though writing from within different traditions, are guilty of underplaying the role of human agency in their accounts of technology-and-society. But there is another aspect to this, namely that new technologies and systems should be seen as over-determined by social forces. Information technology may itself be a semi-independent factor within social change. When British Rail computerized their freight yards for instance, the new system had quite unpredictable consequences for management structures.

Rejecting the determinism latent in 'information society' thinking means that the concept may be opened up into a forum for the consideration of alternative futures. If social and personal choice are involved, then their role should be highlighted. At the same time, those choices, and their motivations, will not always be unambiguous. The impulse behind the timing of data protection law in the UK, for instance, was not concern over privacy as such, but fear of losing important information markets on the continent because British law was out of step with the European Convention.

Fourthly, and following from the previous point, the problem of the information society is a political as well as an analytical one. Social analysis has a role within IT policy. I am thinking of such 'policy' at different levels, from international fora, through national government planning, to the level of the firm and the school, and even the neighbourhood organization. What currently passes as policy frequently lacks an ethical dimension and social awareness.

Within today's political climate, overshadowed as it is by technology policy (whether to remain economically competitive or militarily secure), strenuous attempts are made to co-opt social science for technological ends. Research money is available for those willing to investigate the conditions under which new technology may be adopted, and people adapted to it, successfully. To question social goals, to explore the possibilities for emancipatory, appropriate technology, to examine the ethics or cultural dimensions of new technology, these are not perceived to be priorities.

The task ahead involves a reassertion of the classic role of social inquiry, which is to act as a form of 'public philosophy'.[37] Social analysis has unavoidable moral dimensions, and is concerned in profound ways with the 'human condition'. This is why issues of the magnitude of the social shaping and social consequences of information technology may not be siphoned off into mere social engineering. Social scientists dare not sell their moral and analytical birthright for a mess of technological pottage. Social analysis must remain in, but not of, the 'information society'.

Notes

Preface

1 Critical theory's best known exponent is Jurgen Habermas. See *Knowledge and human interests* (Boston: Beacon Press, 1971), *Theory of communicative action, volume 1* Cambridge, MA: MIT Press, Cambridge: Polity Press (1984). 'Public philosophy' is Robert Bellah's term for a revival of Alexis de Tocqueville's approach in *Democracy in America*. It is described in (1984) *The habits of the heart* (Berkeley: University of California Press).

2 I explore this further in (1983) 'Valuing in social theory: postempiricism and Christian responses' *Christian Scholars' Review* 12 (4), pp. 324–38 and (1983) *Sociology and the human image* Downers Grove IL, and Leicester: Inter-Varsity Press. I comment on the ethical critique of new technology in (1986) *The silicon society* Tring: Lion Publishing/Grand Rapids MI: Eerdmans, and in 'Being human in the information society', forthcoming in P. Blokhuis and G. Groenewoud (eds) *Being human* Amsterdam: Vrije Universiteit. Authors significant for the development of this perspective include Jacques Ellul, Bob Goudzwaard, Egbert Schuurman and Nicholas Wolterstorff (see bibliography).

3 Frank Webster and Kevin Robins (1986) *Information technology: a Luddite analysis* Norwood, New Jersey: Ablex, p. 347.

Chapter 1 Introduction: the roots of the information society idea

1 Steve Wozniak (1986) *Equinox*, Channel 4 (TV) November.

2 NEDO (1984) *Crisis facing information technology* London: National Economic Development Office, August.

3 Christopher Evans (1982) *Mighty micro: impact of the computer revolution* London: Gollancz; Geoffrey Simons (1985) *Silicon shock* Oxford: Basil Blackwell; John Wicklein (1981) *Electronic nightmare: the home communications set and your freedom* Boston: Beacon Press; Ian Reinecke (1984) *Electronic illusions* Harmondsworth: Penguin.

4 James Martin (1978) *The wired society* Harmondsworth: Penguin.

5 Alvin Toffler (1980) *The third wave* London: Pan.

6 Science Council of Canada (1982) *Planning now for the information society: tomorrow is too late* Ottawa: Science Council.

7 Daniel Bell (1974) *The coming of postindustrial society: a venture in social forecasting* Harmondsworth: Penguin, p. 14.

8 Daniel Bell (1980) 'The social framework of the information society' in Tom Forester (ed.) *The microelectronics revolution* Oxford: Basil Blackwell, and also in Michael Dertouzos and Joel Moses (eds) (1980) *The computer age: a twenty year view* Cambridge MA: MIT Press.

9 Bell 'Social framework' p. 533.

10 Ibid. p. 545.

11 Alain Touraine (1969) *La Société post-industrielle* Paris: Editions Denoël; English translation (1974) *The postindustrial society* London: Wildwood House.

12 Touraine, *Postindustrial society* pp. 28, 61.

13 Mark Poster (1984) *Foucault, Marxism and history* Cambridge: Polity Press p. 168.

14 Tom Stonier (1983) *The wealth of information* London: Thames-Methuen p. 202.

15 Martin *Wired society* p. 4.

16 Stonier *Wealth of information* p. 202.

17 Jean Voge (1985) 'The new economic information order' in *International information economy handbook* Springfield VA: Transnational Data Reporting Service pp. 39–40.

18 Japan Computer Usage Development Institute (1971) *The plan for information society: a national goal towards the year 2000* Tokyo.

19 Yoneji Masuda (1981) *The information society as postindustrial society* Bethesda MD: World Futures Society.

20 Ibid. p. 3.

21 Ibid. p. 29.

22 James Beniger (1986) *The control revolution: technological and economic origins of the information society* Cambridge MA and London: Harvard University Press. Unfortunately Beniger does little to locate this 'control revolution' within a theory of social power relations.

23 This is discussed with particular reference to telecommunications in William H. Dutton, Jay G. Blumler and Kenneth L. Kraemer (eds) (1987) *Wired cities: shaping the future of communications* Boston: G. K. Hall.

24 Philip Abrams (1982) *Historical sociology* Shepton Mallet: Open Books p. xv.

25 Marc Porat (1977) *The information economy: definition and measurement* Washington DC: US Government Printing Office.

26 Krishan Kumar (1978) *Prophecy and progress: the sociology of industrial and postindustrial society* Harmondsworth: Penguin.

27 Patrick Dawson and Ian McLoughlin (1986) 'Computer technology and the redefinition of supervision: a study of the effects of computers on railway freight supervisors' *Journal of Management Studies* 23 (1) 116–32.

28 This phrase comes from Ian Miles and Jonathan Gershuny (1986) 'The social economics of information technology' in Marjorie Ferguson (ed.) *New communications technologies and the public interest* London and Beverly Hills: Sage.

29 See, for instance, Ben Barber (1984) *Strong democracy* Berkeley CA: University of California Press.

30 This example comes from Herbert Schiller (1986) 'The erosion of national sovereignty' in Michael Traber (ed.) *The myth of the information revolution* London and Beverly Hills: Sage p. 28.

31 Quoted in Schiller 'Erosion of national sovereignty' p. 23.

32 Stonier *Wealth of information* p. 73. See also Toffler *The third wave* and Jacques Servan-Schrieber (1980) *Le défi mondial* Paris: Fayard.

33 Juan Rada (1982) 'A third world perspective' in Günter Friedrichs and Adam Schaff (eds) *Microelectronics and society: for better or for worse* London: Pergamon p. 216.

34 Stonier *Wealth of information* p. 32.

35 Kumar *Prophecy and progress* p. 229.

36 Edward Feigenbaum and Pamela McCorduck (1984) *The fifth generation* London: Pan p. 289.

37 Bell *Coming of postindustrial society* p. 188.

38 Ibid. pp. 114–15.

39 David Bolter (1984) *Turing's man: Western culture in the computer age* London: Duckworth and Chapel Hill: University of North Carolina Press.

40 Ibid pp. 8–9.

41 Ibid p. 13.

42 Bell *Coming of postindustrial society* p. 188.

43 See Cees Hamelink (1983) *Cultural autonomy in global communications* New York: Longman.

44 Such issues are raised by Mark Poster in *Foucault, Marxism and history*.

45 See Michael Shallis (1984) *The silicon idol* Oxford: Oxford University Press.

46 Cees Hamelink (1986) 'Is there life after the information revolution?' in Traber *The myth of the information revolution*.

47 Bryan Nicholson's speech, recorded in *The Guardian* 16 September 1986.

48 Jacques Ellul (1976) *The new demons* London: Mowbray or Shallis *The silicon idol*.

49 See Nicholas Abercrombie and John Urry (1980) *The dominant ideology thesis* London: Allen and Unwin.

50 Jennifer Daryl Slack (1984) 'The information revolution as ideology' *Media Culture and Society* (6) p. 250.

51 Pessimistic statements of Luddism include David Noble (1983) 'Present tense technology' *Democracy* Spring (8–24), Summer (70–82) and Fall (71–93), and Shallis *The silicon idol*.

Chapter 2   A marriage of convergence? The shaping of IT

1 Kenneth Baker (1982) in Niels Bjørn-Andersen et al. (eds) *Information society: for richer, for poorer* Amsterdam and Oxford: North-Holland p. 77.

2 B. O. Evans (1980) 'Computers and communications' in Michael Dertouzos and Joel Moses (eds) *The computer age: a twenty year view* Cambridge MA and London: MIT Press.

3 See Rob Kling and Suzanne Iacono (forthcoming 1987) 'Computing as a by-product of social movements' in R. Gordon (ed.) *Microelectronics in transition* Norwood NJ: Ablex.

4 Jacques Ellul (1964) *The technology society* New York: Vintage, discusses 'self-augmenting technology'. See also Langdon Winner's critique in (1977) *Autonomous technology: technics-out-of-control as a theme in political thought* Cambridge MA and London: MIT Press.

5 Ernest Braun and Stuart MacDonald (1982) *Revolution in miniature: history and impact of semiconductor electronics* Cambridge: Cambridge University Press.

6 Ibid. p. 52.

7 G. P. Dineen and F. C. Frick (1977) 'Electronics and national defence: a case study' *Science* (195) 18 March p. 1151.

8 Ibid. p. 1152.

9 John Keller (1981) *The production worker in electronics: industrialization and labour development in California's Santa Clara Valley* Ann Arbor MI: University of Michigan (PhD thesis).

10 Braun and MacDonald *Revolution in miniature* p. 71.

11 Ibid. p. 95.

12 Marjorie Sun (1983) 'The Pentagon's ambitious computer plan' *Science* (222) 16 December p. 1214.

13 Michael Dempsey (1985) 'SDI software won't work says dissident professor' *Datalink* 12 September p. 11.

14 Jon Turney (1985) 'Computer scientists send 'Star-Wars' protest to Bush' *Times Higher Educational Supplement* 5 July.

15 Anthony Tucker (1985) 'Who really needs Eureka?' *The Guardian* 1 August.

16 Jill Hills (1984) *Information technology and industrial policy* Beckenham: Croom-Helm p. 244.

17 Sir Ieuan Maddock (1983) *Civil exploitation of defence technology* London: National Economic Development Council.

18 Ian Wray (1986) 'How defence weakens Britain' *Management Today* August pp. 38–43, 76.

19 Jill Hills (1986) 'British industrial policy and the information technology sector' forthcoming in Frank Gregory (ed.) *Information technology: the public issues* Manchester: Manchester University Press.

20 M. F. Smith (1985) 'UK IT – 1990s' *Information Technology Training* 3 (3) p. 70.

21 'Big Blue books its long-distance call' *The Sunday Times* 30 June 1985.

22 'Mr Sugar gets help from little green man' *The Guardian* 3 November 1986.

23 'The silicon crisis' *The Sunday Times* 9 June 1985.

24 Ian Macintosh (1986) *Sunrise Europe: the dynamics of information technology* Oxford: Basil Blackwell.

25 Kevin Robins and Frank Webster (1986) 'The revolution of the fixed wheel: information, technology, and social Taylorism' in Philip Drummond and Richard Paterson (eds) *Television in transition* London: British Film Institute; see also Frank Webster and Kevin Robins (1986) *Information technology: a Luddite analysis* Norwood NJ: Ablex.

26 Kling and Iacono 'Computing as a by-product'.

27 Tarja Cronberg (1986) 'Consumer influence on new technology: real potential or false hopes?' *Journal of Consumer Policy* 9 (3) pp. 335–43.

28 Hills 'British industrial policy'.

29 'Even the air-waves are up for sale' *The Guardian* 18 November 1986.

30 Quoted in John Howkins (1982) *New technologies: new policies?* London: British Film Institute p. 34.

31 See Jon Woronoff (1985) 'Japan and the 21st century' *Oriental Economist* September.

32 Woronoff 'Japan and the 21st century'.

33 Simon Nora and Alain Minc (1981) *The computerisation of society* Cambridge MA: MIT Press p. 110.

34 Her Majesty's Stationery Office (1983) *The development of cable systems and services* London: Cmnd 8866 p. 69.

35 Hills 'British industrial policy'.

36 This point is also stressed by, e.g., Frank Webster and Kevin Robins *Information technology*.

37 The phrase is Langdon Winner's. See note 4.

38 See Thomas Misa's contribution to Merritt Roe Smith (ed.) (1985) *Military enterprise and technological change: perspectives on the American experience* Cambridge MA and London: MIT Press.

Chapter 3 A new economy: new classes?

1 Quoted in Krishan Kumar (1978) *Prophecy and progress* Harmondsworth: Penguin pp. 35–6.

2 Bob Dylan (1972) *Tarantula* London: Panther p. 77.

3 Charles Jonscher (1983) 'Information resources and information productivity' *Information Economics and Policy* (1) pp. 13–35.

4 Donald MacKenzie argues against the common assumption that this is a statement of classic technological determinism in his (1985) 'Marx and the

machine' *Technology and Culture* (25), pp. 473–502. S. Marglin (1974) argues that in fact things happened the other way round: capitalism gave us the steam mill. 'What do bosses do? The origins and functions of hierarchy in capitalist production', *Review of Radical Political Economics* 6 (2).

5   Jonscher 'Information resources' p. 14. 'De-industrialization' is discussed in Frank Blackaby (1978) *De-industrialization* London: Heinemann.

6   Fritz Machlup (1980) *The production and distribution of knowledge in the USA* Princeton NJ: Princeton University Press; Marc Porat (1977) *The information economy: definition and measurement* Washington DC: US Department of Commerce.

7   Peter Drucker (1968) *The age of discontinuity* New York: Harper and Row; Daniel Bell (1974) *The coming of postindustrial society* Harmondsworth: Peregrine; Daniel Bell (1980) 'The social framework of the information society' in Tom Forester (ed.) *The microelectronics revolution* Oxford: Basil Blackwell; Yoneji Masuda (1981) *The information society as postindustrial society* Bethesda MD: World Futures Society.

8   OECD (1981) *Information activities, electronics and telecommunications technologies: impacts on employment and growth in trade* Paris: OECD p. 13.

9   See Kumar *Prophecy and progress*.

10   Ibid. p. 203.

11   Ian Miles and Jonathan Gershuny (1986) 'The social economics of information technology' in Marjorie Ferguson (ed.) *New communication technologies and the public interest* London: Sage; see also Jonathan Gershuny and Ian Miles (1983) *The new service economy* London: Frances Pinter.

12   This is discussed in ch. 4.

13   Jonscher 'Information resources' p. 21.

14   Tom Stonier (1983) *The wealth of information* London: Thames-Methuen pp. 33–48. Note that Jonscher in 'Information resources' argues for only two sectors, production and information.

15   See, e.g., Ray Pahl (1984) *Divisions of labour* Oxford: Basil Blackwell.

16   Christopher Freeman (1984) in Pauline Marstrand (ed.) *New technology and the future of work and skills* London: Frances Pinter.

17   Anthony Giddens uses the 'leapfrog' image in (1973) *The class structure of the advanced societies* London: Hutchinson p. 261.

18   Patricia Arriaga (1985) 'Towards a critique of the information economy' *Media Culture and Society* (7) pp. 271–96.

19   Again, Miles and Gershuny 'Social economics' refers to this, but so does Daniel Bell 'Social framework' without apparently questioning its salience to other aspects of his work.

20   Jonscher 'Information resources' p. 16.

21   H. P. Gassman (1981) 'Is there a fourth economic sector?' *OECD Observer* (113) November.

22 Bell 'Social framework' p. 516.
23 Miles and Gershuny 'Social economics' p. 23.
24 Trevor Jones (1980) 'A new society? The social impact of microprocessor technology' in Trevor Jones (ed.) *Microelectronics and society* Milton Keynes: Open University Press.
25 Miles and Gershuny 'Social economics' p. 24.
26 Bell 'Social framework' p. 543.
27 Julian Newman and Rhona Newman (1985) 'Information work: the new divorce?' *British Journal of Sociology* 36 (4) pp. 497–515.
28 Ibid. pp. 508–9.
29 Cynthia Cockburn (1985) *Machinery of dominance: women, men and technical know-how* London: Pluto Press p. 225. See also Anne Lloyd and Liz Newell (1985) 'Women and computers' in Wendy Faulkner and Erik Arnold (eds) *Smothered by invention: technology in women's lives* London: Pluto.
30 Department of Trade and Industry (1982) *Information technology: the age of electronic information* London: DTI.
31 Michael Beenstock (1982) *The world economy in transition* London: Unwin is cited by Samuel Brittan (1983) 'The myth of the Kondratieff' *Financial Times* 7 April. See also Angus Maddison (1982) *Phases of capitalist development* Oxford: Oxford University Press.
32 Tom Kitwood (1985) 'A farewell wave to the theory of long waves' *Education Culture and Society/Universities Quarterly* 58 (2) pp. 158–78.
33 John Naisbitt (1982) *Megatrends* New York: Warner, ch. 8.
34 Ibid. p. 212.
35 Andrew Neil (1983) 'The new freedom will mean the end of old-fashioned capitalism and socialism' *The Listener* 23 June.
36 Bell *Coming of postindustrial society* p. 162.
37 Bell 'Social framework' p. 543.
38 Alvin Toffler (1980) *The third wave* London: Pan p. 449.
39 David Albury and Joseph Schwartz (1982) *Partial progress: the politics of science and technology* London: Pluto pp. 138–9.
40 Karl Marx (1973) *Grundrisse* Harmondsworth: Penguin p. 706.
41 Karl Marx *Capital* vol. 1, ch. 15, sect. 5.
42 See Tom Bottomore (1985) *Theories of capitalist society* London: Allen and Unwin pp. 61–2.
43 See, e.g., Frank Webster (1986) 'The politics of new technology' *Socialist Register* (ed. R. Miliband) London: Merlin pp. 385–413.
44 Vincent Mosco (1982) *Pushbutton fantasies* Norwood NJ: Ablex, p. 163.
45 Nicholas Garnham (1982) 'New communications technologies' in Liam Bannon et al. (eds) *Information technology: impact on the way of life* Dublin: Tycooly p. 285.
46 Kevin Robins and Frank Webster (1986) 'The revolution of the fixed wheel:

information, technology, and social Taylorism' in Phillip Drummond and Richard Paterson (eds) *Television in Transition* London: British Film Institute.

47 Bell *Coming of postindustrial society* p. 15.

48 Ibid. p. 33.

49 Bell 'Social framework' p. 543.

50 Toffler *Third wave* p. 449.

51 Serge Mallet (1963) *The new working class* Nottingham: Spokesman; André Gorz (1964) *Strategy for labour* Boston: Beacon Press.

52 Marx *Grundrisse* p. 705.

53 Cited in Graeme Salaman (1981) *Class and the corporation* Glasgow: Fontana p. 92.

54 Duncan Gallie (1978) *In search of the new working class* Cambridge: Cambridge University Press.

55 Barbara and John Ehrenreichs (1979) 'The professional-managerial class' in Pat Walker (ed.) *Between capital and labour* Brighton: Harvester p. 45.

56 Nicholas Abercrombie and John Urry (1983) *Capital, labour and the middle classes* London: Allen and Unwin.

57 Alain Touraine (1974) *The postindustrial society* London: Wildwood House, p. 17.

58 Alain Touraine (1977) *L'Après Socialisme* Paris: Editions Gallimard.

59 Herbert Marcuse (1964) *One-dimensional man: studies in the ideology of advanced industrial society* London: Routledge and Kegan Paul.

60 Jacques Ellul (1964) *The technological society* New York: Vintage.

61 John Goldthorpe (1982) 'On the service class, its formation and future' in Anthony Giddens and Gavin MacKenzie (eds) *Social class and the division of labour* Cambridge: Cambridge University Press.

62 Joan Rothschild (1981) 'A feminist perspective on technology and the future' *Women's Studies International Quarterly* 4 (1) p. 70.

63 This is to extend Touraine's analysis somewhat. His concept of the 'programmed' society refers to the modern phenomenon of societies acting upon themselves, not necessarily to surveillance as discussed here.

64 Mark Poster (1984) *Foucault, Marxism and history* Cambridge: Polity Press, p. 169.

Chapter 4   New technology, employment, work and skills

1 William Morris 'How we live and how we might live' in Asa Briggs (ed.) (1962) *William Morris: selected writings and designs* Harmondsworth: Penguin pp. 163, 177.

2 Gene Bylinsky (1985) *Silicon Valley: high tech window on the future* San Francisco: Arthur Young p. 27.
3 Colin Hines (1978) *The chips are down* London: Earth Resources Research.
4 Mike Norton (1984) 'Where IT may not build jobs' *Computing, the Magazine* 6 December, pp. 13–14.
5 Simon Nora and Alain Minc (1980) *The computerisation of society* Cambridge MA: MIT Press p. 37. Admittedly, some of the more alarming predictions of job-loss due to the adoption of IT have not been fulfilled. However, new technology *is* often used rather than replacing workers who have left for some other reason, see W. W. Daniel (1987) *Workplace industrial relations and technical change* London: Frances Pinter.
6 See, e.g., John Bessant et al. (1985) *IT futures: what forecasting literature says about the social impact of IT* London: NEDC.
7 Colin Gill (1985) *Work, unemployment and the new technology* Cambridge: Polity Press pp. 89–90.
8 Warwick University Institute of Employment Research report summarized in *The Times* 10 July 1986, p. 21, Heather Menzies (1981) *Women and the chip: case studies of the effects of informatics on employment in Canada* Montreal: Institute for Research on Public Policy.
9 Charles Handy (1984) *The future of work* Oxford: Basil Blackwell p. 16.
10 See J. Northcott (1986) *Microelectronics in industry: promise and performance* London: Policy Studies Institute, and Ian Macintosh (1986) *Sunrise Europe* Oxford: Basil Blackwell.
11 Ian Miles and Jonathan Gershuny (1986) 'The social economics of information technology' in Marjorie Ferguson (ed.) *New communications technologies and the public interest* London and Beverly Hills: Sage p. 28.
12 Jenny Mill (1985) '*L'informatique*: France fights for its future' *Computing* 24 October pp. 7–8.
13 Clive Jenkins and Barrie Sherman (1981) *Leisure shock* London: Eyre Methuen.
14 Tom Stonier (1983) *The wealth of information* London: Thames-Methuen p. 212.
15 André Gorz (1982) *Farewell to the working class* London: Pluto Press.
16 The phrase is Frank Webster's (1985) 'IT: More service jobs, more leisure, or more of the same?' Ealing College of H.E. Occasional Paper.
17 See Tony Walter (forthcoming) *Basic income: the reasons why* London: Marion Boyars, and John Keane and John Owens (1986) *After full employment* London: Hutchinson.
18 Charles Handy (1984) p. 42.
19 This example appears in David Boddy and David Buchanan (1985) 'New technology with a human face' *Personnel Management* April pp. 28–31.
20 See the account in E. P. Thompson (1968) *The making of the English working class* Harmondsworth: Penguin, but also M. I. Thomis (1970) *The Luddites*

London: David and Charles, and Robert Reid (1986) *Land of lost content* London: Heinemann.

21 Harry Braverman (1974) *Labour and monopoly capital* New York: Monthly Review Press.

22 The phrase comes from Craig Littler and Graeme Salaman (1982) 'Bravermania and beyond: recent theories of the labour process' *Sociology* 16 (2) pp. 251–69.

23 Barry Wilkinson (1983) *The shopfloor politics of new technology* London: Heinemann pp. 65–7.

24 Ibid. p. 86.

25 David Noble (1979) 'Social choice in machine design' in A. Zimbalist (ed.) *Case studies in the labor process* New York: Monthly Review Press; repr. in Donald MacKenzie and Judith Wacjman (1985) *The social shaping of technology* Milton Keynes: Open University Press.

26 Howard Rosenbrock (1984) 'Must skills be lost?' in Pauline Marstrand (ed.) *New technology and the future of work and skills* London: Frances Pinter.

27 Council for Science and Society (1981) *New technology: society, employment and skill* London: CSI.

28 See Bryn Jones (1982) 'Destruction or redistribution of engineering skills: the case of CNC' in Stephen Wood et al. (eds) *The degradation of work?* London: Hutchinson.

29 Diane Werneke (1983) *Microelectronics and office jobs: the impact of the chip on women's employment* Geneva: International Labour Office, repr. in Tom Forester (ed.) (1985) *The information technology revolution* Oxford: Basil Blackwell p. 404.

30 Rosemary Crompton and Stuart Reid (1982) 'The deskilling of clerical work' in Stephen Wood et al. (eds) *The degradation of work?* London: Hutchinson.

31 Stephen Bevan (1985) *Secretaries and typists: the impact of office automation* University of Sussex: Institute of Manpower Studies.

32 See Bessant et al. *IT futures*.

33 P. M. B. Dawson and I. P. McLoughlin (1986) 'Computer technology and the redefinition of supervision' *Journal of Management Studies* 23 (1) January.

34 Peter Cressey, John Eldridge and John McInnes (1985) *Just managing: authority and democracy in industry* Milton Keynes: Open University Press p. 51.

35 See Thomas Peters and Robert Waterman (1984) *In search of excellence* New York: Harper and Row.

36 See Boddy and Buchanan 'New technology'.

37 Gill *Work, unemployment and the new technology* p. 120.

38 Jenny Mill (1986) 'Utopia: the only alternative to violence at Wapping?' *Computing Magazine* 10 July pp. 18–19.

39 Wilkinson *Shopfloor politics* p. 93.

40 Gill *Work, unemployment and the new technology* p. 131.

41 W. W. Daniel (1987) *Workplace industrial relations and technical change*.

42 R. Williams and R. Moseley (1982) 'The trades unions response to informa-tion technology' in Bannon et al. (eds) *Information technology* p. 243.

43 Bernhard Rosellen (1984) 'Effects of new technologies' *Social and Labour Bulletin* (3/4) September–December pp. 381–3.

44 Monica Elling (1985) 'Remote work/telecommuting: a means of enhancing the quality of life or just another means of making business more brisk?' *Economics and Industrial Democracy* 6 (2) pp. 239–49.

45 Catherine Hakim (1984) 'Homework and outwork' *Employment Gazette* January pp. 7–12.

46 Walter Baer (1985) 'IT comes home' *Telecommunications Policy* 9 (1) March pp. 3–22.

47 Ursula Huws (1984) 'New technology homeworkers' *Employment Gazette* January pp. 13–17, and Elia Zureik (1985) 'The electronic cottage: old wine in new bottles?' Paper presented at conference on technology and culture, University of Ottawa, May.

48 Linda Thompson (1985) 'The electronic cottage: haven or nightmare?' *International Management and Data Systems* January–February p. 22.

49 Carla Lipsig Mumme (1983) 'The renaissance of homeworking in developed economies' *Relations industrielles* 38 (3).

Chapter 5   Information, democracy and the state

1 Ithiel de Sola Pool (1983) *Technologies of freedom* Cambridge MA and London: Harvard University Press.

2 Ecclesiastes 5, verse 8 (New International Version).

3 Alvin Toffler (1980) *The third wave* London: Pan p. 439.

4 Quoted in Vincent Mosco (1982) *Pushbutton fantasies* Norwood NJ: Ablex p. 108.

5 Yoneji Masuda (1981) *The information society as postindustrial society* Bethesda MD: World Futures Society pp. 101–3.

6 'Hi-tech: the ayes have it' *The Sunday Times* 15 September.

7 See, e.g., Jacques Vallee (1984) *The networking revolution* Harmondsworth: Penguin.

8 John Garrett and Geoff Wright (1980) in Tom Forester (ed.) *The micro-electronics revolution* Oxford: Basil Blackwell pp. 488–96.

9 de Sola Pool *Technologies of freedom*.

10 Ibid. p. 10.

11 T. Tannsjo (1985) 'Against freedom of expression' *Political Studies* (33) pp. 547–59.

12 John Street (forthcoming) 'Taking control? Some aspects of the relationship between IT, government policy and democracy' in Frank Gregory (ed.) *Information technology: the public issues* Manchester: Manchester University Press.

13 Ben Barber (forthcoming) 'Pangloss, Pandora or Jefferson? Three scenarios for the future of democracy and technology' in Frank Gregory (ed.) *Information technology*; see also Ben Barber (1984) *Strong democracy* Berkeley: University of California Press.

14 Quoted in *New Scientist* 2 June 1983 p. 634.

15 'Mindless minorities and murderous micros' *Computing* 14 March 1985.

16 Herbert Schiller (1981) *Who knows? Information in the age of the Fortune 500* Norwood NJ: Ablex p. 74.

17 'Booking in for the new technology' *The Sunday Times* 28 September 1986.

18 Schiller *Who knows?* p. 80.

19 James Carey and John Quirk (1970) 'The mythos of the electronic revolution' *The American Scholar* 39((2) p. 225.

20 Ithiel de Sola Pool (1983) *Forecasting the telephone* Norwood NJ: Ablex p. 71.

21 Abbe Mowshowitz (1980) in Lance Hoffman (ed.) *Computers and privacy in the next decade* New York: Academic Press p. 99.

22 John Haber (1986) 'Black tracking' *The Guardian* 30 December.

23 'Protests at computer ID cards' *The Guardian* 1 March 1986.

24 'Germans computerise identity cards' *New Scientist* 20 February 1986.

25 Cited in Duncan Campbell and Steve Connor (1986) *On the record* London: Michael Joseph p. 255; Sue Baker (1984) 'The spy under the road' *The Observer* 28 October.

26 David Burnham (1983) *The rise of the computer state* New York: Vintage/ London: Weidenfeld and Nicholson, Kenneth Laudon (1986) *The dossier society* New York: Columbia University Press.

27 'Reagan scrambles to curb electronic eavesdropping' *The Guardian* 30 December 1986.

28 'On-line credit: mixed blessing?' *Computing, the Magazine* 8 November 1984.

29 John Wicklein (1981) *Electronic nightmare: the home communications set and your freedom* Boston: Beacon Press.

30 Anthony Giddens (1979) *A contemporary critique of historical materialism* London: Macmillan/Berkeley: University of California Press pp. 169ff.

31 Anthony Giddens (1984) *The constitution of society* Cambridge: Polity Press pp. 127ff.

32 Michel Foucault (1977) *Discipline and punish* Harmondsworth: Penguin pp. 201–2.

33 Ibid. p. 296.

34 Mark Poster (1984) *Foucault, Marxism and history* Cambridge: Polity Press p. 103.

35 Ellie Scrivens (1985) 'IT and the civil service' *Political Quarterly* 56 (1) 81–4.

36 Jacques Ellul (1964) *The technological society* New York: Vintage p. 100 (quoted in Burnham *Rise of the computer state* p. 154).

37 Ellul *Technological society* p. 284.

38 Ibid.

39 See Patricia O'Brien (1982) *The promise of punishment: prisons in nineteenth century France* Princeton: Princeton University Press, to which Poster *Foucault, Marxism and history* p. 111 refers.

40 'Protection of privacy and ethical dilemmas in computer applications in social work' *Computer applications in social work and allied professions* 3 (1) 1986 p. 17.

41 Kenneth Laudon (1980) 'Privacy and federal data banks' *Society* January/February p. 50.

42 Quoted in Schiller *Who knows?* p. 175.

43 Kenneth Laudon, *Dossier society*; William Dutton, review of Laudon forthcoming in *The Library Quarterly*.

44 Duncan Campbell and Steve Connor (1986) 'The battle against privacy' *New Statesman* 9 May; see also Campbell and Connor *On the record*.

45 Paul Dolan (1983) 'Protecting data or protecting people?' *Community Care* 1 September pp. 15–16.

46 Geoffrey Brown (1985) 'Privacy and information: a new moral problem?' *Culture Education and Society/Universities Quarterly* 39 (2) p. 122.

47 Brown 'Privacy and information' p. 125.

48 Ellul *Technological society* p. 286.

49 Claus Offe (1984) 'Reflections on the welfare state and the future of socialism' (interview with John Keane and David Held) in *Contradictions of the welfare state* (ed. John Keane) London: Hutchinson.

50 Abbe Mowshowitz (1980) in Hoffman *Computers and privacy* p. 101.

51 Michael Goldhaber (1986) *Reinventing technology: policies for democratic values* London and Boston: Routledge and Kegan Paul pp. 135–6, 157–8; Shirley Williams (1985) *A job to live* Harmondsworth: Penguin pp. 210ff.

Chapter 6   The global dimension

1 Edward Ayensu (1982) *International Management* September, quoted in Brian Murphy (1983) *The world wired up* London: Comedia p. 119.

2 Anthony Smith (1980) *The geopolitics of information: how Western culture dominates the world* London: Faber p. 176.

3 John Bessant and Sam Cole (1985) *Stacking the chips: IT and the global division of labour* London: Frances Pinter.

4　Tom Stonier (1983) *The wealth of information* London: Thames-Methuen pp. 26–8.

5　Ibid. p. 204.

6　Yoneji Masuda (1981) *The information society as postindustrial society* Bethesda MD: World Futures Society p. 118.

7　Jean-Jacques Servan-Schrieber (1980) *Le Defi mondial* Paris: Fayard.

8　Alvin Toffler (1980) *The third wave* London: Pan p. 338.

9　Daniel Bell (1979) 'Communications technology: for better or worse' *Harvard Business Review* 57 (3) p. 76, and (1980) 'The social framework of the information society' in Tom Forester (ed.) *The microelectronics revolution* Oxford: Basil Blackwell p. 544.

10　Daniel Headrick (1981) *The tools of empire: technology and European imperialism in the nineteenth century* New York: Oxford University Press.

11　Juan Rada (1985) 'IT in the third world' in Tom Forester (ed.) *The information technology revolution* Oxford: Basil Blackwell.

12　E. J. Hobsbawm (1969) *Industry and Empire* Harmondsworth: Penguin, p. 13.

13　Smith *Geopolitics of information* p. 76.

14　James Carey (1980) 'Culture, geography, and communications: the work of Harold Innis in an American context' in William Melody (ed.) *Culture, communication and dependency* Vancouver: Simon Fraser University.

15　Anthony Giddens (1981) *A contemporary critique of historical materialism* London: Macmillan/Berkeley: University of California Press p. 190.

16　Smith *Geopolitics of information* p. 30.

17　Daniel Lerner (1958) *The passing of traditional society* Glencoe, New York: Free Press.

18　Smith *Geopolitics of information* p. 64.

19　Ian Roxborough (1979) *Theories of underdevelopment* London: Macmillan p. 60.

20　Willy Brandt et al. (1980) *North–South: a programme for survival* London: Pan.

21　Frank Barnaby (1982) 'Microelectronics in war' in Günter Friedrichs and Adam Schaff (eds) *Microelectronics and society: for better or for worse* London: Pergamon p. 264.

22　Quoted by Herbert Schiller (1986) in Michael Traber (ed.) *The myth of the information revolution* London and Beverly Hills: Sage p. 22.

23　'IBM-ulators harass Big Blue' *The Sunday Times* 2 November 1986.

24　Aktar Mahmud Faruqui (1986) 'Science and technology: the Third World's dilemma' *Impact of Science on Society* 36 (1) p. 11.

25　L. McCartney (1983) 'Our newest hi-tech export: jobs *Datamation* May.

26　Rachel Grossman (1979) comments on this in *South-East Asia Chronicle* (66) January–February.

27　Stephen Maxwell (1985) 'International perspectives: Malaysia's electronics industry' in Howard Davis and David Gosling (eds) *Will the future work?* Geneva: WCC p. 70.

28 Rada 'IT in the Third World'.

29 Simon Nora and Alain Minc (1980) *The computerisation of society* Cambridge MA: MIT Press pp. 68ff.

30 Armand Mattelart (1985) 'Infotech and the Third World' *Making waves: politics of communication* London: Free Association Books p. 31.

31 Ibid. p. 32.

32 Cees Hamelink (1983) *Cultural autonomy in global communications* New York: Longman p. 9.

33 Herbert Schiller (1986) 'Strengths and weaknesses of the new international information empire' in Philip Lee (ed.) *Communication for all* New York: Orbis p. 20.

34 Jeremy Tunstall (1977) *The media are American* New York: Columbia University Press pp. 39–40.

35 A. Sivanandan (1979) 'Imperialism and disorganic development in the silicon age' *Race and Class* 21 (2) pp. 111–26.

36 Tom McPhail (1981) *Electronic colonialism* London and Beverly Hills: Sage p. 20.

37 This kind of argument is used by Herbert Schiller (e.g. in 'Strengths and weaknesses'). But see also Roxborough *Theories of underdevelopment* pp. 55ff.

38 Hamelink *Cultural autonomy* p. 5.

39 Frank Ugboajah (1984) in 'The debate over the US decision to withdraw from UNESCO' *Journal of Communication* 34 (4) p. 105.

40 Quoted in Lema Forje and John Forje (1986) 'The multinational and underdevelopment in Africa' *Impact of Science on Society* 36 (1) p. 48.

41 Sean MacBride (ed.) (1980) *Many voices: one world* Paris: UNESCO.

42 The debate is well documented in Smith *Geopolitics of Information* pp. 13–18.

43 MacBride *Many voices*, p. 41.

44 Mina Ramirez (1986) 'Communication as if people mattered' in Michael Traber (ed.) *The myth of the information revolution* London and Beverly Hills: Sage pp., 106f.

45 Gaston Roberge (1986) 'Communication and the church in India' in Philip Lee (ed.) *Communication for all* New York: Orbis p. 125.

46 Nicholas Ashford (1981) 'Pressures grow on Reagan to block UNESCO's international information order' *The Times* 20 July.

47 Smith *Geopolitics of information* p. 174.

48 Carolyn Dempster (1986) 'Ideals versus ideology' *Times Higher Educational Supplement* 7 November p. 10.

49 Mattelart 'Infotech and the Third World' p. 32.

50 Faruqui 'Science and technology' p. 13.

51 See Paul Ansah (1986) in Michael Traber (ed.) *The myth of the information revolution* London and Beverly Hills: Sage pp. 64–83.

52 Schiller 'Strengths and weaknesses' p. 32.

Chapter 7   Information, meaning and culture

1 Quoted in Lewis Mumford (1934, preface to 1964 edition) *Technics and civilization* New York: Harcourt Brace Jovanovich.

2 Sherry Turkle (1980) 'Computers as Rorschach' *Society* January–February p. 15.

3 Walter Ong (1982) *Orality and literacy: the technologizing of the word* London and New York: Methuen.

4 The work of both Jürgen Habermas and Alain Touraine, in different ways, points up this trend.

5 Andrew Neil (1986) *The TV explosion* BBC2 (TV) 10 November.

6 Quoted by Richard Collins (1984) 'Will choice be extended by cable?' *Telecommunications Policy* March p. 9.

7 Ibid. p. 10.

8 Peter Golding and Graham Murdock (1986) 'Unequal information: access and exclusion in the new communications marketplace' in Marjorie Ferguson (ed.) *New communications technologies and the public interest* London and Beverly Hills: Sage.

9 Jeremy Tunstall (1985) 'Deregulation is politicisation'.

10 Graham Murdock, Paul Hartmann and Peggy Gray (1983) *Everyday innovations* Leicester: Centre for Mass Communications Research.

11 Jay Blumler (1984) 'The politics of cabling policy in Britain' paper presented at the International Forum on the Public Policies of New Communications Technologies, Paris 15–16 May.

12 Kevin Robins and Frank Webster (forthcoming) 'Public service broadcasting in the UK: a defence' *Screen*.

13 Vincent Mosco (1982) *Pushbutton fantasies* Norwood NJ: Ablex p. 117.

14 Anita Rind and Charles Vial (1986) 'Minitel's "special services" alarm French jurists' *The Guardian Weekly* (from *Le Monde* 11 September) 19 October p. 14.

15 Mosco *Pushbutton fantasies* p. 115.

16 Lyn Champion (1985) 'Too tight a test for a free-thinking medium' *The Guardian* 9 September.

17 Mark Poster (1984) *Foucault, Marxism and history* Cambridge: Polity Press p. 166.

18 Michael Goldhaber (1986) *Reinventing technology* London and Boston: Routledge and Kegan Paul p. 76.

19 Ibid. p. 77 and David Bolter (1984) *Turing's man: Western culture in the computer age* London: Duckworth/Chapel Hill: University of North Carolina Press p. 186.

20 Donald Michie and Rory Johnson (1985) *The knowledge machine: artificial intelligence and the future of man* New York: Morrow p. 244.

21 Quoted in Frank Rose (1984) *Into the heart of the mind* New York: Harper and Row p. 209.

22 Donald Michie (1980) 'The social aspects of AI' in Trevor Jones (ed.) *Microelectronics and society* Milton Keynes: Open University Press p. 115.

23 Steve Woolgar (1985) 'Why not a sociology of machines?' *Sociology* 19 (4) p. 568.

24 In an interview with Marion Long (1985) *New Age Journal* December p. 50.

25 Herbert Dreyfus (1979) *What computers can't do* New York: Harper Colophon.

26 Quoted in Tom Athanasiou (1985) 'Artificial intelligence' in Tony Solomonides and Les Levidow (eds) *Compulsive technology: computers as culture* London: Free Association Books p. 33.

27 Ibid. p. 11.

28 Bolter *Turing's man* p. 14.

29 Mumford *Technics and civilization* p. 14.

30 See, e.g., British Computer Society (1986) *People and computers: design for usability* Cambridge: Cambridge University Press.

31 Sherry Turkle (1984) *The second self: computers and the human spirit* London: Granada/New York: Simon and Schuster p. 313.

32 Turkle 'Computers as Rorschach', pp. 17–18.

33 See, e.g., David Sudnow (1983) *Pilgrim in the microworld* London: Heinemann/New York: Warner Books; Tracy Kidder (1982) *The soul of a new machine* Harmondsworth: Penguin/New York: Little Brown and Company; Steven Levy (1984) *Hackers: heroes of the computer revolution* Garden City NY: Anchor-Doubleday.

34 Bolter *Turing's man* p. 236.

35 This is discussed in Anthony Giddens (1981) *A contemporary critique of historical materialism* London: Macmillan/Berkeley: University of California Press, and in David Landes's elegant (1983) *Revolution in time* Cambridge MA: Harvard/Belknap Press.

36 Norbert Elias (1982) *The civilizing process* Oxford: Basil Blackwell.

37 Helga Nowotny (1982) 'The information society: its impact on the home, local community and marginal groups' in Niels Bjørn-Andersen et al. (eds) *Information society: for richer, for poorer* Amsterdam, New York and Oxford: North-Holland p. 100.

38 Poster *Foucault, Marxism and history* p. 166.

39 John Naisbitt (1984) *Megatrends* New York: Warner p. 42.

40 See National Economic Development Council Taylor Nelson Monitor Report quoted by Peter Large (1986) 'Britain's new people show work ethic is old hat' *The Guardian* 18 September.

41 Daniel Bell (1974) *The coming of postindustrial society* Harmondsworth: Penguin p. 298.

42 Quoted in Kathleen Woodward (ed.) (1980) *The myths of information: technology and postindustrial culture* London: Routledge and Kegan Paul p. 78.

43 Judith Larsen and Everett Rogers (1984) *Silicon Valley fever* London: Allen and Unwin/New York: Basic Books p. 265.

44 James Danziger (1985) 'Social science and the social impacts of computer technology' *Social Science Quarterly* (66) p. 14.

45 Sara Keisler et al. (1984) 'Social psychological aspects of computer-mediated information *American Psychologist* 39 (10) p. 1126. It is interesting to compare contemporary concern about new electronic media with the forecast effects of the early telephone systems. See Ithiel de Sola Pool (1983) *Forecasting the Telephone* Norwood NJ: Ablex.

46 James Carey (1975) 'Canadian communications theory: extensions and interpretations of Harold Adams Innis' in Gertrude Robinson and Donald Theall (eds) *Studies in Canadian Communications* Montreal: McGill.

47 Joseph Weizenbaum (1976) *Computer power and human reason* New York: W. H. Freeman and Company/Harmondsworth: Penguin (1984).

48 Ibid. (1984 edn) p. 50.

49 Herbert Marcuse (1964) *One-dimensional man: studies in the ideology of advanced industrial society* London and Boston: Routledge and Kegan Paul; Theodore Roszak (1973) *Where the wasteland ends: politics and transcendence in postindustrial society* London: Faber and Faber and (1986) *The cult of information* Cambridge: Lutterworth/New York: Pantheon.

50 Jacques Ellul (1964) *The technological society* New York: Vintage.

51 Michael Shallis (1984) *The silicon idol* Oxford: Oxford University Press.

52 Ibid. p. 169.

53 The phrase is Tunstall's (from 'Deregulation is politicisation'); further details are available, e.g., in Larsen and Rogers *Silicon Valley fever*.

54 Marshall Sahlins (1976) *Culture and practical reason* Chicago and London: University of Chicago Press.

55 Ibid. p. 221.

56 Jacques Ellul (1980) *The technological system* New York: Continuum.

57 See George Grant (1986) 'The morals of modern technology' *The Canadian Forum* October pp. 11–17.

58 Carl Mitcham (forthcoming) 'From ethos to ethics and from mythos to religion' *Technology in society*.

59 Cees Hamelink (1986) 'Is there life after the information revolution?' in Michael Traber (ed.) *The myth of the information revolution* Beverly Hills and London: Sage.

60 Morris Berman (1984) *The re-enchantment of the world* New York.

Chapter 8 Information, ideology and utopia

1 A. N. Whitehead (1985) *Science and the modern world* London: Free Association Books (orig. pub. 1925) p. 254.

2 W. H. Auden (1955) 'Vespers' from *Collected shorter poems 1927–1957* London: Faber.

3 Information technology advisory panel (1986) *Learning to live with IT* London: Her Majesty's Stationery Office.

4 See Ruth Levitas (1982) 'Dystopian times? The impact of the death of progress on utopian thinking' *Theory, Culture and Society* 1 (1) pp. 53–61.

5 Arnold Pacey (1983) *The culture of technology* Oxford: Basil Blackwell, p. 178.

6 Evelyn Fox-Keller (1985) *Reflections on gender and science* New Haven and London: Yale University Press pp. 36, 42.

7 See, e.g., Lynn White (1978) *Medieval religion and technology* Berkeley: University of California Press.

8 Carl Mitcham (1983) 'The religious and political origins of modern technology' in Paul Durbin and Friedrich Rapp (eds) *Philosophy and technology* New York and Frankfurt: Reidel Publishing Company.

9 See Krishan Kumar (1978) *Prophecy and progress* Harmondsworth: Penguin.

10 Howard Segal (1985) *Technological utopianism in American culture* Chicago and London: University of Chicago Press.

11 Howard Segal (1978) 'American visions of technological utopia 1883–1933' *The Markham Review* 7 (Summer) p. 66.

12 Marshall McLuhan (1964) *Understanding media* London: Routledge and Kegan Paul, the original edition of which began by asserting that we are in 'the electronic age whose media substitute all-at-onceness for one-thing-at-a-timeness' (see James Carey and John Quirk (1970) 'The myths of the electronic revolution' *The American Scholar* 39 (3) p. 401).

13 Anthony Giddens discusses 'ideological aspects' in (1979) *Central problems in social theory* London: Macmillan pp. 193ff.

14 Jürgen Habermas (1971) *Towards the rational society* London: Heinemann.

15 Cees Hamelink (1986) in Michael Traber (ed.) *The myth of the information revolution* London and Beverly Hills: Sage p. 11.

16 Bob Goudzwaard (1975) *Aid for the overdeveloped West* Toronto: Wedge p. 4.

17 Alan Storkey (1986) *Transforming economics* London: SPCK p. 203.

18 Michael Shallis (1984) *The silicon idol* Oxford: Oxford University Press p. v.

19 Quoted in Ursula Huws (1982) *Your job in the eighties* London: Pluto Press p. 9.

20 E. P. Thompson (1968) *The making of the English working class* Harmondsworth: Penguin.

21 Robert Reid (1986) *Land of lost content* London: Heinemann p. 283.

22 Frank Webster and Kevin Robins (1986) *Information technology: a Luddite*

analysis Norwood NJ: Ablex, p. 4, and David Albury and Joseph Schwartz (1982) *Partial progress: the politics of science and technology* London: Pluto Press.

23 Anthony Giddens (1985) *The nation-state and violence* Cambridge: Polity Press p. 318.

24 Cynthia Cockburn (1983) *Brothers: male dominance and technological change* London: Pluto Press p. 230.

25 Herbert Schiller (1981) *Who knows? Information in the age of the Fortune 500* Norwood NJ: Ablex p. 176. See also the negative Luddism of David Noble in his articles on 'Present tense technology' in *Democracy*, Spring, Summer and Fall 1983.

26 Shallis *Silicon idol* pp. 176–8.

27 William Morris (1890) *News from nowhere* in Asa Briggs (ed.) (1962) *William Morris: selected writings and designs* Harmondsworth: Penguin.

28 Hans Jonas (1984) *The imperative of responsibility* London and Chicago: University of Chicago Press.

29 Geoffrey Brown (1985) 'Privacy and information: a new moral problem?' *Education, Culture and Society/Universities Quarterly* 39 (2) pp. 114–26.

30 This is an extension of the views expressed in, e.g., Nicholas Abercrombie and John Urry (1983) *Capital, labour and the middle classes* London: Allen and Unwin; Alain Touraine (1974) *The postindustrial society* London: Wildwood House; and Alain Touraine (1981) *The voice and the eye* Cambridge: Cambridge University Press.

31 See, e.g., Council for Science and Society (1981) *New technology: work, employment and skill* London: CSI.

32 Paul Ansah (1979) 'Problems of localising radio' in *Ghana Gazette* 25 (4) pp. 1–16.

33 Robin McCron (1984) 'New technologies: New opportunities?' *Journal of Educational Television* 10 (1) pp. 7–18.

34 Bernd-Peter Lang et al. (1982) *Sozialpolitische Chancen der Informationstechnik* Frankfurt and New York: Campus Verlag (cited in *Communication Research Trends* 5 (2) 1984 p. 9), Elisabeth Gerver (1986) *Humanizing technology* New York: Plenum.

35 M. F. Smith (1985) 'UK information technology: 1990s' *Information Technology Training* 3 (3) pp. 69–71.

36 William Melody (1985) 'Implications of the information and communications technologies: the role of policy research' *Policy Studies* 6 (2) p. 49.

37 The term comes from Robert Bellah et al. (1984) *Habits of the heart* Berkeley: University of California Press; see also William Sullivan et al. (eds) (1983) *Social science as moral inquiry* New York: Columbia University Press.

Select bibliography

Abercrombie, Nicholas and Urry, John (1983) *Capital, labour and the middle classes*. London: Allen and Unwin.

Albury, David and Schwartz, Joseph (1982) *Partial progress: the politics of science and technology*. London: Pluto Press.

Arriaga, Patricia (1985) 'Towards a critique of the information economy', *Media, Culture and Society* (7) 261–96.

Bannon, Liam et al. (eds) (1982) *Information technology: impact on the way of life*. Dublin: Tycooly.

Barber, Ben (1984) *Strong democracy*. Berkeley: University of California Press.

Barnaby, Frank (1982) 'Microelectronics in war' in Friedrichs and Schaff (eds) *Microelectronics and society*.

Barrett, William (1986) *Death of the soul: from Descartes to the computer*. New York: Anchor Press.

Bell, Daniel (1974) *The coming of postindustrial society: a venture in social forecasting*. Harmondsworth: Penguin.

Bell, Daniel (1980) The social framework of the information society in Tom Forester (ed.) *Microelectronics revolution*.

Beniger, James (1986) *Control revolution: the technological and economic origins of the information society*. Cambridge, MA: Harvard University Press.

Bessant, John and Cole, Sam (1985) *Stacking the chips: information technology and the global division of labour*. London: Frances Pinter.

Bessant, John et al. (1985) *IT futures: what forecasting literature says about the social impact of IT*. London: NEDC.

Bjørn-Andersen, Niels et al. (eds) (1982) *Information society: for richer for poorer*. Amsterdam and London: North-Holland.

Bolter, David (1984) *Turing's man: Western culture in the computer age*. London: Duckworth; Chapel Hill NC: University of North Carolina Press.

Bottomore, Tom (1985) *Theories of capitalist society*. London: Allen and Unwin.

Braun, Ernest and MacDonald, Stuart (1982) *Revolution in miniature: the history and impact of semiconductor electronics*. Cambridge: Cambridge University Press.

Braverman, Harry (1974) *Labor and monopoly capital: the degradation of labor in the 20th century*. New York: Monthly Review Press.

Brown, Geoffrey (1985) 'Privacy and information: a new moral problem?' *Culture, Education and Society/New Universities Quarterly* 39 (2).

Burnham, David (1983) *The rise of the computer state*. New York: Vintage; London: Weidenfeld and Nicholson.

Campbell, Duncan and Connor, Steve (1986) *On the record: surveillance, computers and privacy*. London: Michael Joseph.

Carey, James (1975) 'Canadian communications theory: extensions and interpretations of Harold Adams Innis' in Gertrude Robinson and Donald Theall (eds) *Studies in Canadian communications*. Montreal: McGill University Press.

Carey, James and Quirk, John (1970) 'The mythos of the electronic revolution' *The American Scholar* 39 (2) 219–41 and (3) 395–424.

Cockburn, Cynthia (1983) *Brothers: male dominance and technological change*. London: Pluto Press.

Cockburn, Cynthia (1985) *Machinery of dominance: women and technical know-how*. London: Pluto Press.

Cooley, Mike (1980) *Architect or bee? the human/technology relationship*. Slough: Langley Technical Services.

Council for Science and Society (1981) *New technology: society, employment and skill*. London: CSI.

Cressey, Peter, Eldridge, John and McInnes, John (1985) *Just managing: authority and democracy in industry*. Milton Keynes: Open University Press.

Cronberg, Tarja and Sangregorio, Inga-Lisa (1981) 'More of the same: the impact of information technology on domestic life in Japan' *Development Dialogue* (2) 68–78.

Daniel, W. W. (1987) *Workplace industrial relations and technical change*. London: Frances Pinter with the Policy Studies Institute.

Danziger, James (1985) 'Social science and the social impacts of computer technology' *Social Science Quarterly* (66).

Danziger, James, Dutton, William, Kling, Rob and Kraemer, Kenneth (1982) *Computers and politics*. New York: Columbia University Press.

Dawson, Patrick and McLoughlin, Ian (1986) 'Computer technology and the redefinition of supervision: the effects of computerization on railway freight supervisors' *Journal of Management Studies* 23 (1) 116–32.

Dertouzos, Michael and Moses, Joel (eds) (1980) *The computer age: a twenty year view*. Cambridge MA: MIT Press.

Dreyfus, Herbert (1979) *What computers can't do*. New York: Harper Colophon.

Dutton, William, Blumler, Jay G. and Kraemer, Kenneth (eds) (forthcoming 1987) *Wired cities: shaping the future of communications*. Boston: G. K. Hall.

Elias, Norbert (1982) *The civilizing process*. Oxford: Basil Blackwell.

Elling, Monica, 'Remote work/telecommuting: a means of enhancing the quality of life or just another means of making business more brisk?' *Economics and Industrial Democracy* 6 (2) 239–49.

Ellul, Jacques (1964) *The technological society*. New York: Vintage.

Ellul, Jacques (1980) *The technological system*. New York: Continuum.

Faruqui, Aktar Mahmud (1986) 'Science and technology: the Third World's dilemma' *Impact of Science on Society* 36 (1).

Feigenbaum, Edward and McCorduck, Pamela (1984) *The fifth generation*. London: Pan.

Ferguson, Marjorie (ed.) (1986) *New communications technologies and the public interest*. Beverly Hills and London: Sage.

Forester, Tom (ed.) (1980) *The microelectronics revolution*. Oxford: Blackwell.

Forester, Tom (ed.) (1985) *The information technology revolution*. Oxford: Blackwell.

Foucault, Michel (1977) *Discipline and punish*. Harmondsworth: Penguin.

Fox-Keller, Evelyn (1985) *Reflections on gender and science* New Haven, Connecticut and London: Yale University Press.

Francis, Arthur (1986) *New technology at work*. Oxford: Oxford University Press.

Freeman, Christopher (1984) 'Keynes or Kondratiev?' in Pauline Marstrand (ed.) *New Technology*.

Friedrichs, Günter and Schaff, Adam (eds) (1982) *Microelectronics and society: for better or for worse*. London: Pergamon.

Gallie, Duncan (1978) *In search of the new working class*. Cambridge: Cambridge University Press.

Gershuny, Jonathan and Miles, Ian (1983) *The new service economy*. London: Frances Pinter.

Gerver, Elisabeth (1986) *Humanizing technology: computers in community use and adult education*. New York: Plenum Press.

Giddens, Anthony (1979) *A contemporary critique of historical materialism*. London: Macmillan; Berkeley: University of California Press.

Giddens, Anthony (1984) *The constitution of society*. Cambridge: Polity Press.

Giddens, Anthony (1985) *The nation-state and violence*. Cambridge: Polity Press.

Giddens, Anthony and MacKenzie, Gavin (eds) (1982) *Social class and the division of labour*. Cambridge: Cambridge University Press.

Gill, Colin (1985) *Work, unemployment and the new technology*. Cambridge: Polity Press.

Goldhaber, Michael (1986) *Reinventing technology: policies for democratic values*. London and New York: Routledge and Kegan Paul.

Goldthorpe, John (1982) 'On the service class, its formation and future' in Giddens and MacKenzie (eds) *Social class*.

Gordon, R. (forthcoming 1987) *Microelectronics in transition*. Norwood NJ: Ablex.

Gorz, André (1982) *Farewell to the working class*. London: Pluto Press.

Goudzwaard, Bob (1979) *Capitalism and progress*. Grand Rapids: Eerdmans.

Grant, George (1986) 'The morals of modern technology' *The Canadian Forum* October 11–17.

Gregory, Frank (ed., forthcoming 1987) *Information technology: the public issues*. Manchester: Manchester University Press.

Habermas, Jürgen (1971) *Towards the rational society*. London: Heinemann.

Hamelink, Cees (1983) *Cultural autonomy in global communications*. New York: Longman.

Handy, Charles (1984) *The future of work*. Oxford: Blackwell.

Headrick, Daniel (1981) *The tools of empire: technology and European imperialism in the nineteenth century*. New York: Oxford University Press.

HMSO (1983) *The development of cable systems and services*. London: Cmnd 8866.

Hills, Jill (1984) *Information technology and industrial policy*. Beckenham: Croom Helm.

Hines, Colin (1978) *The chips are down*. London: Earth Resources Research.

Hoffman, Lance (1980) *Computers and privacy in the next decade*. New York: Academic Press.

Howkins, John (1982) *New technologies: new policies?* London: British Film Institute.

Information Technology Advisory Panel (1986) *Learning to live with IT*. London: HMSO.

Innis, Harold Adams (1964) *The bias of communication*. Toronto: University of Toronto Press.

Jones, Alwyn (1987) 'The violence of materialism in advanced industrial society: an eco-sociological approach' *Sociological Review* (1) 19–47.

Jones, Barry (1982) *Sleepers awake! Technology and the future of work*. Brighton: Wheatsheaf.

Jones, Trevor (ed.) (1980) *Microelectronics and society* Milton Keynes: Open University Press.

Jonscher, Charles (1983) 'Information resources and information productivity' *Information Economics and Policy* (1) pp. 13–35.

Keisler, Sara et al. (1984) 'Social-psychological effects of computer-mediated information' *The American Psychologist* 39 (10).

Kling, Rob (1980) 'Social analyses of computing: theoretical perspectives in recent empirical research' *Computing Surveys* (12) pp. 61–110.

Kling, Rob and Iacono, Suzanne (forthcoming 1987) 'Computerisation as a by-product of social movements' in R. Gordon (ed.) *Microelectronics in Transition*. Norwood NJ: Ablex.

Kumar, Krishan (1978) *Prophecy and Progress: the sociology of industrial and post-industrial society*. Harmondsworth: Penguin.

Kumar, Krishan (1987) *Utopia and anti-utopia in modern times*. Oxford: Basil Blackwell.

Landes, David (1983) *Revolution in time*. Cambridge MA: Harvard University Press.

Lang, Bernd-Peter et al. (1982) *Sozialpolitische Chancen der Informationstechnik*. Frankfurt: Campus Verlag.

Larsen, Judith and Rogers, Everett (1984) *Silicon Valley fever*. New York: Basic Books, London: Allen and Unwin.

Laudon, Kenneth C. (1986) *Dossier society: value choices in the design of national information systems*. New York: Columbia University Press.

Lee, Philip (ed.) (1986) *Communication for all: new world information and communication order*. New York: Orbis.

Lloyd, Anne and Newell, Liz (1985) 'Women and computers' in Wendy Faulkner and Erik Arnold (eds) *Smothered by invention: technology in women's lives*. London: Pluto Press.

Lyon, David (1986) 'From postindustrialism to information society: a new social transformation?' *Sociology* 20 (4) 577–88.

Lyon, David (1987) 'The information society and public policy' forthcoming in Frank Gregory (ed.) *Information technology: the public issues*. Manchester: Manchester University Press.

MacBride, Sean (1980) *Many voices, one world*. Paris: UNESCO.

Machlup, Fritz (1980) *The production and distribution of knowledge in the USA*. Princeton NJ: Princeton University Press.

MacIntosh, Ian (1986) *Sunrise Europe*. Oxford: Basil Blackwell.

MacKenzie, Donald (1985) 'Marx and the machine' *Technology and Culture* (25) 473–502.

MacKenzie, Donald and Wacjman Judith (eds) (1985) *The social shaping of technology*. Milton Keynes: Open University Press.

McCron, Robin (1984) 'New technologies: new opportunities?' *Journal of Educational Television* 10 (1) 7–18.

McPhail, Tom (1981) *Electronic colonialism*. London and Beverly Hills: Sage.

Marstrand, Pauline (ed.) (1984) *New technology and the future of work and skills*. London: Frances Pinter.

Marx, Karl (1973) *Grundrisse*. Harmondsworth: Penguin.

Masuda, Yoneji (1981) *The information society as postindustrial society*. Bethesda MD: World Futures Society.

Maxwell, Stephen (1985) 'International perspectives: Malaysia's electronics industry' in Howard Davis and David Gosling (eds) *Will the future work?* Geneva: WCC.

Melody, William (1985) 'Implications of the information and communications technologies: the role of policy research' *Policy Studies* 6 (2).

Menzies, Heather (1981) *Women and the chip: case studies of the effects of informatics on employment in Canada*. Montreal: Institute for Research on Public Policy.

Mercier, P. A., Plassard, F. and Scardigli, V. (1984) *La société digitale: les nouvelles technologies au futur quotidien*. Paris: Editions du Seuil.

Miles, Ian and Gershuny, Jonathan (1986) 'The social economics of information technology' in Ferguson (ed.) *New communications technologies*.

Mitcham, Carl (1983) 'The religious origins of modern technology' in Paul Durbin and Friedrich Rapp (eds) *Philosophy and Technology*. New York and Frankfurt: Reidel Publishing Company.

Monsma, Stephen et al. (1986) *Responsible technology*. Grand Rapids: Eerdmans.

Mosco, Vincent (1982) *Pushbutton Fantasies*. Norwood NJ: Ablex.

Moseley, Russell (1980) 'Microelectronics and policy: who's running the revolution?' *International Journal of Social Economics* 7 (1) pp. 47–54.

Mumford, Lewis (1934, 1964) *Technics and civilization*. New York: Harcourt Brace Jovanovich.

Murdock, Graham, Hartman, Paul and Gray, Peggy (1983) *Everyday innovations*. Leicester: Mass Communication Research Centre.

Murphy, Brian (1983) *The world wired up*. London: Comedia.

Newman, Julian and Newman, Rhona (1985) 'Information work: the new divorce?' *British Journal of Sociology* December.

Noble, David (1979) 'Social choice in machine design' in Zimbalist (ed.) *Case Studies* and also in MacKenzie and Wacjman (eds) *Social shaping*.

Noble, David (1983) 'Present tense technology' *Democracy* Spring, 8–24, Summer, 70–82, Fall, 71–93.

Noble, David (1984) *Forces of Production: a social history of industrial automation*. New York: Knopf.

Nora, Simon and Minc, Alain (1980) *The computerisation of society*. Cambridge MA: MIT Press.

OECD (1981) *Information activities, electronics and telecommunications technologies: impacts on employment and growth in trade*. Paris: Organization for Economic Cooperation and Development.

Pacey, Arnold (1983) *The culture of technology*. Oxford and New York: Basil Blackwell.

Pahl, Ray (1984) *Divisions of labour*. Oxford: Basil Blackwell.

Porat, Marc (1977) *The information economy: definition and measurement*. Washington DC: US Dept of Commerce.

Poster, Mark (1984) *Foucault, Marxism and history: mode of production versus mode of information*. Cambridge: Polity Press.

Reid, Robert (1986) *Land of lost content*. London: Heinemann.

Reinecke, Ian (1984) *Electronic Illusions*. Harmondsworth and New York: Penguin.

Rose, Frank (1984) *Into the heart of the mind*. New York: Harper and Row.

Rosenbrock, Howard (1984) 'Designing automated systems: need skills be lost?' in Pauline Marstrand (ed.) *New technology*.

Roszak, Theodore (1986) *The cult of information*. New York: Pantheon; Cambridge: Lutterworth Press.

Rothschild, Joan (1981) 'A feminist perspective on technology and the future', *Women's Studies International Quarterly* 4 (1) pp. 65–74.

Roxborough, Ian (1979) *Theories of underdevelopment*. London: Macmillan.

Sahlins, Marshall (1976) *Culture and practical reason*. Chicago and London: University of Chicago Press.

Sayer, Andrew (1986) 'Industrial location on a world scale' in Allen J. Scott and Michael Storper (eds) *Production, work, territory: the geographical anatomy of industrial capitalism*. Boston, London, Sydney: Allen and Unwin.

Schiller, Herbert (1981) *Who knows? Information in the age of the Fortune 500*. Norwood NJ: Ablex.

Servan-Schrieber, Jean-Jacques (1980) *Le défi mondial*. Paris: Fayard. *The world challenge*. New York: Simon and Schuster.

Schuurman, Egbert (1980) *Technology and the future: a philosophical challenge*. Toronto: Wedge Publishing Foundation.

Science Council of Canada (1982) *Planning now for the information society: tomorrow is too late*. Ottawa: SCC.

Segal, Howard (1985) *Technological utopianism in American culture*. Chicago and London: University of Chicago Press.

Shallis, Michael (1984) *The silicon idol*. Oxford: Oxford University Press.

Smith, Anthony (1980) *The geopolitics of information: how Western culture dominates the world*. London: Faber.

Smith, Merritt Roe (ed.) (1985) *Military enterprise and technological change: perspectives on the American experience*. Cambridge MA, and London: MIT Press.

Sola Pool, Ithiel de (1983) *Technologies of freedom*. Cambridge MA, and London: Harvard University Press.

Solomonides, Tony and Levidow, Les (eds) (1985) *Compulsive technology: computers as culture*. London: Free Association Books.

Stanley, Manfred (1978) *The technological conscience: survival and dignity in an age of expertise*. Chicago and London: University of Chicago Press.

Stonier, Tom (1983) *The wealth of information*. London: Thames-Methuen.

Storkey, Elaine (1985) *What's right with feminism*. London: SPCK/Grand rapids, Michigan: Eerdmans.

Street, John (1987) 'Taking control: some aspects of the relationship between IT, government policy and democracy' forthcoming in Gregory (ed.) *Information technology: the public issues*.

Sudnow, David (1983) *Pilgrim in the microworld*. New York: Warner Books/ London: Heinemann.

Sullivan, William et al. (eds) (1983) *Social science as moral inquiry*. New York: Columbia University Press.

Thompson, Linda (1985) 'The electronic cottage: haven or nightmare?' *International Management and Data Systems* Jan–Feb.

Toffler, Alvin (1980) *The third wave*. London: Pan.

Touraine, Alain (1974) *The postindustrial society*. London: Wildwood House.

Touraine, Alain (1977) *L'Après Socialisme*. Paris: Editions Gallimard.

Touraine, Alain (1981) *The voice and the eye*. Cambridge and New York: Cambridge University Press.

Traber, Michael (ed.) (1986) *The myth of the information revolution*. London and Beverly Hills: Sage.

Tunstall, Jeremy (1985) 'Deregulation is politicization'. *Telecommunications Policy* September pp. 203–14.

Turkle, Sherry (1984) *The second self: computers and the human spirit*. London: Granada; New York: Simon and Schuster.

Vallee, Jacques (1984) *The network revolution*. Harmondsworth: Penguin; USA: And/Or Press Inc.

Vanderberg, Willem (1985) *The growth of minds and cultures (Technique and culture* vol. 1). Toronto, Buffalo and London: University of Toronto Press.

Webster, Frank and Robins, Kevin (1986) *Information technology: a Luddite analysis*. Norwood NJ: Ablex.

Weizenbaum, Joseph (1984) *Computer power and human reason*. Harmondsworth: Penguin; New York: W. H. Freeman and Company (1976).

Werneke, Diane (1983) *Microelectronics and office jobs: the impact of the chip on women's employment*. Geneva: International Labour Office; reprinted in Tom Forester *Information technology revolution*.

Wicklein, John (1981) *Electronic nightmare: the home communications set and your freedom*. Boston: Beacon Press.

Wilkinson, Barry (1983) *The shopfloor politics of new technology*. London: Heinemann.

Williams, Raymond (1980) *Problems of materialism and culture*. London: Verso.

Williams, Shirley (1985) *A job to live*. Harmondsworth: Penguin.

Winner, Langdon (1977) *Autonomous technology: technics-out-of-control as a theme in political thought*. Cambridge MA and London: MIT Press.

Winner, Langdon (1984) 'Mythinformation in the high-tech era' *IEEE Spectrum* 21 (6) 90–6.

Wolterstorff, Nicholas (1981) *Reason within the bounds of religion*. Grand Rapids: Eerdmans.

Wood, Stephen et al. (eds) (1982) *The degradation of work?* London: Hutchinson.

Woodward, Kathleen (ed.) (1980) *The myths of information: technology and post-industrial culture*. London: Routledge and Kegan Paul.

Woronoff, Jon (1985) 'Japan and the 21st century' *Oriental Economist* September.

Zimbalist, A. (ed.) (1979) *Case studies in the labor process*. New York: Monthly Review Press.

Index